FROM BOTTOM TO

TOP TIER

IN A DECADE

WAGNER COLLEGE 1988-2002

SECOND EDITION WITH UPDATES 2024

by

NORMAN R. SMITH

PRESIDENT EMERITUS, WAGNER COLLEGE

PRESIDENT EMERITUS, ELMIRA COLLEGE

PAST PRESIDENT, SUFFOLK UNIVERSITY BOSTON

PAST PRESIDENT, RICHMOND AMERICAN INT'L UNIVERSITY LONDON

FORMER ASS'T. DEAN, HARVARD UNIVERSITY

GRADUATE SCHOOL OF EDUCATION

&

JOHN F. KENNEDY SCHOOL OF GOVERNMENT

iUniverse®

FROM BOTTOM TO TOP TIER IN A DECADE
THE WAGNER COLLEGE TURNAROUND YEARS

iUniverse books may be ordered through booksellers or by contacting:

iUniverse
1663 Liberty Drive
Bloomington, IN 47403
www.iuniverse.com
844-349-9409

ISBN: 978-1-4502-4309-4 (sc)
ISBN: 978-1-4502-4311-7 (hc)
ISBN: 978-1-4502-4310-0 (e)

Print information available on the last page.

iUniverse rev. date: 11/22/2023

NORMAN R. SMITH has logged over 30 years, of his more than 50 years in higher education, as a college and university president. Most recently, he has served as interim president at several institutions including Suffolk University Boston and Elmira College in New York. His first presidency was at Wagner College in New York where, during his decade and a half tenure, the then near bankrupt College evolved from *US NEWS* BEST COLLEGES bottom tier ranking to TOP TIER achieving capacity enrollment, fiscal stability, and record fund raising. Smith went on to be President of Richmond The American International University in London, England. Earlier in his career, he was Assistant Dean of two Harvard University graduate schools: Education and then the John F. Kennedy School of Government. He was a Fellow of the Harvard Philosophy of Education Research Center. He earned his doctorate from Harvard University and a BS & MBA from Drexel University. He is the 2018 recipient of the American Association of University Administrators' Stephen Trachtenberg annual award for Leadership in Higher Education. Other awards have included the New York University Presidential Medal for Educational Leadership and the Drexel University Alumni Award for Professional Achievement and Contributions to the Advancement of Higher Education. Presently he is the Board Governance and Leadership Team Leader for the Registry Advisory Service's cadre of veteran presidents offering counsel to Trustees and Presidents. For additional background information and to contact, visit:

www.normansmith.org

TABLE OF CONTENTS

PREFACE

The events in this memoir are based on my recollections of the fourteen-years I served as president of Wagner College (1988–2002). While data and dates were checked against appointment calendars, trustee meeting minutes, and President's Reports that were prepared for the Board of Trustees on a quarterly basis, some events are based on my memory, as much as over twenty years later when this book was originally written and now nearly twice that amount of time.

As you will discover, the book features dozens of media accounts, mostly from *The Staten Island Advance*, a daily Newhouse newspaper that is the original publication of the Newhouse empire. I included them to corroborate my account of events. As these articles were originally published between 1988 and 2002, they precede the era of online archives and were therefore scanned from original hard copies I saved. As such, their resolutions, except for headlines, are difficult to read when reduced to the size of this book. I have therefore transcribed many of the articles and posted them on the page following the original newspaper image.

PROLOGUE

In 2002, my fourteen-year tenure as president of Wagner College on Staten Island, New York ended on what was almost universally viewed as a very high note. Wagner College, at the time of my departure, had successfully evolved from a bottom-ranked college to become a top-tier institution. Enrollments exceeded capacity with academically promising students. *The Princeton Review* would soon judge Wagner to be the most beautiful campus in America and had already singled out Wagner's musical theatre program to be the best in undergraduate higher education.

In less than a decade and a half, Wagner College had realized perhaps the most remarkable turnaround that any college or university had ever managed.

In the late 1980s when I arrived, conventional wisdom viewed Wagner to be on its deathbed. The college had been under-enrolled for years. Admissions standards were fundamentally nonexistent, and most of the residence halls were nearly empty. The campus was in dreadful disrepair, earning the nickname "seedy old Wagner" and "The Wag."

I first visited Wagner in September of 1987 shortly after the search for a new president had been publicly announced.

I couldn't help but notice the sorry condition of the campus (litter, graffiti, overgrown bushes and grass, etc.) but I also was impressed.

Here were nearly one hundred acres of land on what I learned was one of the two highest elevations on the eastern seaboard of the United States. Although the East Coast lacks grand seaboard elevations from Maine to Florida, Wagner's Grymes Hill perch gave it one of the most breathtaking panoramic views anywhere in the country. From various vantage points throughout the campus, the Manhattan skyline, the Statue of Liberty, the New York harbor, the Verrazano-Narrows Bridge, and the Atlantic Ocean were visible.

Before Wagner's founding in 1883, the campus was divided into the private estates of several shipping magnates including Sir Edward Cunard, of England's Cunard Ocean Liners, and Cornelius Vanderbilt, both of whom presumably could survey their shipping empires from the porches of their homes.

I was mesmerized and puzzled. How on earth could a private, residential college within the city limits of New York City, the world's richest and most powerful capital, *not* be flourishing on a campus like this Grymes Hill hidden treasure? My almost immediate assessment was that Wagner long ago should have established itself as New York City's version of what Williams and Amherst are to Massachusetts, or what Haverford and Swarthmore are to Philadelphia. There was no other small, private, residential college within the Big Apple's borders able to claim that status.

The New York City mantle was Wagner's for the taking ... but it had failed to seize the opportunity and instead faced demise.

I felt that the opportunity for greatness still existed and proceeded to throw my hat into the presidential candidate ring.

I was only forty-one years old at the time, which, if I were to succeed in becoming president, would make me one of the youngest college presidents in America. I had hoped that my credentials (most notably my Harvard doctorate and deanships at two Harvard graduate schools) might help me get through at least the first door, giving me the opportunity to make my case for Wagner's future.

In the early stages, I didn't fully realize why Wagner was in such dire straits, or how close the ship was to crashing into the rocks.

Wagner College in foreground atop Grymes Hill overlooking Manhattan and the Statue of Liberty Circa late 1990s

Wagner was founded as a Lutheran seminary, in Rochester, New York, in the late 1800s. The seminary was moved to Staten Island in the 1920s and evolved into a four-year Lutheran college that remained quite small through World War II. Like many colleges in America, the post-WWII GI Bill greatly expanded enrollments. Wagner rode the GI-Veteran Bill Wave, experiencing growth that would continue through the baby boom of the 1960s.

I was never able to find reliable data, except for alumni recollection, but there appears to be every indication that Wagner was flourishing throughout the 1960s, especially following the opening of the Verrazano-Narrows Bridge in 1964, which brought the rest of New York City more readily onto Staten Island. This new access to Staten Island, however, would prove to be both a bonanza and a deterrent to securing the success that other geographically remote colleges were achieving.

During the salad days of the baby boom, so many New Yorkers sought to attend Wagner that there was no need for the college to broaden its geographic reach. The baby boom years were also a time when low-interest funding was available from the New York State "Dormitory Authority" funding agency. Wagner took full advantage of the financial opportunity, building not only dormitories but also other facilities including a student center, a library, and additional classrooms. Alumni from this era recall a flourishing college from where they obtained a good education and for which they have fond memories.

So, what went wrong? Two events, both in the post-baby boom 1970s, gored Wagner's "business" model.

First, in 1971, a small women's institution nearly across the street from Wagner, Notre Dame College, became a branch of the city's prominent St. John's University, thereby providing local students with a Catholic alternative to what was then Wagner Lutheran College. Both Staten Island and Brooklyn (where most Wagner students had been hailing) were heavily populated with Irish and Italian heritage Catholics, who, from that time on, heavily opted for St. John's instead of Wagner.

Then, in 1976, a brand-new public university, CUNY Staten Island, opened its doors within a mile or so of Wagner College. Because of the baby boom surge, both the State University of New York (SUNY) and the City University of New York (CUNY) had been building new campuses throughout the city and the state. Staten Island got its turn thanks to a powerful state senator, John Marchi.

Within five years, during the first half of the 1970s, Wagner found itself literally sandwiched between two formidable competitors. One took away big chunks of Wagner's Catholic cohort while the other took away students with limited financial wherewithal. CUNY's tuition and fees were a small percentage of Wagner's private college rates. Wagner needed to quickly retool itself and reach beyond the local enrollment pool it had been enjoying without competition. Instead, Wagner opted to compete with CUNY and St. John's attempting to take back the traditional local enrollment it owned throughout the fifties and sixties.

Wagner should have recognized the obvious: that, among the three, it was the only institution with student residence halls and should therefore recruit students in the way that most private, residential colleges in less-populous venues had been doing much earlier; namely, students aspiring to live away from home and in a big city.

Wagner overlooked Manhattan! What better motivation for academically promising students wanting to be where top of the ladder opportunities are located?

For the next decade or so after the arrival of St. John's and CSI (CUNY Staten Island), up to the time they announced their search for a new president in 1987, Wagner struggled in vain to attract the traditional local student enrollment. They failed in every way.

Enrollments plummeted. Wagner's appeal to the CUNY-bound students was that Wagner was not as expensive as might appear to be the case because generous scholarships were available. In its attempt to fulfill this claim, Wagner discounted its tuition to levels that virtually matched CUNY's heavily government-subsidized rates, but with the consequence of not having enough money to operate at even a minimal level of acceptability. They were "selling" Wagner College for less than it was costing to "make" Wagner College.

After a decade of decline, Wagner had deteriorated in the mid-1980s to an under-enrolled, financially strapped college in disrepair and in financial crisis. Morale was low, including among students who had come to nickname the college "The Wag"—intended in the most unflattering way.

By the mid-1980s a new contingent of trustees joined the board, including a 1967 alumnus, Jay Hartig, a Price Waterhouse partner who had been enrolled during Wagner's salad days. Hartig became chairman of the board and, along with the vice chairman, another Wagner alumnus and lawyer, Howard Meyers '63, would lead an administration-supported initiative to start leasing campus properties that were being "underutilized."

The college's largest residence hall, a high-rise overlooking Manhattan, was in the process, during the presidential transition, of being leased in the long term to the local Eger Lutheran Nursing Home for needed expansion to accommodate a surge in old age populations. Perimeter acreage, including land adjacent to existing playing fields, was being offered to the U.S. Navy as a housing site for enlisted sailors working in the New York harbor ports.

No one in a position of power at the college appeared to have an ambitious outlook for Wagner. Wagner had failed to win back the local enrollments from St. John's and CSI. No one seemed to believe that students from anywhere else could ever find Wagner attractive. So, the "powers-that-be" concluded the only option was to downsize even further and generate alternative rental revenues that might keep the college afloat.

The local media, among others including the borough political leadership, reacted very negatively to the leasing initiatives which would significantly alter the character of the College. The leasing plans signaled what many saw as the beginning of the end for Wagner. A 1940 Wagner alumnus, Les Trautman, was editor in chief of the *Staten Island Advance*, and a nearby resident of the campus. He launched a prominent media campaign to prevent the demise of his alma mater.

Unknown to Wagner leadership at the time, St. John's University had already approached the borough president, Ralph Lamberti, for help in acquiring Wagner when it closed ... which was viewed as inevitable. Since Wagner and St. John's Staten Island were virtually across the street from each other, the merger would be a natural for St. John's. It would give the university a powerhouse presence on Staten Island that could conceivably eclipse its main campus in Queens.

In addition to launching a campus leasing initiative, the new trustee leadership had also determined the need for new presidential leadership. While the search was underway, they promoted the Vice President for Academic Affairs, Carlyle Haaland, on an interim basis.

If the board had not known at the time of the interim appointment, they soon discovered that Haaland sought the presidency permanently and he reportedly had the support of many board members who wanted the next president to be of Lutheran heritage. I picked up on the likelihood that Haaland would probably be selected, which diminished my expectation of success before I had even become a serious candidate. But I was young and concluded that the experience would be at least a good training ground for subsequent attempts at presidencies elsewhere.

I was puzzled by the way in which the new generation of trustees was forwarding such a defeatist attitude. Wagner was being viewed, it seemed to me, like a bankrupt corporation that had no choice but to start liquidating its assets. That approach, however, doesn't work very well in private higher education, unless the college in question is coming to an end and will be replaced by whatever comes next. I was especially concerned that the trustees were choosing to forgo assets that a more viable future Wagner would need to be competitive.

In my view, Wagner's only hope for a better tomorrow required a strategy to expand the out-of-state student enrollment, which would require the provision of the residence halls that were in the process of being turned over to long term renters. Without housing, Wagner would have to remain the local commuting college that it should have already concluded was not viable. The campus rental strategy was dooming Wagner and therefore had to be prevented.

The Trustee leadership, most notably Board Chair Hartig and Vice Chair Meyers, defended the leasing plans as putting to use land and properties not needed by the College. They noted that the leases were limited to 20 years and that the College would continue to own the properties. And the revenue generated for Wagner would be in the tens of millions over two decades, money greatly needed by the College.

A partial image of the Harborview dormitory that was being leased to the Eger Nursing Home is on the extreme left of this image which shows the view of Manhattan seen from many of the rooms creating a very desirable home for prospective students.

The Harborview high rise that was being turned over to Eger Nursing Home, however, was the most attractive student housing option on campus. While it wasn't needed at the time due to the diminished enrollments in 1987, it was a valuable enrollment marketing tool if the College aspired to return to enrollment health. To be denied access for at least 20 years would make it impossible for the College to reestablish itself.

The Trustees and the departing President, Sam Frank, declared, however, that the nursing home residents would attend courses and help populate the classes. I didn't see that as a plus, but rather a deterrent to recruiting quality residential, traditional age undergraduates.

My contrary views, however, stood the chance of jeopardizing my candidacy. How would I go about challenging the strategies authored by those who would also be selecting the next president?

Would they shoot the messenger?

Staten Island
nday Advance

Final edition
★ ★ ★
Complete sports

Wagner dorms may house elderly

June 1985

Attempts to lease property for decades began as early as 1985, three years before my arrival. The local media and political leaders opposed the Wagner plans, which helped delay any final action.

The overture to the U.S. Navy occurred less than a year before my presidency and was still an active proposal at the time of my arrival in the spring of 1988. The blackened areas in the newspaper image on the next page show the properties offered to the Navy for housing families. The character of the campus would have been adversely affected and stood the likelihood of deterring a return to a flourishing enrollment of full-time undergraduates.

Staten Island Advance

Thursday, January 21, 1988

North Shore 25 Cents
Home-delivered daily and Sunday $1.50 a week

13 acres of Wagner campus may be used for Navy housing

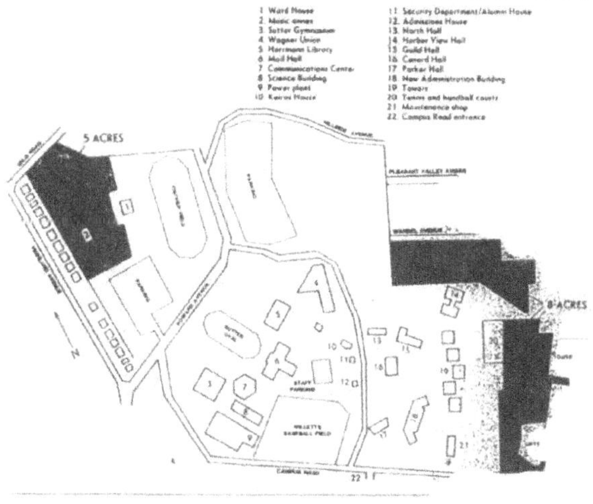

Shaded area indicates where the proposed Navy housing would be built

Builder, trustees want 2 tracts for 200 townhouses

By ANNE FANCIULLO
ADVANCE STAFF WRITER

Nearly 200 units of housing for Navy families assigned to the Stapleton home port are being proposed for two large tracts of vacant land on Wagner College's Grymes Hill campus, principals have disclosed.

College officials declined to reveal any of the financial arrangements involved in the proposal, which is being submitted today to the Navy by developer Kenneth Simons.

The proposed deal had been kept under tight wraps and the information that has now been released came to light only when the Advance learned of it through reportorial sources and pressed for answers.

While Wagner refused to discuss its financial arrangements, informal appraisals obtained by the Advance put the value of the two tracts between $11.4 million and $17.6 million.

However, the Wagner trustees emphasized that if the plan is accepted by the military and goes through, the deal would ensure the college "a significant economic benefit" without its having to relinquish title to its most valuable asset — real estate.

Jay P. Hartig, chairman of Wagner's board of trustees, and Howard Meyers, its vice chairman, told the Advance that the board voted on Monday to endorse the concept of entering into a ground lease with Simons for two large tracts that each could support about 100 attached townhouses.

The college essentially would be renting the land under the proposed houses rather than selling it outright.

The properties include a 5-acre site at the corner of Highland Avenue and Arlo Road, which is commonly referred to as the West Campus, and an 8-acre tract on the college's easternmost side bordering Wardell Avenue and Cedar Terrace.

According to the plan, the houses would be built, owned and managed by Simons and rented to Navy families for the 30-year lifespan of the ground lease.

(See WAGNER, Page A 12)

January 1988

Howard Meyers, left, Jay P. Hartig and Kenneth Simons discuss their plans for Navy housing with Advance reporters.

Staten Island Advance, January 20, 1988

Year ONE 1988–1989

Chapter 1
The Presidential Search

My recounting of the search committee events leading up to my selection as president are largely secondhand. Over the fourteen years of my presidency, many of the committee members shared anecdotes corroborated by each other. I have chosen to report on those that were corroborated by at least two members of the search committee although most are no longer alive.

More than two search committee members told me that I came very close to not having been selected at all. The committee was reportedly divided throughout and could have very easily tilted toward the interim president, Carlyle Haaland, instead of me.

In the late stages, there were three finalists; Carlyle Haaland and I were the leading choices. The third candidate, who, like Haaland, was Lutheran, would subsequently become the last president of Upsala College, another Lutheran institution in East Orange, New Jersey that closed in the 1990s because of financial and enrollment problems not dissimilar to the ones that were also confronting Wagner.

Kevin Sheehy, secretary of the board of trustees and a Wagner alumnus, had revealed to me that there were two different advocacies in the selection committee. One group that included the chairman, vice chairman, and the local Lutheran minister reportedly wanted Carlyle Haaland, partly because of his Lutheran roots but also because of his loyalty during the disruptions of recent years. Some members contended that he was entitled to become the permanent president and not selecting him would represent ingratitude, even betrayal.

An opposing group, however, warned that the closure of the college was a real possibility, and the only hope for survival was to bring in someone new who had ideas that would change the status quo — presuming, of course that she or he also had the ability to see those ideas implemented. This group included Sheehy, a high school biology teacher who was a highly visible community leader and a former unsuccessful candidate for Staten Island's congressional seat. Kevin was bullishly passionate about Wagner and conveyed an infectious and energizing enthusiasm.

Kevin could have passed for NBC's late *Meet the Press* host, Tim Russert. He was upbeat, but also manifested street-smart, politically savvy astuteness. Kevin was driven to optimize life. Those who remembered him as a student recall his persistent drive to break through the envelope... every envelope!

Kevin Sheehy, Wagner's ultimate alumnus and, by his own account, my key to becoming president

When the Verrazano Narrows Bridge opened in 1964, Sheehy managed to get in the front of the line to be the first nonofficial automobile driver to cross the bridge onto Staten Island. His car, full to capacity, followed President Lyndon Johnson's entourage. Johnson was reportedly the first U.S. president to visit Staten Island since President U.S. Grant's visit to a now burned-down house that was part of Wagner's campus ... or so the story goes.

Kevin was loved at his high school, Tottenville, reportedly one of the nation's highest ranked urban public high schools during his time there as a biology teacher and head of the teachers' union. His energy was never ending. I don't know how he found the time to be everywhere at once.

Kevin played a key role throughout my first decade as president of Wagner. He was a great cheerleader for change and for action that resulted in progress. He worked endlessly to find alumni who would sign on to make the college optimize its potential.

Other key trustees in the presidential search included several successful business executives, all alumni of Wagner. The board treasurer, Al Corbin, was a retired shipyard CFO who had graduated in the 1930s but was still very active and particularly aware of the financial difficulties of the college.

Bob Evans, a rare Texan among alumni (class of 1953), was chairman and CEO of Material Sciences Corp. Bob shared Corbin's worries and felt that a new presidential "broom" was needed.

Bob turned out to be one of the steadiest and most supportive trustees I would know throughout my fourteen years. Although he was a consistent member of the Board Executive Committee, and someone who always proved to be forthcoming when called upon, including for meaningful donations, he did not live nearby and was consumed with overseeing a considerable corporation.

His stature and authority were of great value to me. His 2002 honorary degree, one of the last I conferred before departing, was long overdue.

Bob Evans '53 received an overdue honorary doctorate from Wagner in 2002, at my final commencement ceremony. For most of my presidency, he was a key advocate for upgrading the college and making it competitive when many resisted spending for such improvements, instead favoring an endowment first.

Kevin told me that the most aggressive trustee among those wanting someone new at the helm of the college was Brad Corbett, a 1960 alumnus and one-time owner of the Texas Rangers baseball team. He had been encouraged by Sheehy to be part of the selection process.

Brad Corbett '60 *(deceased 2012)*

In addition to trustees, the selection committee included faculty, alumni, and staff, as is typical of college and university presidential searches.

The two veteran faculty members largely agreed with those trustees who were advocating that someone new was preferable to maintaining the status quo. Otto Raths, professor of physics, and Richard Gaffney, professor of arts, both seemed to lean toward me although, to this day, I don't know which way they voted but I am pretty sure they were on my side.

Both Otto and "Gaff" became close friends who always felt free to disagree with and criticize me, which, most of the time, I found very valuable and well-intended.

Jason Jones

Professor Otto Raths, Professor of Physics

Norman Smith

Professor Richard Gaffney, Faculty Chair of Arts & Theatre

Kevin Sheehy said that Brad Corbett was initially unimpressed with me, but subsequently reversed his view and became an intense champion on my behalf. What moment in my interviewing process turned him, I don't know, but I suspect it was when I started talking about what I thought Wagner College could and should aspire to become.

Many on the search committee said that most other finalists, including Haaland, had painted a gloomy picture of Wagner's future that would require downsizing ... like the leasing of "excess" campus properties that was already being attempted. I, instead, talked about growth and a great future ... about refilling the dorms to capacity rather than selling or leasing them.

I have been told the debate between the two sides was intense. Those favoring Haaland saluted his responsible and practical assessment of realities and characterized me as young, naive, and romantic, with "delusions of grandeur" representative of my lack of experience in the real world of tough decisions. When the vote finally took place, I won, so I was told, by only one or two votes.

I certainly cannot say what might have happened had I not been selected, but I strongly doubt that Wagner would have been able to move to the heights it has traveled had the college maintained its course of downsizing. Actually, downsizing was almost impossible to comprehend. The student enrollment was down to 1,180 students whose tuition discount exceeded 50%. Thus, the NET enrollment was under 550 students which was financially unsustainable. The only future that would keep Wagner alive was to upsize.

Without the residence halls, one which was in the process of becoming an on-campus nursing home, Wagner faced a permanent dependence on a local student body that just wasn't there. Without additional playing fields, the NCAA Division I athletic program would probably have had to be abandoned or downgraded. That may have included having to drop the football program— one of Wagner's proudest traditions — that had won a proudly promoted NCAA national championship.

For sure, Wagner College would have become a very different place, and I suspect that would have meant becoming the Staten Island campus of the city's Notre Dame University: St. John's University.

Chapter 2
Winning by a Nose

Like most college presidential searches, the selection process took nearly all of an academic year. I can't pinpoint the exact date, but in mid-May — May 18th, I believe — of 1988 I received a telephone call from Jay Hartig, the chairman of the Wagner College board of trustees. I remember asking him how it was going, and he responded, "Well, good — for you, I guess." I had yet to learn that the outcome was maybe not so good from his perspective, having reportedly preferred Haaland.

The understanding was that I would assume the presidency in July 1988. However, living not far away (in Philadelphia), I decided, with Hartig's approval, that I would drive up to Wagner within a few days to say hello to everyone.

I arrived in mid-afternoon and went directly to the president's suite, located on the top floor of the student union, a modern building with suggestions of Frank Lloyd Wright's cantilevered designs, like the iconic "Falling Water." The union was on a hillside looking out onto the New York harbor.

The first person I encountered was Carlyle Haaland, the acting president and heir apparent throughout most of the search. I sensed he was not happy to see me, which, under the circumstances, was completely understandable. I wandered about and introduced myself, reminding everyone that I would not be officially taking over until July, but wanted to drop by and say hello and maybe get a sense of the pressing issues of the moment.

Ask and ye shall receive.

Some serious financial problems were confronting Wagner that were complicated by the lack of a vice president for Administration and Finance. He had recently left and his deputy, the controller, was trying to hold things together, without much success. Wagner was completely out of money, including from credit lines. The college was two weeks away from payroll distribution, with no cash to cover paychecks. Banks had refused additional credit, so even the imminent May payroll was unfunded.

I questioned how the June, July, and August payrolls (the remainder of the fiscal year), not to mention other expenses, would be funded. Private colleges experience two surges of revenue annually. One is in August/September, representing tuition, room and board payments for the fall semester. The next is in December/January, for the winter/spring semester. All other revenue sources are comparatively minimal. If the two income surges had been exhausted four months before the end of the spending year, there would be no additional revenue to get the college through the final third of its current fiscal year.

If all revenues were exhausted in mid-May, how was the final quarter possible? No new significant revenues would be realized until the fall tuition payments of next year were collected. The plan was to use next year's revenues to pay this year's bills, a practice that had been in effect for several years already. If that was the plan, I asked, where was the money for next year's bills? The answer given to me was that the new president and the next vice president for Administration and Finance would have to figure that out.

Then I was told that enrollments were not looking good for the fall. Also, the Financial Aid director had left, but before doing so had exhausted next year's entire financial aid budget for upper class students, leaving no funds to recruit a new freshman class.

What about fund raising? Any revenues there? Well, the Vice President for Development had also left, so there was no promise for a solution from donations that in recent years had been minimal anyway. Not many donors want to pay delinquent electric bills.

I immediately cancelled my plans to arrive in July and decided, instead, to start immediately ... or to at least create a presence immediately. I phoned Jay Hartig telling him of my assessment. Although I wouldn't put myself on the payroll until July, I hoped that *by* July I would have a way of paying myself — and everyone else.

I asked Carlyle to continue as acting president for the time being so I could focus my attention on finding a revenue stream to fund payroll, two weeks ahead. The next step was to call Al Corbin, treasurer of the board of trustees, to inform him of what I'd discovered. He said he was not surprised, then volunteered to drive over the following morning to brainstorm with me.

My first day at Wagner was coming to an end. I looked out the window at the beautiful view of the Verrazano Bridge and New York harbor, reminding myself, once again, that Wagner was an unpolished jewel. But how was I going to buy the time needed to remove the tarnish? Where was the money going to come from that would buy a couple of years of elbow room?

It was now past five p.m. Judy Lunde, my secretary-to-be, said I had a phone call. I presumed it was from my wife, Susan, since few people knew where I was. Instead, it was Richard Gaffney, the Wagner professor of arts who had been one of the two faculty members on the Presidential Selection Committee.

"I *thought* it was you," he declared, explaining that he had seen an automobile with Pennsylvania tags in the president's parking space. He invited me over to the unofficial "faculty club" in Kairos House; actually, a kitchen in an on-campus house that served as the chapel and chaplain's office.

"Chaplain Guttu and some of the faculty are over here having a drink in your honor, and it would be great if you could join us," proposed Gaffney.

Off I went to what would for years to come be a routine way of maintaining informal lines of communication with the faculty. For the next couple of hours, I learned of a demoralized faculty climate with a prevailing spirit of suspicion combined with anger— directed toward what they considered a history of managerial incompetence that had unnecessarily run the college into the ground. Most of the anger was directed at past leadership, but not at Carlyle Haaland. He had been part of a faculty-led anti-administration "cabal" and had not distanced himself from faculty dissent during his year as acting president.

The chaplain, Lyle Guttu, was the unofficial host, being the virtual landlord of the house. What was once the president's office, originally a large living room, was now the college's chapel. Lyle had been chaplain for decades and was once Dean of Students. He was widely liked and very much a part of the faculty and staff community.

Also a part of the first night gathering was Professor Tony Pfister, a science faculty member who had taken over many of Carlyle Haaland's academic vice-presidential responsibilities without actually being so titled. Tony was open about his support for Carlyle, as he had seen himself becoming the permanent academic vice president were Carlyle to be selected president.

Lyle instantly charmed me. I had tried to meet him during the early stages of the presidential search on the recommendation of Francis Horne, former Wagner College executive vice president in the 1960s. Francis was a mentor of mine and close to Lyle. He went on to become president of not only Gustavus Adolphus College and Pratt Institute, but also of the University of Rhode Island, where he retired as president emeritus in residence.

Fran had characterized Lyle as "one of the most intelligent and nicest people [he] had ever known" and someone who knew where "all the skeletons were buried at Wagner."

Lyle was indeed intelligent. He was a 1958 Harvard graduate, where he had been a full scholarship hockey star. Lyle was heroically characterized in his classmate Eric Segal's (*Love Story*) *The Class,* a recollection of Segal's years at Harvard when Lyle was *his* idol. Lyle was "The Mayor of Wagnertown." A little bit of Mister Rogers with a dash of Mayberry's Sheriff Andy Taylor. A Minnesota Norwegian, there was also a large portion of Lake Wobegon's Garrison Keillor there too.

As my years at Wagner evolved, I built a very close relationship with Lyle. He was an indispensable part of my administration. In addition to serving as chaplain throughout my tenure, he oversaw Student Affairs for a number of years until he became Special Assistant to the President and served as my liaison to parents.

Lyle was Wagner's ambassador without portfolio. He taught classes on occasion. He offered a brief invocation at most college events, including trustee and faculty meetings. His comments would be focused on the most relevant issues of the moment and served to help everyone focus on the fact we were all in this together. A college is indeed blessed when lucky enough to have a senior statesman like Lyle Guttu.

I was devastated when he was killed, at 72, while shopping on Staten Island. He was walking across a street during the Christmas season of 2007, when an SUV turned the corner and hit him. No one will ever replace what Lyle brought to Wagner. After his death, the borough of Staten Island renamed a nearby campus street Lyle Guttu Boulevard.

Jason Jones

The late, great Lyle Guttu

Chapter 3

Congratulations on Your Appointment. Now Close Down the College!

The day following my first day at Wagner — what was to have been a one-day visit and instead became a move-in — Al Corbin arrived early as he promised he would. I summoned the controller, Richard Damon, to learn exactly where we stood, and sure enough, the coffers were bare. The situation was worse than I could have imagined and had been that way for some time. The college was pointed toward yet another major deficit year and, with projected enrollments down for the coming year, the situation seemed certain to get worse — although how do you get wetter when you are already soaked to the skin?

Damon was well-intentioned and appeared to want to be part of the solution. He laid out an assessment that led me to realize that the financial condition was even worse than what had been described a day earlier. Not only was there no money to fund the May payroll, now two weeks away, but there was also well over a half-million dollars in invoices that were over six months delinquent. He anticipated that some creditors, like the food service and bookstore suppliers, would cease to send any more provisions until they were paid for what was already owed. So not only were paychecks at risk, but also feeding students in the dining hall might come to an end before the close of the academic year, which, fortunately, was around the corner. Even the gasoline credit card that fueled campus vehicles was so overdue that the card had been cancelled and no longer worked at the pumps.

I learned that what little endowment the college had on the books had been spent some time ago (internally characterized as a loan) to cover past expenses. This struck me as illegal since some of the monies were restricted endowments that could only be used according to the donor's conditions. I asked if the board had approved this action. Damon said he doubted it. He said that the former vice president for finance, who had resigned a few months earlier, was reaching for straws and took whatever he could find — which may well have been one of the reasons he had abandoned ship. Even though he was board treasurer, Al had not been told about the endowment "loan," so clearly the board had not approved the action. Carlyle Haaland told me he also was learning about the so-called loan for the first time. All financial reports had portrayed those funds as on hand. Their "borrowed" status would not be discovered until the audit of the 1987-1988 fiscal year, which wouldn't be issued until early in 1989.

We didn't successfully come up with any silver bullets that day. My view was that we needed a loan from a guardian angel who would have to already have a relationship with the college; perhaps a benefactor or trustee, although no one came to Al's mind. He said he would put on his thinking cap and get back to me.

My second day featured widespread awareness that I was the next Wagner president. One of the first reactions was from the local daily newspaper headed by a veteran editor who was a 1940 graduate of Wagner, Les Trautmann. I recalled during the interviews that Trautmann, who was a member of a presidential search advisory group, had walked out in the middle of my initial interview. I later learned that he had not supported my selection, reportedly thinking I was too young for the job. Les reminded me of Ben Bradlee (*Washington Post* editor during the Watergate exposé). He wasn't alone in thinking I was the wrong choice, but luckily for me, he didn't represent the majority.

Archival

Les Trautman '40

I quickly recognized that my work was cut out for me if I was to have media support, which the college, and, for that matter, I, needed. Trautmann lived in the neighborhood and often took an evening stroll through the campus. I instructed security to phone me whenever they saw him wandering around and about, so I could walk out and "bump" into him. I would bump into him frequently, always receiving a gracious but somewhat distant response.

As time went by, however, we became closer, and Les ended up becoming my champion. I remember an event on Staten Island a year or so into my presidency where I was the keynote speaker. Les was called upon to introduce me. He declared that he was proud to do so, but even prouder that he was on the selection committee that picked me. He neglected to mention that he opposed my selection — but I much preferred his somewhat revised recollection.

The bad news kept coming in over the next few days. Two particularly monumental blows came from the New York State Commissioner of Higher Education and the president of the Middle States Commission on Higher Education, which oversaw Wagner's academic accreditation. Middle States, I learned, had Wagner College on a deathwatch for some time and were close to rescinding accreditation, or at least placing the college on probation. Their reasons covered every key vital sign including the high attrition rate, low graduation rate, low admissions standards and especially the multimillion-dollar deficits being posted for the past several years.

I was reminded that a ten-year on-site accreditation evaluation was scheduled for 1990, just two years away, and we would have to undertake a self-study the year before the visit. If major improvements didn't occur in the coming year, the likelihood of losing accreditation altogether was virtually certain.

As if that weren't enough of a Damocles sword, the New York State Commissioner of Higher Education wasn't inclined to give me time to improve anything. I received notification within my first week at Wagner. The letter acknowledged my appointment and then ordered me to proceed with the closing of the institution. Their financial monitoring concluded that the college was without the resources to serve the paying students planning to enroll in the fall. It was time, they concluded, for Wagner students to begin looking elsewhere before they paid their tuition bills, only to have that money spent on existing debts rather than on next year's operating costs.

The only thing I could think of doing to avoid compliance with the state order was to request an audience where I could appeal. The commissioner agreed to see me, and I scheduled a visit to Albany within days. I realized, though, that my visit would be for naught unless I could present at least a short-term solution to assure the state that none of the students' 1988-1989 tuition payments would be spent on existing deficits. The only way I could make that assurance would be if I had a source of funds to cover outstanding debts — along with the operating costs through the end of the 1987-1988 fiscal year. May, June, July, and August were still to come.

To the degree that I could ascertain from the dubious financial reports I was reviewing, it seemed that two million dollars would cover everything except the restoration of a meager few million dollars' worth of endowment. Something closer to seven million would be needed for everything, including a modest financial cushion for the coming academic year and a contingency for other problems that might likely arise as bad tidings continued to surface.

Given just days before my visit to Albany, there weren't many realistic solutions that could be found that quickly, if any. Gifts of that proportion, especially to fund deficits, were nowhere in sight. Surveying the list of trustees, it seemed no one on the board had anything close to that kind of wherewithal, and besides, who wants to give millions to fund a deficit?

What did occur to me was a mortgage. The college may be in deficit, but its nearly 100 acres of land must be worth a fortune ... certainly much more than seven million. I called Al Corbin to pose the idea.

Al said that the idea for a mortgage had arisen before, but overtures to banks brought cool responses. Banks were reluctant to take mortgages from financially stressed nonprofits, especially charities, churches, and schools. No matter the value of the land as collateral, banks didn't want the negative publicity that would be associated with having to foreclose on such institutions.

I asked whether there existed some prominent Staten Islanders, maybe like the *Advance* editor, Les Trautmann, who didn't want to see his alma mater disappear. Perhaps there was a cadre of citizens tied to Wagner who could collectively put pressure on the local banks? Al said he had an idea. He cited a particularly successful alumnus of Wagner who might have the influence to make something like that happen.

His name was Don Spiro, the CEO of Oppenheimer Management Company (later renamed OppenheimerFunds), a major mutual fund corporation located in the World Trade Center. Don was a 1949 graduate of Wagner, part of the first wave of GI Bill students flooding colleges and universities in the aftermath of World War II. The son of a general store owner on Staten Island, Don appeared destined upon graduation to take over his father's business. He was married to Evelyn, a graduate of Wagner College's nursing program, who had been the youngest head surgery nurse in the history of Staten Island Hospital. Evelyn encouraged Don to aim higher than his father's general store. So, Don, in the early 1950s, became a mutual fund salesman for Dreyfuss. He told me selling mutual funds in those days was comparable to life selling insurance or encyclopedias. Mutual funds were not yet a commonplace high-finance investment.

Archival

Dr. Donald Spiro, Wagner's "silver bullet"

Chairman of the Board for twelve of my fourteen years

Don was Hollywood casting for a corporate CEO. He reminded me of Cary Grant and Charlton Heston. He was an occasional model in his youth, and I suspect his aura, including his personable charm, greatly contributed to his executive success.

And successful he was. He joined up with one of the legendary Wall Street moguls, Leon Levy, and built Oppenheimer into one of the mutual fund giants, making him perhaps Wagner College's most successful and richest alumnus.

Although Don had been occasionally involved in Wagner alumni events, he was not a trustee and, Al told me, was unaware of the college's dire straits. I called Don and asked for a meeting to introduce myself, which he agreed to offer. I went to his office in the World Trade Center and outlined the financial crisis facing the College. He was alarmed to learn about Wagner's dilemma and most certainly didn't want to see his (and his wife's) alma mater close.

Don had moved off Staten Island decades earlier and wasn't close to any of the local bankers. But he did know Tom Russo, head of a prominent Staten Island law firm who was a fellow 1949 graduate. Tom was very active in the local community and knew all the Island bank presidents, along with most of their board members. Tom was also known for his aggressiveness and for not taking *no* for an answer.

Three local savings banks were approached by Tom and Don, each reluctantly acquiescing to take a piece of a $7 million short term loan. To my disappointment, though, they wouldn't agree to a longer-term mortgage. The term of the loan was two years, giving breathing space to find a more permanent solution elsewhere. The bankers made it clear that they wanted out of the debt relationship quickly, and at least one of the bank presidents expressed great unhappiness at having anything to do with the loan.

Within a day or two, the papers were signed, and we had the money. The process happened so quickly that I wondered whether Don Spiro co-signed the loans. I never fully learned who said what to whom, but the local banks did come through with a seven-million-dollar loan collateralized by the campus real estate ... a lot of campus real estate that was worth much more than the loan amount.

Disappointments about a longer-term solution aside, though, I at least had a short-term financial solution that covered the existing year's expenses without depending on next year's tuition revenues. I had something I could take to Albany in the hope they would rescind their order for me to close Wagner.

The meeting in Albany went remarkably well. The gathering included several lawyers and financial analysts, all of whom seemed to be more familiar with the problems at Wagner than the former management of Wagner had been. After reporting to the group that I had a short-term financial solution that would not require using 1988-1989 revenues for the prior year's unpaid expenses, the pressure to immediately close down Wagner College subsided.

I insisted there was no reason why Wagner shouldn't be successful and flourishing. I shared my assessment of what went wrong, specifically that the St. John's and CUNY campuses took away Wagner's historical local enrollments.

Then I made the case that there was a tremendous potential market for a college in New York City that compared to upstate colleges like Ithaca and Hamilton but also offered the advantage of accessibility to Manhattan. I shared my view that Wagner was a "best of both worlds" setting that could be a very attractive compromise to students and their parents. Parents, I contended, often are concerned about the safety and intensity of attending in-city institutions like NYU, Pace, and Columbia. They would rather see their kids attending a bucolic, rural, and safe institution removed from big city dangers --- like Ithaca or Hamilton.

On the contrary, students want to be where the action is; where opportunities to get a foot in the door exist. Walk through the middle of the campus, I explained, and you would swear you were in upstate New York or rural New England. But look out the window of the dorm room, and there is Manhattan just a ferry ride away. I would try not to overuse the cliché —"the best of both worlds"— but that, essentially, *was* the distinctive niche I wanted prospective students and their families to draw from our marketing strategy. Admittedly, students would opt for NYU's Greenwich Village or Columbia's Upper West Side but would settle for a campus like Wagner that parents could live with — instead of being in a remote, inaccessible rural locale so typical of small, residential colleges.

The state officials bought my characterizations, some noting that they had thought similarly and wondered why Wagner didn't get it. We were granted a stay of execution, but I was warned that the state would continue to monitor progress *very* regularly. I was directed to submit monthly financial reports for the remainder of the current fiscal year and throughout the following year. But Wagner was alive as was my job.

Everyone got a paycheck at the end of May that was honored by the banks. In subsequent gatherings with faculty and staff, I was told that past paychecks had often been hard to cash. One faculty member recounted walking into his bank to deposit his check, only to hear the teller yell out "Are we cashing Wagner checks this week?" Finally, this week at least, the checks were good.

Archival

Al Corbin deservedly would become one of the first honorary degree recipients of my presidency, seen here with Professor Mildred Nelson (left) and Professor Eleanor Rogg (partly obscured, right).

Chapter 4
Staying Alive

Now that Wagner had its stay of execution, granting the college at least one more year, I was faced with figuring out how to minimize the damage for the rest of the existing fiscal year and how to survive the coming year. Enrollments were not looking good, and it was too late in the recruiting year to reverse, or even improve upon, the likely fall outcomes.

All new first-year students had applied to college and made their choices months ago. Virtually no one was going to change their mind and instead come to Wagner for any incentive that came to my mind except if they didn't have to pay a dime in tuition. Wagner often had a summer surge of last-minute applicants, but they were typically students who had failed to locate a college that would admit them, so they were coming to Wagner as a last resort. These students were notorious for being academically unqualified to be in college, typically failing out after the first semester, and leaving delinquent tuition bills unpaid.

That Wagner was spending over a million dollars more than it had been making in the current fiscal year — and would have even less revenue for the next year — made for a bleak prognosis. If I was ever going to start attracting paying customers, I needed to invest a lot of money in campus improvements that had been postponed or neglected for years. But, if I was going to keep the wolves from the door (i.e., the state closure order), I would have to show fiscal restraint and not spend more than we were making. Yet, if some money wasn't invested in campus improvements, how were we going to successfully sell Wagner to the market beyond New York? Additionally, the now-departed financial aid director had allocated the entire aid budget to returning students, leaving nothing as an incentive for new students.

If fiscal restraint meant eliminating at least one million from expenses, how were all the vacant senior positions going to be filled? We needed at least a chief financial officer, an admissions czar, a financial aid wiz, and a fund-raising magician ... all expensive positions if you insisted on qualifications like competence and relevant experience. Even in 1988, these positions, with benefits, could add at least a third of a million dollars to expenses that were already over the top and had to be *cut* by a million dollars. And there were other expenditures as or maybe more important.

Nothing had been painted for a very long time. Graffiti was everywhere. The grounds had been totally neglected. The grass was either overgrown or nonexistent. The prettiest part of the campus was a massive, tree-lined oval the size of a football field that fronted the classic Main Hall, reminiscent of Henry VIII's Hampton Court Palace. Unfortunately, Wagner's oval was almost without grass because the football team used it as a practice field to protect the grass on the playing field for game day. Faculty and staff parked their cars around the oval and on the grass, many even parking their cars nose-in to the front entrance of Main Hall.

In the student union, there was almost no furniture anywhere, just empty rooms. I was told that the students didn't take care of the furniture, so it wasn't replaced. The student lounges in the residence halls were similarly void of furniture for the same reason.

The main dining hall was in the student union, the cantilevered modern building that reminded me of Frank Lloyd Wright's designs.

The dining room was cavernous, with what seemed to be a forty-foot ceiling. One wall was floor-to-ceiling glass with a panorama of the New York harbor and the Verrazano Bridge. Breathtaking — but the atmosphere was bleak. The room was furnished with what looked like army surplus furniture: stackable chairs and folding tables. The ceiling was a waffled concoction with limestone-like leaks that had created a stalactite collection of mineral icicles. Particularly ugly was the lighting — line after line of fluorescent light fixtures, painted orange, that one typically associates with a sweatshop. The overall effect reminded me of the 1930s' James Cagney San Quentin Prison movies where the inmates start a riot in the mess hall.

Then there were the nights. To my astonishment, the first time I walked out of my office onto the campus at night, I could hardly see beyond my nose. Here were nearly one hundred acres in darkness. Well, not entire darkness. A few very tall, amber-hued lights were here and there, making the campus feel as bleak as the dining hall — namely, in this case, the exercise yard of San Quentin, or how Hollywood would imagine it.

Touring the residence halls, I was similarly appalled with their condition. The buildings looked like they hadn't been painted in decades. There was no furniture in any of the student lounges. The bathrooms were rusty and leaking. I suspected prisons might well have had better living conditions. In an era before widespread cell-phone ownership, the residence halls were not wired for telephone service. There was an occasional payphone, but the ones I came across were out of order.

My tour of faculty offices showed the same disrepair. There was only occasional telephone service; many offices were without telephones, relying singularly upon a shared telephone on the department secretary's desk. Faculty would have to run down the hall to the secretarial reception whenever they needed to place or receive a call. As a result, most professors left campus after their classes because they were too isolated in their inadequate offices.

Although 1988 was less than a decade after the advent of the personal computer, Wagner remained in the pre-computer era, without even one PC anywhere. At best, administrative offices had IBM correcting Selectrics, a few with programmable magnetic card readers, the most advanced pre-personal computer typewriter. No computer applications were being used or taught. I was particularly struck that the business school was graduating accounting and finance majors who were presumably being hired, or at least expecting to be, by corporations, although they were untrained in the new personal computer-based financial spreadsheets like EXCEL.

I had been using personal computers, at least for word processing, since 1980 when I was assistant dean of the Harvard University John F. Kennedy School of Government. Harvard was quick to install personal computers, and I remember having one of the first IBM desktops. There was no hard drive, just two floppy disk ports. The left port was for software, like word processing. The right port was to store data and files that were generated. A year later Harvard upgraded to the IBM XT, which boasted a massive (at that time) 20-MB hard drive, a microscopic fraction of what is now available even on a cellular phone or digital camera. We wondered how we would ever need more than 20 megs.

By the time I arrived at Wagner, I had owned a personal computer for at least five years, along with a printer. The printer was more like a typewriter—no automatic feed; each page had to be inserted in the roller platen. This was before ink jet or laser printers, but I thought the technology was incredible and couldn't possibly be improved upon. Wagner's very first computer was my home computer, which I brought into the office. I taught my two secretaries, Judy Lunde and Carol Maniscalchi, word processing.

So much needed to be upgraded to late-twentieth century standards if Wagner was going to be seen as a quality college.

There was little promise that Wagner would sell itself to its potential applicant pool unless it first underwent a complete makeover. Wagner was the right kind of institution in the right place, but it needed to clean up its act and look worth the investment that private college tuition represents. That makeover, though, was going to be costly. We now had enough money to keep our head above water, but there was nothing left for a makeover.

If Wagner had been a business, the obvious source would be venture capitalists who would provide the funding for an enterprise to turn itself around. How do nonprofits do the same or anything comparable? A new for-profit venture can lose money for years until they show a profit. Wagner had maybe a year or two to make money — and no tolerance for losing any.

I nevertheless realized that recovery wasn't possible until the campus itself started looking like the kind of place that paying customers would want to buy. Conventional wisdom within college admissions circles affirmed that the most important moment in a college selection decision is the campus visit and the first impression of the campus grounds. *Committed faculty. Dedication to academic excellence. Personal treatment. Preparation for a lifetime of success.* All these universally used clichés and others are meaningless if the first impression of the campus condition is negative.

And that first impression is a multifaceted one. Sometimes, the location and campus aura fail to fulfill the expectations of college-bound prospects. Wagner didn't face that problem. Even in its motley condition, there were some breathtaking elements. But the conditions were so dire that Wagner conveyed that it was an institution in distress, which didn't appear to be managed well or properly cared for, and thereby certainly not one that families with a choice, including financial wherewithal, would likely choose.

Not having a vice president for administration and finance, I started meeting with the buildings and grounds crews. There were actually quite a few people in this department, although some were in peculiar jobs, given the financial straits of the college.

What most stood out was the presence of a full-time purchasing agent, Stan Shilling. Stan reminded me of Jack Klugman playing Allie McGraw's father in the movie "Goodbye, Columbus." Stan was intense and excitable. I was perplexed that he could stay busy as the purchasing agent for an institution that couldn't afford to buy anything. He more or less acknowledged that he was being underutilized, and I proceeded to share with him my wishes to somehow clean up the campus on a shoestring. I was impressed with the way he picked up on the problem.

Stan's energetic enthusiasm kicked in quickly. He declared that, in his view, there were more than enough people on staff to make a big difference. They just had to be managed properly. I wasn't sure what "properly" meant but kept listening. "Just put me in charge of this gang, and we'll get the job done," promised Shilling. "Hell, most of what you're talking about, Mr. President, like mowing lawns, trimming shrubs, washing off graffiti and painting walls, can be accomplished with blood, sweat, and tears and shouldn't cost any more than what we are now spending."

Archival

Stan Shilling

Stan and I then met with the buildings and grounds crew, about ten people. Most had been with the college for years and represented one of the few labor unions organized at Wagner. I thanked them all for hearing me out and proceeded to share with them my assessment of Wagner's problems and what we needed to do to stay in business. The first hurdle was to clean up the campus so that it sells to paying customers. The cleanup had to be accomplished during the summer, in time for the incoming students in September and in time for the admissions recruiting campus visits from prospective students that would begin in October.

I put Shilling in charge of buildings, grounds, and security. He did see a missing link: the lack of a professional groundskeeper who understood how to care for grass, trees, and foliage. Acres of land were without grass because of neglect and because no one presently working at Wagner had a green thumb. If the campus was ever going to put its best foot forward, grounds expertise was needed. I said OKAY and authorized him to find a green thumb.

Shilling found Walter Earl, a tall, soft-spoken man who had been working for a country club. *Perfect*, I thought. What better place for green thumb experience than caring for a golf course? Earl turned out to be the best first hire I could have made for Wagner. He lived to care for the grounds, and his magical touch transformed the campus. Years later, when "seedy old Wagner" was designated the most beautiful college campus in America, Walter Earl and his crew deserved the lion's share of the credit for that accolade from *The Princeton Review*.

Throughout the summer of 1988, Walter Earl was getting to work on what turned out to be a metamorphosis. I was especially concerned about the horrid condition of the massive Sutter Oval in front of the iconic Main Hall. This would be the first image of Wagner visitors saw, and it clearly had the potential to impress. The only way in which the centerpiece of the campus could look its best was to stop the football team from practicing on it. And cars had to stop parking there. So, the Oval was closed to cars, much to the consternation of faculty and staff accustomed to parking close to their offices.

Actually, there was plenty of parking at the college, but the parking lots were about one hundred yards away — an unreasonable distance in the minds of many. I recalled my experience at Harvard, where parking was very limited. For the first two years, I had to park at a street meter and run out to feed it coins every couple of hours. When I finally got an official parking spot, for which I had to pay a substantial annual fee, it was six blocks away from my office, but I was delighted — and envied by others faced with having to continue feeding the meters. Wagner faculty and staff paid nothing for parking. Everything is relative.

While Walter Earl and his crew were attending to the grounds all summer, Shilling was mobilizing the rest of the buildings and grounds crew to upgrade the buildings, inside and out. The cleaning crews first removed graffiti; a task that had not been done for years. The prevailing view was that removing such vandalism was pointless because the graffiti "artists" would just return and do it again. To the contrary, I hoped people would be inclined to take care of something in good condition and that graffiti vandals would eventually give up if their handiwork was routinely and immediately removed.

Shilling appointed a younger member of the unionized buildings crew to be supervisor. He was Dominick Fontano, who had been working at Wagner since his late teens. Dom was a second-generation employee; he'd known all the veteran crewmembers since childhood. Dom's appointment was a good move on Shilling's part. I learned that Stan's aggressive approach to getting the job done had distanced him from the union personnel. Dom was able to form a buffer that worked extremely well. He had a very calm and even-tempered personal style that was an essential key to getting everyone to row in the same direction.

Archival

Dominick Fontano

During my years as president, Dom grew to assume overall authority for buildings, grounds, and security. Like eyesight and good health, the excellent condition of the campus was something I came to take for granted, thanks to Dom. I was always able to rely upon him to competently handle any building and grounds problem that arose, and, as a result, I rarely needed to be brought in to help resolve any such difficulties. Dom never complained about lacking resources or staff. He just got the job done with a dedicated staff that always rose above and beyond the call of duty.

As the summer proceeded, I wandered through the campus buildings on an almost-daily basis. Wherever I went, someone was painting something. Invariably, Stan Shilling was rolling up his sleeves and painting himself. Thankfully, the unions turned their heads the other way on this potential management violation. We were all in this together, and I sensed that most everyone bought into that spirit.

By the time the fall came around, the place was starting to look at least respectable enough to start selling to a more discriminating clientele.

Wagner crews keeping area spotless

By DON GROSS
ADVANCE STAFF WRITER

For the past several months, Wagner College employees have been raking leaves, trimming tree limbs and picking up trash, which is what maintenance workers do all the time -- except the property they work on doesn't belong to the Grymes Hill school.

In fact, Stanley R. Shilling, the school's director of auxiliary services, doesn't know who owns the land that runs from Campus Road down Howard Avenue to Clove Road and from Clove to the Staten Island Expressway. And it doesn't matter to him.

What does matter is that the land, once the property of Augustinian Academy, is -- or was -- a mess.

And that, he said, was unacceptable to Wagner president Norman Smith, who is trying his best to change the school from a college with a regional reputation into one of the nation's premier small, liberal arts colleges.

According to Shilling, the property was an unofficial city dump. "You can't believe what we found out here," he said. "There were washing machines, and refriger-

It's good news!

ators, TVs and tires. We even found dresses."

The mess was also widespread, extending from Narrows Road North and Clove Road all the way to the college grounds. And that, said college president Smith, was what set him off.

"Studies show that the single most significant factor in making up a parent's mind as to whether his child will attend a college is the campus visit and the conditions of the facility," he said.

Smith spent the first months of his presidency putting the campus in shape. In November, as the college prepared for its first open house during his tenure, he drove the paths prospective parents would take to the college and knew the conditions would reflect on the college.

"They wouldn't know that we didn't own the land," he said.

But after the open house, he insisted the conditions be maintained. "I just feel this is a good, neighborly thing to do," he said. "If everyone would clean up 50 yards around their house, this city would be spotless."

Smith's feelings of responsibility for the neighborhood's appearance is part of his Canadian upbringing, he said.

"In Toronto, nobody would think of dropping a piece of paper on the ground. They'd carry it until they found a trash can," he said.

New Yorkers, on the other hand, often drop litter on the street even when they're right next to a trash basket. "I saw someone drop a lunch bag out a car window when he was parked right next to a trash can," Smith said.

Smith's response was to go over, pick up the bag and dispose of it properly. "I didn't say a word to them," he said. "And the driver just stared at me and pulled away laughing."

The reponse to Wagner's cleanup efforts on Grymes Hill has been more appreciative, however.

Maintenance department foreman Walter Earl said that when work started, people stopped and stared at the crews. But lately, he added, people have come out of their houses and expressed gratitude for the cleanup.

According to Shilling, one woman who lives in an apartment at Clove Road and Howard Avenue called to say that she had kept her window blinds closed for years because of the accumulation of trash in the lot.

"She said she keeps them open now," Shilling said.

Achieving this hasn't been easy.

Earl, who until this summer was the groundskeeper at the LaTourette Golf Course, said at least three men work along Howard Avenue every day restoring the area. Curves once shrouded in dead shrubbery are now clear for the first time, giving drivers an unimpeded view of traffic on the steep, winding hill.

"We've taken away between 30 and 40 truckloads of junk," he said.

And while three-man crews work eight-hour shifts doing intensive clean up on the property, others "police" the area three times a week, just keeping the area clear of trash left behind by illegal dumpers, Shilling said.

Come spring, the effort to keep the area beautiful will intensify. The Wagner College sign standing at the foot of Grymes Hill on Clove Road will be surrounded by flowers, said Shilling. And the land along the wooded side of Howard Avenue will be seeded to provide the area with some fresh greenery.

Dominick Fontano, the college's director of maintenance said the area looks better than it has in his 21 years with the college. "And we're going to keep it that way," he added.

Two members of the Wagner College maintenance crew spruce up the area around a sign at Howard Avenue and Clove Road.

Staten Island Advance March 1989

Transcript of "Wagner Crews keeping area spotless"

For the past several months, Wagner College employees have been raking leaves, trimming tree limbs and picking up trash which is what maintenance workers do all the time --- except the property they work on doesn't belong to the Grymes Hill school. In fact, Stanley R. Shilling, the school's director of auxiliary services doesn't know who owns the land that runs from Campus Road to the Staten Island Expressway. And it doesn't matter to him.

What does matter is that the land, once the property of the Augustinian Academy is ...or was...a mess. And that, he said, was unacceptable to Wagner president Norman Smith who is

trying his best to change the school from a college with a regional reputation into one of the nation's premier small liberal arts colleges.

According to Shilling, the property was an unofficial city dump. "You can't believe what we found out here," he said. "There were washing machines and refrigerators, TVs and tires. We even found dresses." The mess was also widespread extending from Narrows Road North and Clove Road all the way to the college grounds. And that, said college president Smith, was what set him off. Studies show that the single most significant factor in making up a parent's mind as to whether his child will attend a college is the campus visit and the condition of the facilities," he said.

Smith spent the first months of his presidency putting the campus in shape. In November, as the college prepared for its first open house during his tenure, he drove the paths prospective parents would take to the college and knew the conditions would reflect on the college. "They wouldn't know that we didn't own the land," he said. But after the open house, he insisted the condition be maintained. "I just feel this is a good neighborly thing to do," he said. "If everyone would clean up 50 yards around their house, this city would be spotless."

Smith's feelings of responsibility for the neighborhood's appearance is part of his Canadian upbringing," he said. "In Toronto, nobody would think of dropping a piece of paper on the ground. They'd carry it until they found a trash can," he said. "New Yorkers, on the other hand, often drop litter on the street even when they're near to a trash basket. I saw someone drop a lunch bag out a car window when he was parked right next to a trash can," Smith said. Smith's response was to go over, pick up the bag and dispose of it properly. "I didn't say a word to them," he said. "The driver just stared at me and drove away laughing."

The response to Wagner's clean-up efforts on Grymes Hill has been more appreciative, however. Maintenance department foreman Walter Earl said that when work started, people stopped and stared at the crews. But lately, he added, people have come out of their houses and expressed gratitude for the cleanup. According to Shilling, one woman who lives in an apartment at Clove Road and Howard Avenue called to say that her window blinds were closed for years because of the accumulation of trash in the lot. "She said she keeps them open now," Shilling said.

Achieving this hasn't been easy. Earl, who until this summer was the groundskeeper at the La Tourette Golf Course, said at least three men work along Howard Avenue every day restoring the area. Curves once shrouded in dead shrubbery are now clear for the first time, giving drivers an unimpeded view of traffic on the steep winding hill. "We've taken away between 30 and 40 truckloads of junk," he said. And while three-man crews work eight-hour shifts during intensive clean up on the property, others "police" the area three times a week just keeping the area clear of trash left behind by illegal dumpers, Shilling said.

Come spring, the effort to keep that area beautiful will intensify. The Wagner College sign standing at the foot of Grymes Hill on Clover Road will be surrounded by flowers, said Shilling. And the land along the wooded site of Howard Avenue will be seeded to provide the areas with fresh greenery.

Dominick Fontano, the college's director of maintenance said the area looks better than it has in his 21 years with the college "And we're going to keep it that way," he added.

Chapter 5
Running on Fumes

While Walter Earl, Stan Schilling, and Dom Fontano were attending to campus beautification, I had other problems to address during the summer of 1988 that prevented me from spending too much of my time on paint and greenery... although I did make it a point to set aside time as frequently as I could to wander about and let the crews know their efforts were making a difference. I got to know the names of everyone involved in the transformation and hoped that my ongoing involvement and compliments kept energy levels high on this most important, and too often thankless, undertaking.

College fiscal years typically end on June 30th. Wagner's ended on August 31st, which was not my doing but made a lot of sense to me. I have always questioned the June thirtieth ending for colleges because a new fiscal year beginning July 1 is two months before the beginning of the next school year. Thus, spending throughout the summer is based on enrollment tuition revenue anticipated for September but not realized until spending is well underway. If enrollments fall short of expectations, the spending already incurred during the summer based on unrealized revenues cannot be corrected and the academic year starts in financial trouble.

By beginning the new fiscal year in September, spending more closely coincides with actual enrollment income. For most colleges and universities that are over 90% dependent on enrollment revenues, budget adjustments are more feasible when the money hasn't already been spent. With the summer coming at the end of the fiscal year, summer spending projects can be cancelled if fall and spring enrollment revenues fall short of budget.

The wisdom of the Wagner fiscal-year cycle, however, didn't prevent the college from overspending each year — but at least we had the summer to recraft the 1988-1989 budget before the spending year began in September. We had to find at least two million dollars in budgeted expenses that could be cut to assure that the coming year had a chance of balancing. Wagner wasn't overspending; rather, it was '*under-revenuing.*' Short of a windfall multimillion-dollar gift for operating expenses, there were no other possible revenue increases for the coming year. The enrollment recruiting cycle was past and it looked like fewer than budgeted, not more, students were expected. And there was no way in June and July to increase those numbers in any meaningful way. So, the choice was to cut expenditure somewhere.

Upon surveying the budget, the first item that jumped out was the high level of scholarship aid, better labeled as "discounts" at an unendowed institution like Wagner, where scholarships are not being allocated from a fund but rather represent forgoing income. Wagner enrolled an unusually high number of staff and faculty children. In fact, it seemed like just about every clerical staff member had at least one child enrolled for a full tuition remission. Staff turnover was high and almost directly correlated with whether a child was enrolled. This, along with admissions recruiting aid, resulted in the college realizing less than 50% of the tuition it was charging. Over time, that level of discounting had to be brought down, but it wasn't likely for the coming year since commitments had already been made and could not legally be rescinded. As time went on, a variety of new controls were implemented that, over a decade, brought the discount level to under 30%, much more in line with comparable institutions.

Having quickly hired a professional financial aid director, Beatrice

Snyder, her audit of financial aid was already revealing some ways in which the problem could more immediately be addressed. She discovered, for example, that none of the staff or faculty were submitting applications for federal and state grants that their income levels often made them eligible to receive. Such grants added no financial burden to the faculty or staff member (i.e., they weren't loans), but did provide the college with some of the revenue being lost because of employee dependents who paid nothing. We implemented the requirement immediately and generated several hundred thousand dollars in additional revenues just like that.

Also discovered was a very high level of delinquent accounts. The controller, Richard Damon, explained that the college had not been aggressive in collecting delinquent tuition payments, fearing students would withdraw if they were being pursued to pay up or were charged interest for late payments. Some students were over two years in arrears and had not been charged any delinquent fees. Additionally, no one was prevented from enrolling, from moving into the dorms or from food service ... no matter how much they owed.

Bills for tuition usually go out twice a year, once in the summer for the fall semester, and once in December for the spring semester. I was told that less than 20% of the bills were paid on time. There were no incentives for early payment and no penalty for late payment. We changed that. The bills for the fall had not yet been sent out, so we inserted a note stating that on-time payments would be rewarded with a $200 bookstore credit. Late payments would accrue interest effectively immediately after the due date. Further, any delinquent accounts that exceeded a semester would result in being denied registration, room, and board.

Upon further digging, Bea Snyder discovered that a surprisingly large number of well-funded grant aid students were achieving very low grades. Many were on probation. Again, Richard Damon acknowledged that many students with high delinquencies eventually dropped out and never paid their bills — one of the contributing reasons, he surmised, for deficits — and certainly for the lack of cash.

Also participating in this budget review was a veteran assistant to the president, Dr. Norbert Leeseberg, someone I found to be enigmatic. A man of few words, at least when around me, "Leese" was seen by many as the man behind the scenes who really ran the college. Reverend Lyle Guttu had explained to me that the previous two presidents had both been very dependent on Leese to serve as chief of staff with authority comparable to an executive vice president or chief operating officer.

To me, Leese was a man of few words, close to the vest, and minimally forthcoming. I don't recall ever seeing him smile or say anything humorous, although many who had known him longer assured me there was another side to him that I wasn't experiencing.

Leese's office was down the hall from mine. It was a relatively small space crammed with trophies and plaques along with several hundred turtles. None of the turtles were alive, although one massive stuffed turtle startled first-time visitors with its realism. Leese was active throughout the Staten Island community, including the zoo. When a legendary large turtle died, Leese won possession and had it stuffed.

The plaques and trophies were all from Staten Island civic groups, primarily honoring Leese, and sometimes Wagner College. Every group from the zoo to Kiwanis to the Knights of Columbus had at one time or other made him their man of the year. "These awards are really for the college," he told me, noting that for decades he had been the college's town-and-gown link, maintaining what he thought were important and obligatory ties. I asked him if any of his efforts benefited the college financially. That is, did these groups ever donate anything to the college?

The man of few words would only respond by saying "Wagner benefits greatly from all this." Most certainly, Leese did. He was known throughout Staten Island as "Mr. Wagner" as I learned everywhere I went on my meet-the-community visits.

At some point, away from Leese's ear, Richard Damon came to me with a budget savings he thought would be substantial if I dared to take it on. He revealed that a massive amount of Wagner money was spent, via Leeseberg, on community civic groups. Every time a civic group had a dinner or fundraiser, Leese would volunteer Wagner as a benefactor.

Whole tables would be bought at luncheons and dinners, routinely selling for $800 for a table of eight, and sometimes much more. Full-page Wagner ads were bought in every fundraising journal. Many groups had their monthly dinner meetings at Wagner. Leeseberg would offer both the meeting rooms and the food, often banquets, compliments of the college — all in the spirit of fostering good community relations.

Damon estimated that several hundred thousand dollars a year, maybe more, in such town-and-gown goodwill activities were distributed by Leeseberg. All this money was unbudgeted, the actual costs buried in administrative accounts throughout the budget. This contributed to the massive deficits that prevented payment of delinquent bills for gasoline, books, and food.

To my disappointment, I learned that virtually no Staten Island organization donated to Wagner, and none of the groups receiving support from Wagner were solicited in college fundraising campaigns. Leeseberg seemed to view Wagner as having a corporate-like financial responsibility to the community, rather than viewing the college as the same kind of nonprofit entity as all the groups seeking and receiving Wagner largess. In fact, some of the groups were more profit driven than Wagner. The Chamber of Commerce, for example, was one of Leese's benefactors that instead should have been a donor *to* Wagner.

I told Leese that while his intentions to position the College in good standing with the community were appreciated, the generosity had to end, at least until Wagner was extremely well footed financially. I knew from my past, for instance, that Harvard University would donate substantial amounts to the city of Cambridge to help underwrite, among other things, police, and fire services — even though Harvard had its own police and fire department. But Harvard also had a multibillion-dollar endowment. Wagner couldn't even pay its bills or payroll. Until it could, the college would no longer donate to any organization on Staten Island or elsewhere. Anyone wishing to use the college's facilities and food should either pay for it or donate an amount that covered the costs, or both. The Wagner "foundation" was closed.

Leese warned I was making a terrible mistake that would alienate the college from the community. I retorted that I had a responsibility, first and foremost, to the students and their families, from whose pockets this generosity came, often with a struggle that meant sacrifices for the family. Tuition payments had to first pay for what it cost to provide students with their education — not for community organization banquets.

Hopefully, if Damon was right, another quarter-million dollars had been sliced from next year's budget. We were making progress.

Another big expenditure was an Austrian campus run by Wagner that was a College pride and joy. Each semester dozens of Wagner students would fly to Bregenz, Austria, a small resort town on Lake Constance near both Switzerland and Germany. Everyone who ever went invariably recalled the semester as one of the most memorable facets of their Wagner education. The costs of this program were viewed as minimal; the Bregenz government provided the facility for a trifle, and the students lived with local families. That was earlier on. In more recent years, the families no longer housed students because the town had become a yuppie resort and was much more expensive than decades earlier. As for cost, the tuition, room, and board revenues that would otherwise stay on the Staten Island campus were sent to Bregenz to cover staff and instructional costs there.

Upon closer examination, $500,000 a year was sent to Bregenz. But it was worse than that. Most of the students attending Bregenz were faculty and staff children who were paying nothing to attend Wagner. Thus, the majority of the money being sent over came from the tuition payments of other students who weren't attending Bregenz. As much as I advocated study-abroad experiences, Wagner couldn't justify the double-dip subsidization of nonpaying attendees. We therefore inaugurated a policy that no grant aid, including employee tuition remission, would be sent to Bregenz. Thus, a student with a 50% Wagner grant would have to pay that 50% extra for the Bregenz semester. Fully remitted staff dependents would pay the full semester's tuition, room, and board.

This policy would either reduce the number of students participating, thereby concurrently reducing the amount of lost revenues, or it would increase revenues from nonpayers. Either way, the budget was better off. What did happen was that the program closed within two years. Few came forward to pay the cost of attending Bregenz, especially faculty and staff freebies, and enrollments disappeared.

The program was destined to end anyway. In the fall of 1988, Bregenz town officials wanted their building back. There was no replacement facility available, except at a very high cost. We subsequently affiliated with the Institute of International Education, a large New York-based study-abroad organization offering semester study-abroad programs in all the major capitals of the world, thereby greatly expanding the choices available to students while saving Wagner over $500,000 annually.

Whenever a college budget is being assessed for savings, it is almost impossible not to look at personnel costs. Colleges are very labor intense, making salaries the largest expense item. But there weren't excess personnel that could generate cost savings. The administration wasn't particularly top heavy. In fact, the fundraising staff was minuscule and not even what was needed to start working on major improvements in donations. The admissions staff wasn't large, nor was the business office or registrar.

Where I did notice some overstaffing was in certain areas of the faculty that had not downsized to accommodate enrollment declines, some of which had dropped by half or more in the last decade. Nursing had as many full-time faculty as the business program — which enrolled three times as many majors. The religion faculty was much larger than the number of courses being offered. Some faculty, as a result, had very light teaching loads compared to others.

Terminating underutilized faculty is not easy, and probably not advisable under any circumstances for a new president. Besides, the faculty was heavily tenured, with veteran faculty that had been there for decades. During the enrollment declines of the 1970s and 80s, too many of the best younger faculty began to see the handwriting on the wall and moved on to greener pastures. The older, more entrenched faculty didn't want to start over again, and stayed around. To start terminating these folks now would most certainly launch AAUP

(American Association of University Professors) censure and greatly bring down morale at a time when morale needed a boost.

At the same time, there were several important, and expensive, administrative positions that needed to be filled. The vice presidents of administration and finance, development, and admissions all were open and couldn't be left vacant without consequence. The registrar was retiring and most certainly needed to be replaced.

Then it occurred to me ... Could underutilized faculty fill any of the open positions, even for a couple of years until there was more money, and, for that matter, until top administrators could be recruited to the college? I started to look through the faculty for people who might work.

The first place I looked was the under-enrolled nursing program, where I found two bright and delightful veterans who would remain administrators for my entire fourteen years. Professor Mildred Nelson became a first-rate registrar who also assumed the interim provost's job when such an appointment became necessary a few years later. She was a great colleague and a counselor I routinely sought and respected. I couldn't have found anyone better anywhere.

Connie Schuyler, also a nursing professor, joined the administration, becoming Mildred's associate in the registrar's office while also overseeing graduate programs. Connie was a bright, upbeat can-do administrator who took on whatever she was asked to do and did it exceptionally with a smile.

I very much wanted to launch an academic awards program, for example, which culminated in a parent-student dinner each year. Up until then, the only annual awards gathering was for athletes. Connie took care of the entire program, which became one of the highlights of the college year. I am forever grateful to Mildred and Connie.

Moving Connie and Mildred to the administration also represented two less budgeted salaries in the overstaffed nursing faculty by now filling two administrative posts, thereby eliminating the need for those budget lines. Their combined costs represented another six-figure budgetary solution.

We were getting remarkably closer than originally seemed possible to finding the two million dollars savings we needed for the coming year's budget.

Archival

Mildred Nelson (left) and Connie Schuyler being lauded at Commencement

Chapter 6
A Tough Sell

Along with campus improvements and budget redesign, the other major priority during my first summer as president was to get admissions better positioned in time for the recruitment of the fall 1989 freshman class, a process that begins at least one year earlier, in this case the fall of 1988. The process starts even earlier because marketing materials have to be ready for distribution in the fall and therefore have to be prepared by the summer.

Meeting the admissions staff was at the top of my agenda, and I was alarmed with what I discovered. Here was a most beleaguered group of sales personnel, reminiscent of the haunting David Mamet play *Glengarry Glen Ross*, depicting a team of burned-out salesmen trying to talk naïve prospects into buying retirement homes on yet-to-be-developed land in the middle of nowhere.

In fairness, the admissions staff's defeated spirit could be explained considering what they'd had to accomplish for years. Given the condition of Wagner College, the admissions recruiters may not have been wrong in their assessment that they had nothing to sell. Too many times, they had taken prospective students and families on tours of the dirty, unkempt campus, going into classrooms that were comparable to urban ghetto schools and dorm rooms that wouldn't be suitable for interned felons. Except for the great hilltop views, there was little else, perhaps nothing else, to showcase.

The promised dawning of a new day was only achievable with a surge of 'can-do' adrenalin from admissions. While they nodded hopefully, I feared this group might not be able to revitalize itself. They needed new leadership. Where could we find someone good enough who could/would come on board for the fall recruiting season at this late date — especially to a risky venture like Wagner? And that someone was needed immediately if there was any hope of better outcomes by the fall. Until new leadership was found, I decided to personally oversee the preparation of new marketing materials, which had been delegated to a consulting firm that was charging a substantial fee for their services. I didn't like any of the admissions materials they had prepared. By my standard, the materials were not impressive and didn't even convey graphic quality. The photographs were grainy, the color second rate.

I had never heard of the consulting firm, which will remain nameless, and I knew no one in higher education who had ever hired them. Their only clients appeared to be among the Lutheran-founded institutions. Upon meeting them, I was even more convinced that they were wrong for Wagner College. Unfortunately, the firm had negotiated a multiyear contract that would represent another $150,000 consulting fee for the coming year. That was an amount that could represent *other* meaningful savings if there was a way of cancelling because there was nothing of value likely to come from yet another year of their services.

The consultants became aware of my disapproval and started to appeal to contacts they had within the college. Within a week or two of my first confrontation, I received a call from a former colleague at Moore College in Philadelphia, where I had been executive vice president earlier in my career. The call was from an admissions officer whom I knew well. She told me that she had received a call from a consulting company, and did I know anything about them? I said that Wagner had a contract with them. She reported that the owner of the company told her she had been recommended to them as a particularly talented admissions executive who might be interested in doing some lucrative consulting on the side for a considerable fee.

I encouraged her to express an interest in knowing more about the "opportunity," and a meeting was arranged. At the meeting, the conversation quickly reverted to me. She was asked what she thought of me and whether I had been an effective executive vice president. They were probing her with questions about whether I was popular or if anyone disliked me.

The consulting firm, it seemed, was hoping to find a skeleton in the closet that might challenge my credibility to continue as president of Wagner, perhaps even lead to my ousting, thereby securing their continued revenue stream. In some ways, their action may well have been a godsend. I was able to confront them, and they willingly agreed to cancel the contract for the coming year if I agreed not to challenge their professional integrity. It was a deal. Another $150,000 was saved from next year's budget.

Although I had taken a hands-on role in the admissions marketing materials, I knew I wasn't going to have time to manage the staff throughout the fall. Could we find a Mildred Nelson or a Connie Schuyler within the faculty who could take on the admissions job? The nursing faculty had given up two winners, but no one else there seemed right — or interested — in the admissions job.

Throughout the summer of 1988, I was on Staten Island without my wife Susan, who remained in Philadelphia as dean of admissions and financial aid at Moore College of Art. We were without the housing we thought we needed, and I was living out of a suitcase. I seized the opportunity to let it be known to faculty and staff that I would welcome invitations to dinner. Many called me, which proved to be a great way to launch close relationships that would be cemented in the next decade and a half.

One omnipresent faculty member was a religion professor, Dr.

Joseph (Joedy) Smith. Smith had an impressive academic background with something like four or five degrees from Yale University. I don't remember the details, but he stayed at Yale for years accumulating one degree after another. Joedy was unique. He was very articulate and always impeccably dressed. He was an ordained minister, although I never saw him perform a service or do anything I would consider pastoral. Joedy had opinions about everything. I was drawn to his interest in Wagner and his attentiveness. I started talking to him about the admissions challenge, and he was animated in his views. He seemed to have good taste, knew all the students and staff, and presented himself in a way that had the potential of making a good impression with prospective students and their parents. His Yale background was another plus for the parents I was hoping to interest in Wagner.

Maybe Joedy might want to take a shot at the admissions job, at least for the coming year.

As a religion professor with an elective course teaching load, his teaching load wasn't essential to anyone majoring in a discipline, so his use in admissions could also be a financial offset to the operating budget, as he, like Mildred and Connie, wouldn't have to be replaced on the faculty. He might just be a short-term solution until funds became available to recruit a top shelf admissions dean.

The admissions staff reacted favorably to the prospect of Joedy's leadership, as he was already involved in admissions recruiting as a faculty spokesperson. Joedy was often called upon by admissions to make presentations to prospective students when they wanted to show off an erudite articulate faculty member. By all reports, Joedy did a laudable job selling Wagner to prospective families. That was good enough for me — particularly considering the lack of options I had available. I decided to take a chance.

We now had admissions leadership, I hoped, while also saving another major position cost in the coming year's operating budget.

Chapter 7
My First Fall Semester

September 1988 marked little more than three months into my presidency, yet much was different at Wagner College already. Carlyle Haaland, who had returned to the academic vice presidency after I fully assumed presidential responsibilities, was now leaving altogether to join the educational division of the Lutheran church. Understandably, he had not been happy returning to his old job as academic vice president. With Lyle's assistance, I met with the education director of the Lutheran Church, Jim Unglaube, who crafted a role for Carlyle that appealed to him. Wagner helped fund the launch of the position and all was well that ended well. Carlyle would go on to become the president of Thiel College, a small Lutheran college in Pennsylvania, from where he retired.

With Carlyle Haaland now departed, the academic vice presidency also had to be filled, and I had been pondering how to proceed. An external appointment seemed out of the question without an interim for the existing academic year. External searches for senior academic positions, especially presidents and academic vice presidents, typically take an entire academic year. Recruiting a top-rate academic leader to an institution that remained precariously fragile might reduce the candidate pool, but the larger problem was the need to maintain fiscal balance after having taken two million dollars out of an already lean budget. There were no provisions for high executive salaries. So, shopping around the faculty once again seemed most practical.

I assembled a faculty advisory group to recommend someone, and they proceeded to go through the possibilities. During this time, several people were individually passing along their suggestions to me. One professor frequently cited was Eleanor Rogg, a sociology professor with a big smile and an unswerving enthusiasm for just about everything.

Ellie, as she was known, was a professor of sociology who was trusted and liked by virtually everyone I consulted. Ellie was also very popular with students and received high grades in faculty evaluations. No one on the faculty seemed threatened by her, and a lot of folks thought she would make a good academic leader, although most saw her as an interim vice president, not a permanent one. She would be the first female VP at Wagner, which also appealed to me.

So, we met to talk about the job. She expressed an almost immediate interest, which sounded good to me. The faculty advisory group seemed fine with the prospect of appointing Ellie. I felt the prevailing sentiment was that she was not a threat — she had no enemies and therefore would be the best choice until Wagner could afford to recruit and hire a properly experienced chief academic officer. That she had spent her entire career at Wagner was seen as a problem for the long term. What Wagner needed was an academic leader from an institution that Wagner would want to emulate. Finding such a person, much less affording the salary, was a project somewhere into the future. I decided to go with Ellie with the understanding that we would take it a semester at a time and hope for the best.

As expected, the enrollments were down for the fall, but the budget had been successfully readjusted during the summer to find two million dollars in savings. Most of the vacant senior positions were being filled—at least temporarily—by underutilized faculty. The grant aid budget was being adjusted by placing minimum academic standards on grant recipients, which proved to be a one-million-dollar savings. Consulting fees had been saved. Largess to community groups was over. Delinquent payments would no longer be tolerated.

Everyone noticed the changes to the campus that we had spent the summer working to accomplish. Most notably, the grounds looked much better thanks to Walter Earl and his crew. Graffiti was nowhere to be seen, and most high-traffic buildings had been painted and were now at least presentable. Cars no longer parked on the grass or against the front doors of buildings. Students were particularly grateful for the improved dormitory conditions, although much was still needed there. A new Wagner was in the making, and many were beginning to think that something better might just actually happen.

Throughout the summer, and now into the fall, I continued my efforts to build relationships with trustees, faculty, staff, and community.

I spent many evenings wandering the campus in search of the *Staten Island Advance* editor, Les Trautman who was becoming a friend and advocate. He could see that the campus was looking much better, which even made his evening walks more enjoyable. Les started sending me notes of advice and invited me to write a college advice column for the newspaper, something I did weekly for years.

Al Corbin was a regular visitor and was very supportive of the new operating budget, understandably his greatest concern.

One of my highest priorities was Don Spiro, who had agreed to join the board of trustees and whom I already had started promoting to become the next chairman. Part of Wagner's future potential was going to be its ability to build a stronger foundation, and that included a more effective giving program.

As the old saying goes, "the fish smells from the head down," meaning, obviously, that the example, good or bad, is set by the top leadership, which then becomes the standard for the rest of the organization. Major gifts were not likely if the chairman of the board wasn't setting an example for others to emulate.

Someone like Don was needed, not only as a giving example, but also as a trustee exemplar. Power attracts power. Wagner needed a board of trustees with lots of Don Spiros.

Don was interested in taking the helm and agreed with me that we needed to find a new cadre of trustees who could open doors. One of the first people Don found was Phil Dusenberry, chairman of BBDO advertising agency. Phil hadn't graduated from college and therefore had no alma mater courting him. He was one of the legendary superstars of advertising. His firm had many of the largest advertising accounts in the country, and he had created several iconic campaigns including the Michael Jackson Pepsi commercials — well before Jackson became the controversial celebrity until his death. Phil also wrote the screenplay for the Robert Redford movie, *The Natural.*

Wagner hopes its new trustee will make everything 'ad' up

BBDO chief Dusenberry a star in advertising world

... most important of all (Phil Dusenberry) has advertising and marketing advice to offer Wagner College. (Dusenberry) said Wagner could benefit from the type of TV and newspaper advertising that helped Hofstra University on Long Island increase its enrollment.

Staten Island Advance

We wanted to find an opportunity to award Phil an honorary degree, making Wagner his only alma mater, not to mention, of course, honoring his career achievements. Don asked Phil to join the board of trustees and he agreed. The board building process was underway.

I proceeded to lobby with Trustees to build support for Don Spiro to become chairman. The board officers are re-elected annually, so the changeover to Spiro seemed doable in the spring 1989 elections. Al Corbin and Kevin Sheehy, the board's treasurer and secretary, were both bullish about the prospect and committed themselves to lining up the votes. Jay Hartig, the current chair, seemed ready to step down, agreeing that the college could greatly benefit from Don's leadership, even though Howard Meyers, the vice chair, had reportedly expected to succeed him.

Jay and Howard were among those trustees who continued to advocate the long term renting of 'excessive' campus, a "strategy" I did not support. I continued to insist that the enrollment could double, and the existing campus and residence halls would someday be anything but excessive. Thankfully, Don and others were supportive of my vision of building a great college that would need all the land it presently had, and maybe more.

My first truly uplifting moment since arriving at Wagner was perfectly timed, although coincidentally, to correspond with my forty-second birthday. On that eve, the *Staten Island Advance* published a large feature article with the headline:

"New Wagner optimism credited to Smith."

The article read:

Wagner College's new president, Norman R. Smith, seems to have taken the Grymes Hill campus by storm and sparked an infectious optimism about the school's ability to rout the financial problems that have beset it for the past several years.

An informal survey of faculty, non-teaching staff and students over the past three months shows a complete elimination of the air of pessimism that pervaded the 106-year-old school at the end of the 1987-88 school year. Student leaders and professors then not only questioned the school's leadership, but whether the school would survive.

Smith has also served as a healer, drawing together factions that only last year were fighting bitterly as the school went through a turbulent search for a new president. In interview and interview, Smith was singled out as the cause of the sudden burst of hope and commitment energizing the campus. Egon Wendel, chairman of the school's education department said "there's no doubt" that the changed atmosphere was emanating directly from the president. Smith, he said, has spread "a lot of good will" on the campus. According to Wendel, Smith was keeping the faculty fully "aware of what's going on in the administration."

C. Carlyle Haaland, the school's former vice president for academic affairs, who had served as provost and chief executive for the year the college was without a president, had been criticized for his inaccessibility and for failing to involve faculty and students in the decision-making process. Haaland, who resigned shortly after Smith was selected, had been considered to have the inside track on the job. His candidacy for the college's presidency was strongly supported by some professors while vehemently opposed by others.

Dr. Eleanor Rogg, the acting vice president for academic affairs, said Smith more than makes himself available for faculty and student input. He seeks it out. "He's almost never in his office." she said. "He's out walking around the campus, stopping people and talking to them." Student government association president Joseph Watson said he had seen Smith stop students to simply ask their names and find out if they were satisfied with the school's new food service or their dormitory accommodations. This concern with what others think and feel about the college, Ms. Rogg said, has released a current of energy as everyone pitches in to help the school.

During recent renovations of the Wagner dorms, a focal point of students' complaints about the school last year, school administrators were seen splashing paint on the walls while contractors installed new tile in the showers to meet tight deadlines. "It was like a dam burst," she said. "Everyone had ideas that just came pouring out."

But at the same time, she said, Smith was not garnering the same reputation as Sam Frank, who was well liked but considered by some to be an ineffectual executive. "He challenges us," she said. An example of the demands placed on the staff came at the outset of Smith's official tenure in July when he ordered the massive rehabilitation of all areas used by students within 80 days. Student government president Watson said the efforts to improve student housing were immediately noticed --- and appreciated.

One faculty member told of yet another angle. He was told Smith wanted to meet with him, so he suggested 11 am. "Oh," he was told, "that's when he will be fundraising on Wall Street." The time shortly after lunch was arranged.

Smith also appointed two faculty members --- Ms. Rogg, who headed the sociology-anthropology department, and Joseph D. Smith (no relation), an associate professor of religious studies --- to interim administrative positions left open when dean of admissions James Keating and Haaland resigned. Joseph D. Smith and Ms. Rogg will serve until permanent replacements are found by search committees. When Norman Smith announced Ms. Rogg's appointment to the administrative post, he noted that one of his reasons was her ability to serve as a bridge between faculty factions. "My loyalty has been to the college as an institution," she said. Both Joseph Smith and Ms. Rogg say they are not interested in holding administrative offices permanently. Yet both also see their new duties as a challenge. Ms.

Rogg said she hopes to institute several new academic programs that will help re-establish the school's academic reputation.

But even those professors not playing an active role in the College's renewal say the mood has improved. Artist Athos Zacarias said his contact with the new president has been infrequent, but meaningful. I believe he is going to be very good for the college," he said

Island news — STATEN ISLAND SUNDAY ADVANCE ■ SUNDAY, OCTOBER 23, 1988

New Wagner optimism credited to Smith

By DON GROSS
ADVANCE STAFF WRITER

Wagner College's new president, Norman R. Smith, seems to have taken the Grymes Hill campus by storm and sparked an infectious optimism about the school's ability to rout the financial problems that have beset it for the past several years.

An informal survey of faculty, non-teaching staff and students over the past three months shows a complete elimination of the air of pessimism that pervaded the 106-year-old school at the end of the 1987-88 school year. Student leaders and professors then not only questioned the school's leadership, but whether the school would survive.

Smith has also served as a healer, drawing together factions that only last year were fighting bitterly as the school went through a turbulent search for a new president.

In interview after interview, Smith was singled out as the cause of the sudden burst of hope and commitment energizing the campus.

Egon Wendel, chairman of the school's education department said "there's no doubt" that the changed atmosphere was emanating directly from the president.

Smith, he said, has spread "a lot of good will" on the campus.

According to Wendel, Smith was keeping the faculty fully "aware of what's going on in the administration."

C. Carlyle Haaland, the school's former vice president for academic affairs, who had served as provost and chief executive for the year the college was without a president, had been criticized for his inaccessability and for failing to involve faculty and students in the decision-making process.

Haaland, who resigned shortly after Smith was selected, had been considered to have the inside track on the job. His candidacy for the college's presidency was strongly supported by some professors while vehemently opposed by others.

Dr. Eleanor Rogg, the acting vice president for academic affairs, said Smith more than makes himself available for faculty and student input, he seeks it out.

"He's almost never in his office," she said. "He's out walking around the campus, stopping people and talking to them."

Student government association president Joseph Watson said he had seen Smith stop students to simply ask their names and find out if they were satisfied with the school's new food service or their dormitory accommodations.

This concern with what others think and feel about the college, Ms. Rogg said, has released a current of energy as everyone pitches in to help the school.

During recent renovations of the Wagner dorms, a focal point of student complaints about the school last year, school administrators were seen splashing paint on the walls while contractors installed new tile in the showers in order to meet tight deadlines.

"It was like a dam burst," she said. "Everyone had ideas that just came pouring out."

But at the same time, she said, Smith was not garnering the same reputation as Sam Frank, who was well liked but considered by some to be an ineffectual executive.

"He challenges us," she said.

An example of the demands placed on the staff came at the outset of Smith's official tenure in July when he ordered the massive rehabilitation of all areas used by students within 80 days.

Student government president Watson said the efforts to improve student housing were immediately noticed — and appreciated.

One faculty member told of yet another angle. He was told Smith wanted to meet with him, so he suggested 11 a.m. "Oh," he was told, "that's when he will be fund-

ADVANCE PHOTO/FRANK J. JOHNS

Norman R. Smith

raising on Wall Street." A time shortly after lunch was arranged.

Smith also appointed two faculty members — Ms. Rogg, who headed the sociology-anthropology department, and Joseph D. Smith (no relation), an associate professor of religious studies — to interim administrative positions left open when dean of admissions James Keating and Haaland resigned. Joseph D. Smith and Ms. Rogg will serve until permanent replacements are found by search committees.

When Norman Smith announced Ms. Rogg's appointment to the administrative post, he noted that one of his reasons was her ability to serve as a bridge between faculty factions. "My loyalty has been to the college as an institution," she said.

Both Joseph Smith and Ms. Rogg say they are not interested in holding administrative offices permanently. Yet both also see their new duties as a challenge.

Ms. Rogg said she hopes to institute several new academic programs that will help re-establish the school's academic reputation.

Joseph Smith, in the meantime, has hired an entirely new admissions staff that is actively going out to high schools recruiting prospective students.

But even those professors not playing an active role in the college's renewal say the mood has improved.

Artist Athos Zacharias said his contact with the new president has been infrequent, but meaningful.

"I believe he's going to be very good for the college," he said.

Staten Island Advance October 23, 1988

In an accompanying editorial, *Advance* editor Les Trautmann wrote:

"Norman Smith came to campus like a strong, fresh breeze on a smotheringly (sic) hot summer's day. He revived the life, rallied the troops, gave new hope, and beautified the campus and the immediate neighborhood. Wagner indeed has a leader again. Tough problems remain and dog him, but he has wiped away fears that they won't be overcome."

Les' articles inspired everyone to believe that Wagner could be a successful college. Too many people had been through endless tough and discouraging years and had lost hope. That spirit adversely affected their productivity and the way in which they spoke of Wagner to others. Even the admissions recruiters had lost the will to cheerlead for Wagner, but the *Advance* coverage of hopeful news affirmed what everyone was seeing — and from a more credible source than anything we could have published internally.

As fall started, I had tired of living out of a suitcase in a tiny bungalow called the President's House. Past president John Satterfield had acquired the house by selling a much larger president's house for a quite modest sum. Having spent a few unpleasant weeks in the Satterfield house, I didn't want to move in permanently, and neither did Susan. I didn't think it worked for what I had hoped the president's role would be. Yet with the college needing to watch every penny, a president's house had to rank lower than a lot of other overdue needs.

I shared my concern with my most supportive trustees, including Don Spiro, Al Corbin, and Kevin Sheehy, who all sympathized with me.

The past two presidents, I was told, rarely entertained and, as a result, the fundraising outcomes during their administrations were modest at best. The college had never received a million-dollar gift and rarely saw six figures. Gifts more than $10,000 were few and far between. The campus itself had no grand gathering rooms where social events could take place, with the exception, perhaps, of the president's office, a very large space that, with furniture pushed against the walls, could probably accommodate sixty or seventy standees. I often had receptions there because of the breathtaking panoramic view of the New York harbor and the Atlantic Ocean.

Don Spiro and Tom Russo referred me to a real estate agent, Hank Percurio, who said he knew of a house down the street from the college that had been sitting empty for years. The house was a massive turn-of-the-century mansion less than a mile from Wagner. It sat on nearly two acres of land that had the same overlook as the college. Originally built for a wealthy importer, it was owned by Avery Gross, a personal injury lawyer who had inherited the house with his siblings. Avery had grown up in the house, which, during his childhood, had even been used as a yeshiva. He had occasionally rented it out, once to the pop singer Roberta Flack. For years, though, it was empty.

Hank took me to visit and, although it was 'tired' with an ancient kitchen and original bathrooms 19th century, the main rooms were beautiful with block wood paneling and marble fireplaces. The main front room was large enough to entertain at least one hundred people.

Avery Gross was hoping to eventually sell the property and he wanted two million for it, a massive sum in 1988 for anything on Staten Island. In lieu of sale, he offered a three-year lease at a fixed monthly rate of $5,000, below what he considered market value, on the condition that the college would take care of routine maintenance.

Norman Smith

79 Howard Avenue would be the Wagner College President's House and our home for fourteen wonderful years. It was a great house for entertaining and, as grand as it appears in this photograph. Unfortunately, the college was never able to acquire it, and it was finally sold in 2009 to become an Italian American cultural center.

With board authorization, we leased the house. Susan left Philadelphia to move up to Staten Island with me. Almost immediately, we had faculty and staff gatherings, albeit rather modest events, as we wanted everyone to see the house and hopefully understand how we planned to use it to generate interest in and support of the college. To that end, I hosted the college's first faculty in-service two-day workshop. Most agreed that it helped make a positive statement that was part of what Wagner was trying to become.

The community was also getting excited and supportive about Wagner's progress. The borough president, Ralph Lamberti, was generous in his accolades. Early on, he invited me to Borough Hall and then offered to host a welcoming ceremony, also in Borough Hall, for the entire Wagner faculty and staff. It was an evening gathering, and the turnout was very large.

Ralph made a speech about the dawning of a new day for the college and how he was behind me.

Many faculty and staff remarked that it was one of the most exciting events that had happened for Wagner College for a very long time.

Community welcomes Wagner president

"Community welcomes…" transcript:

Members of the Wagner College community joined civic leaders and Borough President Ralph J. Lamberti last night in Borough Hall to welcome the school's new president, Dr. Norman R. Smith and his wife to the community and to praise a blossoming partnership.

I have said before that Wagner College must reach out to the community, be a part of it, Lamberti said in a welcoming speech before nearly 100 guests. "I couldn't believe that every event I was going to you were there before me," he said with a laugh.

Smith and his wife, Dr. Susan Robinson came to Staten Island seven months ago when he was appointed Wagner's 17th president replacing Dr. Sam Frank who resigned a year and a half ago after serving six years. "There's a real partnership present which makes this a very special place," Smith said earlier in the evening. "That's what we are with Staten Island: partners." Smith and his wife both praised Staten Island's civic leaders for the efforts of welcome and assistance.

"The spirit of support I've received from the borough president has been a key to my energies," Smith said during a conversation just outside the reception area. "It's not a job you can do alone and Wagner, in my judgment, has the potential to be a nationally visible symbol for Staten Island," he added.

The talk throughout the evening was of the optimism brought by Smith to the Grymes Hill college recently beset by financial problems stemming from declining enrollment. "You came to our borough with enthusiasm and excitement we haven't seen in some time," Lamberti said as guests shook their heads in agreement.

He's energized the entire faculty," said Dr. Eleanor Rogg, Wagner's acting vice president for academic affairs over Irish coffee. Dr. Rogg said Smith has made a name for himself by the changes he's made in the physical plant, academic areas and admissions.

"It's going swimmingly. He's given people a sense of the fact that it can be done," said the Rev. Thomas F. Mugavero, pastor of the Trinity Lutheran Church, Stapleton and a member of the college's board of trustees.

Howard G. Meyers, vice chairman of the board of trustees agreed saying Smith has brought long awaited action to the small liberal arts college. "The difference is that we're not talking about the problems anymore. We're addressing them in a very real way," he said, adding that Smith has made an impact on the community through his contacts with it. "People are think there really is something to Wagner College."

The talk always rolled around to Smith, who holds a doctorate in education from Harvard University.

"We're here tonight to tell Wagner College's new president and his wife we open our arms to you. We welcome you to our town," Lamberti said.

Wagner alumni praise school's new direction

Excerpted from "*Wagner alumni praise..*"

Growth and good friends were the key words last night as Wagner College opened its doors to welcome and honor students, faculty and alumni at the Wagner Alumni Association's annual awards and reunion dinner.

Everyone present had praise for Wagner College and especially for Smith. As Donald Spiro, Class of 1949, who will be taking over as Chairman of the Board of Trustees, put it "The attitude and the impression of the people who have returned is amazement at the positive outlook of the school which, of course, is the result of the enthusiastic leadership of Dr. Smith. He's made so many positive changes."

Kevin Sheehy, Class of 1967, who lauded not only Smith, but also Spiro, stated, "The team of Smith and Spiro will lead and expand this college into the 21st century." One of the honored alumni, Mario Esposito, reflected on his former classmates. "This is a great school with great people. With the new president at the helm, it is really growing."

As important as having found an academic leader in Ellie Rogg was the need for a vice president for development. This was a position in need of a superstar who could not only run a good development office, but also help locate and court major donors including a new board of trustees with the resources and wherewithal to think great things for Wagner and not break into a cold sweat when contemplating million-dollar largess.

The development VP was one position that was not going to be found within the faculty. We needed to find someone who had succeeded elsewhere and who could bring that experience to Wagner.

I had no idea where to begin, and then Susan had a suggestion. She recalled the vice president for development of Skidmore College in Saratoga Springs, NY, her undergraduate alma mater. Susan and I had attended Skidmore alumni receptions, including one for the new president at the Franklin Institute in Philadelphia, where we met David Long, Skidmore's venerable chief fundraiser.

David is a quintessential patrician. He is a slighter version, meaning less tall, of Alistair Cooke — without the British accent. David was one of the nationally regarded deans of college fundraising and, I thought, most certainly would know people who could be right for Wagner.

I called David, and he remembered Susan and me. He said had never seen Wagner College and would have trouble recommending anyone to a college he didn't know. I asked him if he was planning to be in New York City anytime soon and he said that he often visited, as many of Skidmore's trustees and donors lived in Manhattan. "The next time you are in the city, let me send a car over to Manhattan, and you can come out and visit," I proposed.

Within a week or two, the date was set for David's visit. Luckily, it turned out to be a beautiful day. The college's panoramic views of the Manhattan skyline and the Atlantic Ocean would be at their best. As I walked David around the campus, he turned to me and said "Norman, this place is breathtaking. Why isn't it rich and famous?" I responded "My feelings exactly. But it's not too late for this place to become rich and famous, and that is my intended destiny for Wagner."

I recounted my version of what had gone wrong and what was needed to get the college reignited. David reminisced about his earlier days at Skidmore and how many similarities he saw between Wagner and Skidmore. "What you have here at Wagner is very much like Skidmore when I first started there," he recounted. "Skidmore had great potential that was realized, and I think you can do the same for Wagner." "I can't do it alone, David," I responded. "Wagner won't be what it can be unless some major benefactors come forward." David said he would put his thinking cap on and try to locate someone who could help me get there.

I asked him how things were at Skidmore now that there was a new president. David had worked for decades in tandem with Joseph Palamountain, a legendary college president who had died two years earlier. During the Palamountain years, Skidmore had built a new campus funded by the impressive outcomes achieved during their fundraising partnership. David responded, somewhat poignantly, that since Palamountain's departure, he felt like he was in a new job at a new institution. He had had a great run with Palamountain, which makes for tough shoes for any successor to fill.

I posed, "If Skidmore is feeling like a new job, why not throw caution to the wind and instead do for Wagner what you did for Skidmore? You might enjoy a few years near Manhattan before your retirement." He quickly shrugged it away with a smile and a gracious *thank you, but no.* I suggested that he think about it and talk to his wife, Jody, who was deputy superintendent of Saratoga Springs schools — and would probably not want to leave that job, David added.

I said I understood but couldn't help but propose what would represent a bonanza for Wagner College. We parted and I didn't hear from David again for a week or so. Then I received a phone call from him. "I talked it over with Jody, and she thinks it might be fun for me to take on the Wagner job. Besides, I think you have what it takes to be Wagner's Joe Palamountain, and I would like to be part of that." That was about the best compliment I had ever received.

Divine Providence was looking over Wagner College. I immediately arranged for David to meet Don Spiro and a few other trustees, all of whom couldn't believe we had hit such pay dirt.

NORMAN R. SMITH

Norman Smith

David Long

Chapter 8
The David Long 'X Factor'

Probably the most important facet of David Long's decision to come to Wagner was that he lent credibility to my "delusions of grandeur." Even my harshest cynics were caught off balance with David's enlistment and appeared to now be acquiescing that maybe, just maybe, I might be right about Wagner's "unlimited" future. Why would someone of David Long's legendary stature risk his career unless Wagner could legitimately reach for the stars?

I felt like I had just bought a rare, classic Rolls-Royce. I wanted to drive David everywhere for all to see. And that is exactly what we did. David hit the ground running and immediately started calling many of his Skidmore non-alumni contacts, something I had hoped he would be willing to do. Soon, we were in Manhattan on a weekly basis making calls on foundations and corporations that had been generous to Skidmore. Often David was assumed by the receptionist to be the president and I must be his vice president. The mistake was completely understandable; David *looked* presidential. I was forty-two and was told I looked even younger. Whatever it took was okay by me. We were gaining access to the rarified air I had been unable to penetrate on my own. David was a rainmaker. I was euphoric.

David also melded very comfortably into the culture of Wagner College. He was the kind of engaging person who worked the crowd and was well liked by everyone, including those whose judgments I most trusted. Lyle Guttu and David became close friends. They both lived on campus and, while David's wife remained in Saratoga, they spent many evenings together.

Most important, the trustees loved David. Don Spiro was especially bullish and agreed with me that David's endorsement was a catalyst for the dreams we had set for Wagner. As I had hoped, David began a search for major donors and trustees from among the alumni population. If Don Spiro had graduated from Wagner, how many other Wagner success stories might there be? Had other alumni found success on Wall Street? We looked for others to join Don in our pursuit of a "rich and famous" future.

The alumni records were in as bad shape as just about everything else. We had to rely on recollections of alumni board members. Kevin Sheehy was especially useful in recalling other Don Spiro success stories. The 1960s had been a particularly flourishing era for Wagner; graduates of that decade were remembered as success stories. We found John Myers, a 1967 graduate who was chairman of GE Investments, the largest corporate portfolio in America. John signed up and became a generous and able trustee who served on the executive committee for over a decade.

David found Bob O'Brien, a 1966 graduate and Vietnam Purple Heart recipient, who had become one of the most powerful investment bankers in the world. Bob had been the Bankers Trust executive who assembled the money for the then-largest LBO in history, chronicled in *Barbarians at the Gate*. The book became a movie starring James Garner.

Bob had not been involved with Wagner after graduation and shared with David and me that he had always been annoyed that his alma mater wasn't even known by any of his colleagues. He was sold on our plans for Wagner's future. Without a doubt, though, he was persuaded more because '*David of Skidmore*' said it was plausible, and not because of '*Norman the Younger.*'

Bob would become an active member of the board of trustees and one of the college's most generous benefactors. He told me on several occasions that David Long's patrician stature was one of the college's greatest strengths. Whatever it took, the Smith–Long duo was beginning to rack up some results. I cared less about who got the credit and more about the outcome.

Bob O'Brien

Another big find was Bill and Margaret "Peggy" Reynolds. The *Staten Island Advance* editor Les Trautmann deserved the finder's fee. Peggy was a 1940s graduate of Wagner as was Les. Les sent me a note challenging me to find Peggy, who had married into the Congressman Elsworth Buck family, only to be widowed in World War II. She later married Bill Reynolds, a lawyer she met on a military ship. He was on his way to prosecute the Nazis at Nuremburg. Bill Reynolds would go on to become CEO of Litton Industries International, based in London.

I shared Les' suggestion with David Long, and he said he would get to work. Per usual, he found them, inviting them to 'high tea' at Wagner. High tea? Well, David reminded me, they *were* Londoners. Staten Island isn't exactly high tea country, but our food service rose to the occasion, offering what I now can affirm (after my subsequent years in London) was a pretty accurate presentation.

When Bill and Peggy arrived in my office, they were very gracious but seemingly not very interested in anything more than a courtesy call. David must have been very persuasive. Bill reminded me of James Stewart and Gregory Peck. Peggy had the aristocratic characteristics of Manhattan arts benefactor Brooke Astor combined with a cheery and engaging spirit. I liked Bill and Peggy a lot, but worried I would never see them again. Although polite and gracious, they appeared to be in a rush to depart.

David seemed right at home dealing with elegant, intelligent people like the Reynolds. He recounted that most of Skidmore's veteran alumni were alumnae (i.e., female), therefore often making Skidmore the second alma mater of couples of that generation. Bill was a University of Virginia and George Washington University Law School graduate who, I was surprised to later discover, had not become engaged with either of his alma maters. David recalled his success in bringing billionaire Leonard Tisch's support to Skidmore even though NYU, Tisch's alma mater, was his first love and where he was Chairman of the Board of Trustees. Skidmore was his wife's ("Billie" Tisch) school and therefore ranked accordingly but substantially.

That nothing developed quickly with Bill and Peggy taught me the validity of the tenet that it takes a long time for an acorn to become an oak tree, while also reminding me that proposing marriage on the first date is almost certain to result not only in no marriage, but also no second date. As time went along, though, Bill and Peggy would become trustees and major donors, enabling some of the college's most notable improvements, including campus beautification and the renovation of Reynolds House into the development and alumni center.

Photo-edited/Norman Smith

Peggy and Bill Reynolds both became trustees. Bill joined the executive committee and became a powerful advocate for my strategies that called for first investing heavily in upgrading the college in every way before worrying about an endowment. As a successful business CEO, he was among those trustees who realized that, first and foremost, the product has to be as good, if not better, than the competition. Bill and Don Spiro were the two most powerful trustees and, to my good fortune, both were with me. Bill would frequently call me to encourage me to stand my ground because there was no question in his mind that I was right.

David Long's first year at Wagner generated more major breakthroughs in fundraising than the College had ever realized.

Both the Calder and the Clark Foundations came through with six-figure grants. Don Spiro, troubled to learn from me that the only computer on the Wagner campus was my own, donated $250,000 to open up a personal computer lab for students.

Wagner gets $250,000 foundation grant

By DON GROSS
ADVANCE STAFF WRITER

Wagner College's endowment has been enriched by $250,000 with its first major foundation grant.

The Grymes Hill school was among six colleges receiving Louis Calder Foundation challenge grants, Wagner President Norman R. Smith announced yesterday. The grant requires Wagner to raise an additional $500,000 on its own over the next three years.

Smith said he expected no trouble in raising the needed scholarship money, noting that fund-raising at the school had increased by more than 60 percent over the last year.

"We raised more than $2 million on our own, and a substantial portion of that went into the endowment," Smith said.

The scholarship money will pay for the education of students with "high academic promise" who live in New York City.

Other schools receiving the grants are Georgetown, Fairfield and Colgate universities and Hamilton and Marymount Manhattan colleges.

"The real benefit in receiving this grant," Smith said, "is in being included with these other colleges. It means we've arrived."

"The real benefit in receiving this grant, Smith said, "is in being included with these other colleges. It means we've arrived."

When Smith took over the Wagner presidency a little more than a year ago, he said the school would need to build a $40 million endowment in order to fund the education of its student.

"I still am aiming for the numbers I was talking about, he said.

Getting that money, however, was made more difficult by a financially troubled past.

"The last year has been difficult," he said. "Much of it was spent introducing a new administration and getting things going."

Winning the Calder grant, Smith said, now gives Wagner the credibility it has needed. "I expect to do an awful lot better in the future," he said.

"Other schools receiving the grants are Georgetown, Fairfield and Colgate universities and Hamilton and Marymount Manhattan colleges."

Not only does the college have major, private gifts in the pipeline, he said, but college officials are working with other foundations seeking the funds to dramatically increase the endowment.

"A lot of the credit goes to David Long," Smith said.

Smith enticed Long to Wagner from Skidmore College in Saratoga Springs, N.Y., where Long had gained a reputation in fundraising by playing a key role in saving that once-bankrupt college.

"His personal credibility has been a tremendous help in closing this deal," Smith said.

The Calder grant also marks the first substantial gift to the school to come from outside the college community. Wagner previously received a $250,000 grant from board of trustees chairman Donald Spiro and his wife Evelyn that was used to open a computer center on campus.

Staten Island Advance

100G gift for Wagner computers

BY ADVANCE STAFF WRITER

The Clark Foundation of New York City has given Wagner College $100,000 for continued improvements to its computer program.

The grant marks the second time in the past two years the college has received a major gift for computer technology from the foundation.

Dr. Norman Smith, president of Wagner College, said the new grant will be used to upgrade the computer system both academically and administratively.

"My goal is to have every student here graduate with fundamental computer literacy," he said. "There isn't a field where computers aren't being used, whether you're a writer or a musician."

Smith said a grant from Wagner alumni Dr. Donald and Evelyn Spiro which funded the $250,000 Spiro Computer Center has resulted in a surge of student interest in computer technology.

The Spiro Center's 50 computer terminals are constantly being used, said Donta Bell, technology center coordinator.

"My goal is to have every student here graduate with fundamental computer literacy."

"Students are using the computers to do everything from classwork to typing up their resumes," Bell said.

The Clark Foundation was established by heirs of the Clark family fortune, which originated in the 1800s with Edward Clark, a Cooperstown, N.Y., lawyer who was one of the founders of the Singer Company.

Staten Island Advance

David was also busy going through the alumni records in search of other Don Spiros. We spent many days in Manhattan visiting prospects for trusteeships

$250,000 gift to fund Wagner computer facility

It's good news!

Donald W. Spiro

By ANN MARIE BRESLIN
ADVANCE STAFF WRITER

Wagner College will open a state-of-the-art computer facility with a $250,000 alumni donation, President Dr. Norman Smith announced yesterday.

Seeing a great need for computer literacy in the workplace, Wagner alumni Donald W. and Evelyn Spiro donated the funds for development of the center.

"My belief is that in order for students to excel in today's market, they're going to have to have a broad background in computers," said Spiro, a member of the board of trustees at the Grymes Hill college and chairman of Oppenheimer Management Corp., Manhattan.

Featuring IBM PS2 personal computers, the system will be equipped for word processing, financial spread sheet analysis, data base management and research methods. It could be linked to a mainframe computer in the future.

The facility, targeted for a spring completion, will be in two classrooms in the college's Communications Center. The classrooms, Smith said, will be divided for teaching but also will be opened completely for student use in the evening and on weekends.

Smith agreed that access to computers will make students' workloads easier but he stressed the value of computer knowledge when they seek employment after graduation.

Computer literacy is a necessity for every field of study, Smith said. "In areas like business it's an absolute prerequisite," he said, adding that computers also are necessary for liberal arts students and science majors.

Students with intentions of attending graduate school will benefit likewise, Smith said. "It strengthens graduate skills, especially research. A student exposed to computers in undergraduate studies will be a better graduate student."

Spiro said he hopes Wagner's computer modernization and urban location will attract major computer manufacturing companies. He also hopes once this program is initiated Wagner will develop one of the most advanced science programs available.

Though he said he has no immediate plans for a computer science program at Wagner, Smith said this project is merely a springboard to future growth.

"I'm looking for a day when dorms will have computers and they'll be in all other places around campus," he said. "As students and faculty grow into it, the demand will be created."

Staten Island Advance 1988

Don Spiro's first gift was the largest ever for Wagner and the beginning of many more to come that were even larger

Shortly after arriving as president, I was told that the Megerle family had notified the development staff that they would no longer be supporting the college. The Megerles were not alumni but were pre-WWII German immigrants who settled on Staten Island. Because of the college's Lutheran roots, they became associated with the founding Sutter family, including Reverend Carl Sutter, the man instrumental in moving Wagner from Rochester, NY, to Staten Island. The patriarch of the Megerle family, Eugene, who died years before I became president, was a chemist. From his Staten Island garage he developed a line of women's cosmetics that became the Wella Balsam Company. Wella Balsam hit its peak of popularity in the 1970s when Farrah Fawcett, an original *Charlie's Angels* and the reigning pinup in America, was the Wella Balsam girl.

At some point, the Megerles sold the company and became independently wealthy. One of the largest gifts Wagner had ever received was from the Megerles in the 1970s, and the college's science classroom building was subsequently named Megerle Hall. But in more recent years, they, like many others, had become appalled with the deterioration of the college and were not going to continue making contributions.

I attempted to persuade them that Wagner was on a new course and that they should stay on board. Throughout the fall, I met with them as often as they would see me. Susan and I even joined them for Thanksgiving dinner at their New Jersey country club, the Knickerbocker.

Martha Megerle, Eugene's wife, was the matriarch of the family that included a daughter and two sons, one of whom did not live nearby. Martha's daughter, Eva, lived with Martha in Teaneck, New Jersey. George was married with grown children and lived nearby.

Martha was a wonderfully animated woman, very bright, with a pronounced German accent. She was the Hollywood casting stereotype for what Maria von Trapp (*The Sound of Music*) could have looked like in her seventies. To my gratification, Martha and I clicked, and we became very close for the rest of her life.

As trustees, George and Eva continued their support annually. George heavily invested in Megerle Hall, renovating many of the labs there. Eva was very interested in the women's athletic program.

The Megerles were key to the college's recovery.

Wagner dedicates chemistry lab

BY ADVANCE STAFF WRITER

Wagner College last night dedicated its refurbished chemistry lab in the Megerle Science Building with a ceremony and reception attended by faculty and friends of the Grymes Hill college.

The refurbished labs are the result of a $175,000 grant from trustees Dr. George Megerle and his wife, Judith. The science building is named for Megerle's father, Eugen, the founder of Wella Corp., who was a major benefactor of Wagner College.

Wagner president Dr. Norman Smith said the Megerles' gift will go a long way toward the future of Wagner and its students. "I am grateful to George and Judith — they gave this together — for their desire to begin a program that strengthens the science programs of the college at an important time."

Renovations, which took place over the summer, were recently completed. Besides starting the year off on a good note, Smith said the new lab will help to recruit students and make a greater impact on their education.

Dr. Donald Spiro, chairman of the board of trustees, spoke on the need for strong science education in today's colleges, so the United States can maintain a competitive edge into the 21st century.

Enjoying the dedication ceremony are, from the left, Dr. Eva Megerle, Wagner president Dr. Norman Smith, and Dr. George Megerle with his wife, Judith, and his mother, Dr. Martha Megerle.

Martha Megerle's (right) daughter Eva and son George became Trustees.

Supporters celebrate Wagner future

By MERLISA LAWRENCE
ADVANCE STAFF WRITER

'Tis the season for giving. And those who have given to Wagner College gathered last night at the Grymes Hill home of Dr. Norman R. Smith, the school's president, to celebrate what they see as a sparkling future.

"These people have been helpful to Wagner over the years, and I hope that they will continue to be," Smith said of the supporters. "An important part of a small college is fund raising."

The people Smith was speaking about are members of the Cunard Society, Wagner College's staunchest supporters.

Outside of their continuous support at Wagner functions, this group gets together annually for this black-tie pep rally.

More excited than the Wagner cheerleaders was Kevin Sheehy, former president of the college alumni association and member of the executive committee of the board of trustees.

"We've gone through some tough times, but those times are in the past," Sheehy said. "We're ready to build a national reputation."

Sheehy's thoughts were echoed throughout the three main rooms in the president's home.

As flames crackled in fireplaces in each room, guests talked about the "good old days" and the better days to come.

"Wagner is on a roll again," said Mildred Olsen, president of Wagner Alumni Association. Swinging a clenched fist, Mrs. Olsen enthusiastically talked about the school's future.

Mrs. Olsen's team spirit was a small sample of the cameraderie evident throughout the house.

Donald Spiro, a member of the board of trustees and a 1949 graduate, said Wagner would someday be known as the top small college of the Northeast.

"And then we'll go after the rest of the country," he said.

"These people have been helpful to Wagner over the years and I hope that they will continue to be."
— Dr. Norman R. Smith

Al Corbin, treasurer and oldest member of the board of trustees, said he has been supporting the college since he was graduated in 1931.

Bob Sbarbaro, a member of the board of trustees and graduate of 1954, said he saw a great deal of promise for the 105-year-old school.

Even those who did not graduate from Wagner were full of school spirit last night.

Jay Hartig, chairman of the board and a 1967 graduate, said the key to this newfound optimism is the arrival of Smith.

"This attitude has spread from him into the faculty and the student body," Hartig said. "People here have really rallied around him."

Dr. Albert B. Accettola Sr., a member of the board of trustees, said Smith has infused the college with a number of new and positive ideas.

"We needed new blood," Accettola said of Smith.

John Braisted, an honorary member of the board, said the college should be on solid ground within five years under Smith.

Smith described those present as a family. There certainly was a feeling of kinship last night. Unlike years past, when this affair was held in restaurants, the celebration took on a warmer flavor in the home of the family's newest member.

Smith and his wife, Dr. Susan Robinson, have been on the Island for several months and said they felt settled, thanks to the people at Wagner College and other Staten Islanders.

Dr. Norman R. Smith, left, Wagner College president, talks with Martha Megerle; his wife, Dr. Susan Robinson, and Donald Spiro, a member of the school's board of trustees.

"The people have made our welcome complete," Ms. Robinson said.

To show their appreciation, the couple opened their home to more than 60 people, including the Wagner College Choir.

No one had lived in the home for more than a year, Ms. Robinson said. But that wasn't evident last night.

The rooms were decorated with green garland and velvet red bows. The centerpiece in the main room was a modestly decorated Christmas tree with toy soldiers, beaded golden garland and other ornaments.

After the guests caught up on old times, they were treated to performances by the Wagner College Choir and members of the school's theater department.

In formal attire, the women in pink and the men in black, the Wagner choir filled the stairway as guests huddled in close to hear them sing.

The Wagner College Choir sings Christmas carols at the Smiths' Grymes Hill home.

Staten Island Advance December 1988

Martha Megerle joined with Don Spiro, Susan, and I for a photo at the first Holiday Black Tie we held for trustees and donors, an event that became an annual tradition and always included a performance by the college's choir.

Excerpted from **"Supporters celebrate..."**

Tis the season for giving and those who have given to Wagner College gathered last night at the Grymes Hill home of Dr. Norman R. Smith, the school's president, to celebrate what they see as a sparking future.

More excited than the Wagner cheerleaders was Kevin Sheehy, former president of the college alumni association and member of the executive committee of the board of trustees. "We've gone through some tough times, but those times are in the past," Sheehy said. Sheehy's thoughts echoed throughout the three main rooms in the president's home.

"Wagner is on a roll again," said Mildred Olsen, president of the Wagner Alumni Association. Mrs. Olsen's team spirit was a small sample of the camaraderie evident throughout the house.

Bob Sbarbaro, a member of the board of trustees and graduate of 1954, said he saw a great deal of promise for the 105-year-old school. Even those who did not graduate from Wagner were full of school spirit last night.

Trustee Jay Hartig said the key to this newfound optimism is the arrival of Smith. "This attitude has spread from him into the faculty and the student body," Hartig said. "People here have really rallied around him.

Trustee Dr. Albert Accettola said Smith has infused the college with a number of new and positive ideas. "We needed new blood," Accettola said of Smith.

Another important benefactor walked into my office on his own accord during the first fall of my presidency. John Lehmann was a 1960s graduate of Wagner who earned his degree in night school while raising a family and working full time as a mailman during the day. He was a veteran Army MP who had served in England and Germany during the Korean War. His father had been a Staten Island policeman.

Upon graduation, John became an accountant for the Butterick Company, when making clothing using Butterick's patterns was still something most housewives did to cut household costs in the days before Walmart, Sims, Kmart, Target, and Marshalls. Such stores made it possible to buy finished garments for less than the cost of a pattern and fabric, thanks to third-world labor.

In the early 1980s, John led a leveraged buyout of the company and then merged it with Vogue Patterns. By his own account, he made a bundle, and was now chairman and CEO of the Manhattan-based company.

John had dropped by to introduce himself and to donate $200,000 in memory of his daughter who had drowned in childhood years earlier — if I was interested in taking it. I was interested.

John was a massive man. One might immediately presume he was a defensive center for a professional football team, but he reminded me that he'd had no time for extracurricular *anything* during his student days. Behind his massiveness, though, was a gentle and warm guy with a heart.

Upon giving me the check, he asked if it would be illegal for me to look up the names of a couple of his classmates. Although our alumni records weren't all that good, I agreed to see what we could find. He then admitted that he was interested in finding a couple of old girlfriends. "They never thought I would amount to much of anything, and I would love them to know that I did all right," he admitted. I don't remember whether we found those names.

Immediately after John left, though, I called up Don Spiro to tell him about this exciting new trustee prospect. The following week, Don, whose corporate headquarters were in the World Trade Center, invited John and me to lunch in the Windows on the World, the top floor restaurant that, until 9-11, was the highest eatery in the world.

Archival

John Lehmann, right, was awarded an honorary doctorate presided over by Don Spiro and me.

John joined the trustees and would later become treasurer and then vice chairman of the board. John and Don became close friends, and the two of them were my rocks for well over a decade. John was a very generous annual benefactor but resigned shortly after I left as president, having completed a twelve-year term limit that required going off the board for one year.

He chose not to return, but visited me regularly when I moved on to England in 2002 (more about that in later chapters), where he had purchased a home and a pub. We remained close friends in regular contact with each other until about 2007 when he went into the advanced stages of Alzheimer's disease.

In retrospect, a remarkable amount of progress had been made in a relatively short period of time.

By the end of the first academic year, fundraising exceeded two million dollars for the first time in the recorded history of the college. The first major foundation gifts had been realized. A computer center was made possible. The trustees were transforming into the powerhouse that was needed to get Wagner to the next level and beyond.

Chapter 9
"Shanghai-ing" an Admissions Dean

As many had advised me from the start, Professor Joedy Smith was proving to be less than ideal as dean of admissions through no fault of his own. His interpersonal skills appeared to be winning over prospective students and parents, but he was not as adept in managing the complex processes involved in the overall operation—processes that were essential to success. There were mass mailings of marketing materials to plan and execute. There was the processing of inquiries and applications. There was follow-up of inquiries to application. All this was a complex logistics job that appeared to be beyond Joedy's areas of expertise.

I was torn because I had gotten Joedy into this situation and didn't want him hurt. No one is good at everything. If someone had asked me to take over as baseball coach, I would have been a disaster. I was getting reports that Joedy's assistant dean, Mike Walsh, was not happy. Mike was a high-energy, personable Wagner assistant coach we transferred to admissions on the recommendation of athletic director, Walt Hameline. Walt was one of the solid-gold plusses at Wagner whom I could take no credit for having discovered.

Walt was justly liked and respected by everyone at Wagner. I sought his view on most anything associated with the college. When we discussed the need for new, can-do blood in admissions, he volunteered Mike Walsh as someone who was his best athletic recruiter, a role he could continue to do within the admissions office. We weren't making any breakthroughs with campus visits. At a campus open house in the early fall of 1988, the turnout was thin, and the academic quality of the group seemed below average. We still weren't attracting any new faces, but rather the same crowd of local students.

There were exceptions. One family from Connecticut struck me as exactly what we were looking for in our future student body. At a typical open house, visitors would gather in the main dining hall, the one with the floor-to-ceiling windows overlooking the harbor. The San Quentin tables and fluorescent lighting had not yet been resolved, nor had the ceiling been repaired. The stalactites were still everywhere. As I was sitting with the mother answering her questions, a massive glob of moist limestone goop fell from one of the stalactites onto the front of her silk blouse, leaving a mark that looked like a pigeon had just flown over leaving a calling card. The stain likely ruined her blouse. We insisted on paying for the dry cleaning, but the damage had been done, including her decision about whether Wagner was worth further consideration. They never came back.

By mid-October, the need for experienced admissions leadership was exceedingly apparent, but that was easier said than done. Enter my wife, Susan, who had finally moved up from our former home in Philadelphia. Susan had resigned her deanship of Moore College where she oversaw admissions and financial aid and had been credited with building a top-shelf staff that had greatly increased applications and enrollments. But she had made me promise that I wouldn't call upon her to do admissions of any sort at Wagner. In fact, Susan had earned her doctorate in human development from Harvard and had never sought a career in admissions.

I told her of the crisis we faced and how our future at Wagner was going to be heavily dependent on turning around the enrollment declines in a period much shorter than should reasonably be expected.

My short-term solutions were not working as well as need be. Could she please at least spend a little time in admissions and see if anything could be done to improve the process while there was still time to generate a better outcome for the following year? A quantitative and systems whiz, Susan needed to initially focus her efforts on the database systems, so the right applicants were not lost in the masses.

She agreed to visit and to volunteer some time. She didn't want a job and she definitely didn't want to replace Joedy. I understood Susan's position. The community reaction to Susan's involvement could hurt both of us. We set up a desk in an intern's area. Joedy, perhaps understandably, didn't seem thrilled having the president's wife on the premises.

Little by little, though, Susan's presence allowed her to start influencing the smoother running of operations. She started by focusing on the logistics of the paperwork processes, including the applicant database, since that part of the operation was not where Joedy appeared to be focusing his attention anyway. People person that he was, Joedy was much more comfortable and effective on the frontline, talking to prospective students and their families.

One of the early initiatives Susan took on was to upgrade the monitoring of the applicant pool. The admissions office had no personal computers. They were dependent, like the entire college, on a fundamentally archaic mainframe computer located in the basement of the Megerle Hall science center, and managed by a veteran faculty member, Jim McCoy.

Jim seemed resistant to personal computers replacing any of the college's administrative functions currently on his mainframe.

Archival

Professor and computer czar Jim McCoy

The mainframe was an old piece of equipment that wasn't responsive to the daily needs of monitoring the applicant pool. On the one hand, Jim McCoy was getting a lot of blood out of the stone, but his pride of ownership was standing in the way of a better mousetrap.

Susan wanted to abandon the mainframe dependence by using the same admissions software she had been employing at Moore College, all of which was personal computer-friendly and could be readily retrieved when needed, as opposed to sometimes having to wait days for an updated printout from McCoy's computer center. Admissions status was not something that could wait days at a time without losing sales.

Susan's instincts and initiatives were greatly improving operations, including the ability of the admissions staff to monitor the more-promising applications. Her volunteer term had now extended to over five months and it was clear that virtually everyone on the admissions team loved Susan and regarded her as the solution.

Joedy was better suited in the faculty, including as a professor whom admissions could showcase during campus visitations. With wide-reaching persuasion that reached far beyond my groveling, Susan reluctantly consented to being shanghaied, but only until such time that a permanent, experienced dean could be found and financed. Joedy returned to the faculty with our genuine gratitude for his earnest efforts.

Susan continued her admissions magic, without pay. In addition to building a first-rate recruiting staff and implementing operating systems that effectively monitored and served the applicant pool, Susan developed what was then an novel approach to awarding financial aid.

In the late eighties, financial aid was largely seen as grants to applicants with significant financial need and/or to the top academic students among the applicants. This need-and-merit system was widely employed and didn't always work well, especially for schools like Wagner that were not heavily endowed and were not always the first-choice institution of academically exceptional students.

The problem with granting too much financial aid to needy students is that even 50% of tuition is often not enough to make enrollment affordable. The financially strapped family still must come up with the other 50%. And 50% of tuition was more than Wagner could routinely afford to forgo. By sending too much financial aid to the needy applicants, Wagner and other colleges were enrolling too many students who really couldn't afford to stay for four years, if even for one year.

As for the academically exceptional, this group was being awarded scholarships elsewhere, often at their first-choice institution. Thus, Wagner's award offers really didn't yield many of the students to whom they were offered.

Susan studied the total applicant pool and noticed that the academic performance and financial wherewithal extremes created a bell curve. That is, the top scholarship applicants represented about 15% of the students at one end of the bell curve, and the very needy students were about 20% of the applicant pool at the other end of the curve. That left two thirds of the applicants who were neither A students nor extremely financially needy.

Among those two-thirds in the middle were a large group of B students from financially comfortable backgrounds who would be ideal for Wagner. However, this middle-of-the-bell-curve group were never offered academic merit financial aid and, because of their middle-class background, rarely applied for need-based financial aid.

Susan pondered what would happen if these B students became the group to whom we offered grants. She created a Presidential Scholars category for the A students we rarely yielded anyway. Then, we created a secondary Dean's Scholar category, thereby giving the B students a scholarship they probably were not being offered elsewhere. That scholarship just might be the magnet that could tilt students toward Wagner.

Sure enough, even though the amount of the scholarship was not significant, sometimes only 15% of tuition, the honor of being offered a scholarship was a source of pride for the student and his/her family. Almost immediately, we started to see a higher yield within this largest cohort of the applicant pool. This practice would become more widely employed in the 1990s and even became a nationally prominent enrollment strategy. I was asked to write a chapter about the methodology for a higher education management book published by Coopers and Lybrand.

Not everyone likes the premise of the strategy we launched. Within academe, there is an understandably prevailing view that financial aid should go to students of academic promise who lack the financial wherewithal to pay for their education. No student should be denied the college of their choice because they are poor. On the other hand, very few private colleges are wealthy enough to forgo having most of their students pay a substantial portion of their tuition, if not all of it. Wagner was among most colleges who needed paying customers.

Enrollment revenue-dependent colleges like Wagner can remain financially viable only if most of the students they are enrolling can pay, on average, about 70% of their tuition. Thus, a substantial portion of students must come from families with financial wherewithal. When Wagner is so heavily endowed that it no longer needs its students to pay tuition, then the admissions decisions can be need-blind. Until then, the admissions strategy must emphasize finding and realizing paying customers.

By the end of the admissions year, full-time equivalent (FTE) enrollments were up for the following fall. Academic quality showed signs of improving. Geographic reach was beginning to widen. Less grant aid was being allocated, thereby increasing net enrollment revenues at a rate that was greater than enrollment headcount. That is, if you recruit 500 students at a 50% discount, you only enroll 250 net students. If you recruit 400 at a 30% discount, you enroll 280 net students, thirty more from a financial perspective. Yet with one hundred fewer heads, your costs are down while your revenues are up.

This was one of the most frustrating concepts I faced having to explain to trustees who were alarmed about an enrollment headcount decline, a mistaken perception that may have contributed to Wagner's problems. Total heads are less important than net revenue heads.

Thankfully, Don Spiro, John Lehmann, Bob Evans, Al Corbin, and other new members of the board were business executives themselves and they did get it.

Susan's "temporary" oversight of Wagner admissions would last for a decade before she departed to become president of the Snug Harbor Cultural Center, a ninety-acre arts center on Staten Island that included a symphony hall, children's museum, botanical garden, outdoor band shell, and modern art gallery.

Over the ten-year period of Susan's leadership, the enrollments at Wagner nearly doubled from 1,188 to 2,100. Discounting dropped from 50% to under 30%. The average SAT of new students increased from under 800 combined to over 1150.

Susan assembled a first-rate team that included her successor, Angelo Araimo, who spent over three decades at Wagner including as President.

She recruited Rob Franek, who had just graduated from Drew University and today is the publisher and editor-in-chief of *The Princeton Review* college ratings. Without Susan's leadership, the skyrocketing enrollments would never have happened, and without the enrollments, both from a revenue and academic quality perspective, Wagner would not have made it. The pace with which she accelerated change exceeded all expectations.

Norman Smith

Susan recruited everyone on the new admissions team including Rob Franek (right of Susan, front left in photo) who would become the publisher of The Princeton Review and Angelo Araimo (top middle) who would serve over 30 years at Wagner and retire as President.

I doubt I would have managed to hang onto my presidency for a decade and a half without my brilliant and able — albeit shanghaied — wife. If ever there was a better half, she was, and remains, the personification of the metaphor.

Staten Island Advance

Lifestyle

Dr. Susan Robinson casts her own shadow

By DON GROSS
ADVANCE STAFF WRITER

When new Wagner College President Norman R. Smith was first formally introduced during graduation ceremonies last May, the campus community got its first hint that the new First Lady of Wagner didn't quite fit the usual mold of college president's wife. Standing beside Smith was a woman also wearing the crimson academic robes of a person holding a doctorate in education from Harvard University.

And while Smith joked that if his tenure as president didn't work out he and his wife would be available as "a matched set of bookends," a talk with Dr. Susan Robinson reveals a person who will cast her own shadow and not live in someone else's.

What form that shadow will take isn't yet clear. Dr. Robinson said the illness of a family member complicated her task of tying up loose ends at the job she just left in Philadelphia and arranging for the move from that city to Grymes Hill.

"I need time to step back and see where I want to go," she said.

If where she has been is an indicator of where Dr. Robinson is headed, her next career step is likely to be interesting.

Her last job was as dean of admissions at Moore College of Art in Philadelphia. The job was exciting, she said, for she was able to see the budding stages of many artists who came bearing portfolios for admissions interviews.

Making the job even more interesting is the fact that the arts play a strong role in her life.

"It isn't just a current," she said. "It's more like a tide."

Her father owned a firm that made supplies for professional artists. She studied music for years with the intention of playing professionally. "We seem to alternate generations," she said. "One is involved in visual arts, the next in performance."

She deviated from the family tradition, she said, because the "practical side of me took over" and pointed the way toward an academic career.

Working with Dr. Robinson at Moore was her husband, who served as the school's vice president during much of her tenure.

"Working together enabled us to stay close," she said. "We both like to work. If one of us had to stay in the office to meet a deadline on a project, the other would stay late so we could walk home together. There was always some project that we could work on."

There were disadvantages, too, she said. By working together, they limited themselves to a small circle of friends. She'd like to see that expand now.

But the family approach to employment isn't something she's going to repeat at Wagner. Part of it is that she would immediately be identified as the president's wife, she said, and she is someone who has her own identity.

"Because we have different names I had time to establish myself before it (their marriage) became common knowledge," Dr. Robinson said.

The other is the conflict of interest she'd encounter with a husband who was also her boss.

Most likely, she said, she'll find her future across the harbor in Manhattan. There, she'll be able to use the knowledge she gained while studying at Skidmore College, where she earned her bachelor's in psychology; at Columbia University's Teachers' College, where she studied special education; or at Harvard, where she obtained her masters in education as well as her doctorate.

It was at Harvard that she met her husband. She was a graduate student sitting in an auditorium looking up at the podium when she first saw Norman Smith, then a youthful dean of students at Harvard's Graduate School of Education.

"I was immediately attracted to him," she said. "And he was to me."

She knows this, she said, because she remembers exactly where she was sitting in the auditorium and Smith remembered spotting her.

But their relationship didn't start until a little over a year later when Smith left the graduate school of education to become dean of students at Harvard's Kennedy School of Government.

Almost immediately, she said, he called asking her out.

The next few years saw both her relationship with Smith and her career blossom. But her degrees weren't much good in helping her get her next job in the community affairs and public relations department of WGBH, Boston's public broadcasting station.

ADVANCE PHOTO IRVING SILVERSTEIN

Dr. Susan Robinson is determined to be her own person

To get her foot in the door, she said, she volunteered her talents, some of which, such as fund raising, she says she'll be able to bring to Wagner.

"I intend to play a very active role at Wagner College," she said, noting that she's already become a one-person cheering section for the school's theater department. "I've been to a dress rehearsal and two performances of 'My Fair Lady,'" she said.

She also intends to be a more active hostess to both faculty and students as her husband and the Wagner College community become acquainted. Also on the list of future dinner engagements will be prospective donors to the endowment the college needs to stabilize its financial situation.

"I already told the board of trustees I'm looking forward to doing that," she said. "After all, Norman and I are partners."

Staten Island Advance circa 1988

I was not surprised that Susan was well received from the start. She should go down in Wagner history as having been key to Wagner's success in every dimension. Within a year of her involvement at Wagner, a tongue-in-cheek question arose about nepotism. Then-chairman of the board, Don Spiro, forwarded the solution, if one was needed. "Wagner needs Susan," Don affirmed. "Thus, if one of you has to go, Norman, I think it will have to be you." I agreed and fortunately got to stay.

Wagner President Angelo Araimo 2022-24

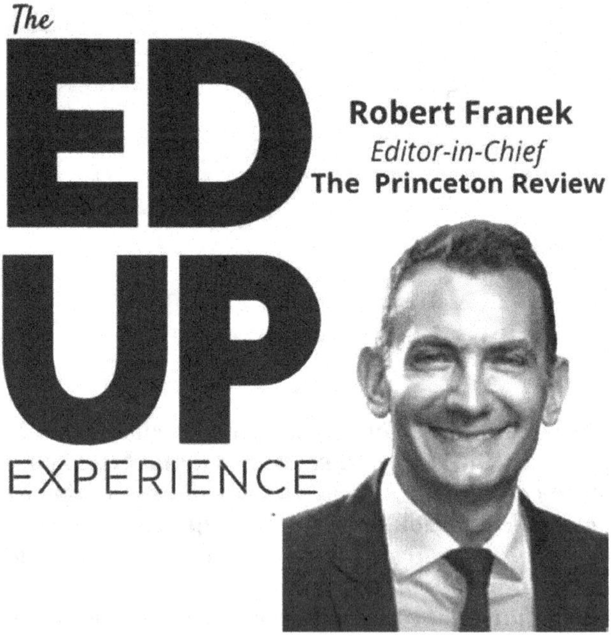

Chapter 10
Faculty Can Make or Break a President

I had learned long before becoming president of Wagner College that faculty can make or break any administration if they put their mind to it, so I committed myself early on to reaching out in every way I could to build solid working and personal relationships. I put out the word during my first summer that my wife Susan hadn't yet moved up and that invitations to dinner at faculty homes were welcome. A gratifying contingent took me up on this, and I experienced many lovely nights with their families.

Most faculty hosts observed that I was the first president who had ever visited their homes. Getting to know spouses and children cemented my relationships with the Wagner faculty that stayed intact throughout my tenure. One of the more attractive facets of smaller colleges is that the president can know the entire faculty on a first-name basis if she or he is willing to devote the time — to me, time that is very well spent.

Lyle Guttu was also a big help in faculty relations. Lyle lived on campus in a small cottage adjacent to the library. The lawn around his house was one of the more bucolic areas of the college, in one direction looking toward the main quad, Sutter Oval, and Main Hall. In the other direction, one could sit under a truly grand oak tree and look out over the New York harbor. Once married, Lyle had divorced years ago and lived alone except for frequent visits from his school-age son and daughter, who spent most of their time at their mother's house about a mile away. As a result of his independence, Lyle's home became almost a walk-in center, at the end of the day, for faculty and staff. Whenever I walked out of my office on summer evenings, I would look up toward Lyle's house to see ten or twelve people sitting in a circle under the oak tree, enjoying the camaraderie and the setting.

Lyle would wave me over to join in what was largely a gathering of faculty members. Lyle was the faculty's most trusted source of *what really was going on* at Wagner. During the early years when rumors abounded about the precariousness of the college, Lyle kept everyone well informed and thus much calmer than might otherwise have been the case. When faculty heard from Lyle that a rumor was untrue, they tended to believe the rumor was untrue. Any president benefits from having someone like Lyle on campus.

Sobered, though, by the way in which a faculty union was assembled and then legally closed, Lyle advised me to seek out several key professors who had been the union leaders and remained distanced since the union had somehow been legally eliminated a number of years ago. Two of the most anti-administration faculty were political science professors Bob Anderson and George Rappaport. I contacted them early on and extended invitations, individually or together, to drop by my office at their convenience.

The first to come by was Bob Anderson. Bob was the soft-spoken quintessence of a small-college professor. As he walked into my office, his head scanned the entire space as he sighed, "So this is the president's office of Wagner College." Bob was not a junior professor who had just recently joined the faculty. "How long have you been at Wagner?" I queried. I remember he said something like twenty-two years—but not less than that. “And you have never been up here before?”

Bob suggested that he wasn’t the only one. In fact, the president’s office, although in the student union, was not in the traffic pattern. Along with other executive offices, the president’s office was on a fourth floor that was accessible only by climbing an unwelcoming stairway closed off by a door. Once on the fourth floor, the office was at the end of a long, narrow hallway. One couldn’t just casually pass by and wave. You had to go out of your way to get there, and, as a result, there weren’t many, if any, casual visitors. I was told it had been designed with inaccessibility in mind. There was even a secret ‘escape’ stairwell within the office should anyone unwelcome charge down the entrance hallway.

Bob was not hostile or pugnacious in any way, but he was also not all that forthcoming. He was polite but close to the vest, listening intently and saying little. I told him that I sought a good relationship with the faculty, that we were all in this together, and that everyone needed to be part of the solution. To that end, I asked his advice on what I should be doing. He said that I appeared to be off to a good start by at least trying to get to know everyone, and he wished me luck.

As he walked away with a smile and a handshake, after maybe an hour of conversation, Anderson passed Norbert Leeseberg who was coming down the hall toward my office. They looked at each other but said nothing. “What was that anarchist doing up here?” a somewhat troubled Leese inquired. Leese then proceeded to characterize Anderson as someone who was not to be trusted and recounted how much damage he had caused during the faculty union strikes. There was clearly a lot of scar tissue.

George Rappaport came by a few days later. George was a high-energy, rapid-fire conversationalist. As everyone had warned me, George was a proud, card-carrying (at least metaphorically) union advocate. He recounted how his mother had been a union organizer and how he passionately supported collective bargaining. I listened and then laid out the same story I had told Bob Anderson a few days earlier. All in all, George was a nice guy, with firm convictions. At the end of the conversation, George took me up on my request for dinner invitations and asked me over to his house. I accepted and visited a week or two later. Throughout the dinner with his wife, Susan, and their very bright children, George kept saying, "I can't believe I'm having the president of Wagner over to my house for dinner... what would my mother say?"

Professor Bob Anderson

Professor George Rappaport

Over the years, George and Bob both became supportive colleagues and, from my vantage point, friends with whom I had fundamentally positive relationships. George often disagreed with me, but I always sensed he knew he could come and visit and express his view without consequence, which he did. Bob, at times, even championed my causes. After several years of living in the new, rented, president's house, Bob came up to me at a reception we were having there and advised "The College should try to buy this house. It is good for the image of Wagner and its president." That coming from Bob was out of character, and I couldn't have been more pleased.

I attended all faculty meetings, sometimes just for the opening moments when I would extemporaneously bring them up to date with my view of the most relevant developments at the college since the last faculty meeting. I would also answer questions before leaving, adding an invitation that everyone was welcome to drop by my office after the meeting for a reception. The faculty meetings usually started at 3:30 so the social gathering rarely was underway before 5:30 and would sometimes last until 7:30. I was always the last to leave so no one felt rushed. Usually, over half of the faculty attended the reception.

Most would laud the way in which they interacted with some colleagues they rarely otherwise saw.

Throughout my time at Wagner, I greatly enjoyed my relationship with the faculty and was lucky to have an unusually positive interaction with most of them. Smaller colleges heavily emphasize teaching effectiveness, and a good teacher must have an engaging personality to be effective. Such was the case at Wagner as I think back on so many wonderful professors from all areas of the school.

In the sciences, I already mentioned Jim McCoy, the math professor who held together a mainframe administrative computer with paper clips and rubber bands until we were able to upgrade. Otto Raths, a veteran physics professor, was always ready to offer an opinion on anything and everything. And there were many others.

John Esser, a professor of sociology who was one of my early recruits, greatly advanced the social sciences faculty while contributing to the community culture of the college in a way that students, faculty, and staff respected. I was also drawn to his experience as an undergraduate at Haverford College, a small and highly regarded institution on the Main Line of Philadelphia that I aspired to see Wagner College emulate.

Anne Schotter was a humanities professor before I arrived at Wagner, and she quickly struck me as an asset. She went on to chair the humanities faculty and was also someone I regularly called upon. She played an instrumental role in the search and selection of all the senior academic leaders we sought during my tenure.

Alison Smith was one of my early recruiting coups. A Vassar College undergraduate and master's degree graduate, she was a Fulbright

Scholar in Italy with a PhD from Johns Hopkins. She had returned to the Vassar faculty when we somehow managed to add her to the Wagner faculty, a decision on her part that was tied to her family demands in New York City. She, like Anne, was one of my trusted academic advisors. She knew what Wagner could be based on her experiences at Vassar. In addition to being a respected colleague, Alison and her family were a valued part of our life on Staten Island.

Tony Carter was the college's business faculty brain trust, and someone I sought for a wide array of challenges including internships and career development. He oversaw the college's largest student major, business, for the latter years of my presidency. Shortly after I left for London, he left Wagner to chair the small-business institute of the University of New Haven while also teaching at Columbia University. I tried to talk him into joining me in London, but his family demands at the time made that impossible. Tony achieved much more at Wagner than most realized, and his departure was a loss for the college. He died in a tragic house fire.

NORMAN R. SMITH

Although there was a flourishing theatre department at Wagner before Christopher Catt, the years he chaired the faculty produced a consistent array of memorable productions that elevated the Wagner theatre program to the *Princeton Review's* "best in American higher education" pinnacle. Christopher honored me with my only casting call when I was the voice of the *How to Succeed in Business Without Really Trying* manual, a role handled by Walter Cronkite on Broadway. I also tried to recruit Christopher to join me in London. Susan called upon him to play a leadership role at the Snug Harbor Cultural Center during her years as president. Sadly, Christopher died a young man in 2009.

Julia Barchitta was yet another member of Wagner's extraordinary nursing faculty whom I mercilessly plundered for leadership assignments within the administration. Julie became dean of the experiential program. In addition to competence, she brought a positive outlook and a can-do attitude. She was a joy. When our daughter Caroline was born in 1992, she and a group of selected Wagner nursing students extended extra care and love at the hospital.

Julie also led the Christmas caroling in our house at every annual faculty/staff holiday party. She died of lung cancer in 2008.

A great deal of what made my years at Wagner so satisfying was this very talented and very human group of professionals.

Chapter 11
Acorns Take Time to Become Oak Trees

My first academic year, 1988–1989, was tough every step of the way. After all, September 1988 was only four months after my arrival, and those first few months were spent frantically addressing a crisis that almost prevented the existence of an academic year at all. Most of what affects a college's enrollment and finances cannot be improved in so short a time. In fact, it can take years to improve enrollments at institutions that have been in a decade-long downslide. What most had to occur was to successfully demonstrate that the college could live within the limits of its resources; that is, there could be no more deficits.

Progress had to be made that would improve revenues—and that progress had to come from enrollment. Wagner had to find a way to attract more paying customers. With empty dorms and minimally enrolled classes, there was plenty of room for growth. If that growth didn't commence quickly, some trustees would continue to advocate leasing out excess property and dorms — a defeatist solution that had to be avoided at all cost.

Our new marketing message aimed to someday sell Wagner College as New York City's version of what Swarthmore and Haverford are to Philadelphia, or what Amherst and Williams are to Massachusetts. While that was nowhere close to reality in 1989, I believed it was not unreasonable for Wagner to aspire to that kind of status a generation or two down the road. In fact, there were no Swarthmore-esque colleges in New York City. The mantle was Wagner's for the taking — something the college should have aspired to decades earlier.

From a marketing perspective, the "best of both worlds" cliché stood the best chance of winning both prospective students and their bill-paying parents. By the 1980s, urban colleges and universities had gained popularity among college-bound students, especially males. Urban settings were rightfully seen as where the action was, where students could get a foot into a future career door while at college.

We also needed new marketing materials, and this is where Susan excelled, having previously overseen admissions at an art college where aesthetics was of the highest standard. Now having advertising guru Phil Dusenberry as a trustee gave us access to his firm's creative expertise, and his first contribution was to design a print ad for Wagner that corresponded to the message we thought would work with our applicant pools — namely, being near Manhattan but also feeling like a more rural campus setting.

We ran Phil's ad in all the usual places, including the educational supplements of major northeastern newspapers: *The New York Times*, the *Boston Globe* and the *Philadelphia Inquirer*. It is always hard to say exactly what part of a marketing campaign generates results, but we were lucky to have the professional touch of Dusenberry's BBDO largely donated because of his status as a trustee and honorary alumnus.

The college still needed to upgrade most of its facilities, as well as its academic programs. The college's ranking in the fourth (bottom) tier of *US News and World Report*'s rankings was a ball and chain. There continued to be a lot of subliminal sentiment that Wagner had too long a road to travel during difficult economic times and not enough positive change was likely to happen during the four years that prospective students would attend.

Sometimes I worried whether we would be given enough time, and resources for that matter, to pull this phoenix out of the ashes.

As each open house progressed, there were a few students and parents who were the kinds of families that Wagner needed to attract, namely, paying customers with academic promise. Such prospects were few and far between.

Susan shared another dilemma when she reported to me that she had met a wonderful student and her parents; exactly the type of student we wanted to recruit. She expressed her guilt in encouraging the student to enroll. "Wagner isn't ready to give a student like her everything she has a right to expect," Susan lamented. "I feel guilty promising her wonderful parents that we are everything they want us to be!"

I shared Susan's moral concern, but also knew that in this chicken-or-the-egg dilemma, we needed paying customers if we were going to have the money to make all the upgrades. It wasn't going to happen the other way around.

"We have a lot of really good faculty members and that, finally, is what a good college education is all about," I rationalized — and believed.

We would do everything to ensure that these truly motivated students were exposed to the college's best. Then, we would move as quickly as we could to make all the other improvements that were needed.

Susan agreed, and we proceeded with the realization of what we had to do and, in the end if we were successful, we wouldn't look back and regret anything.

With a new array of stunning publications developed by Admissions Dean Susan Robinson, complemented by an advertising campaign designed by Phil Dusenberry, Chairman of BBDO and new trustee of Wagner, the College gained wider recognition during the past year.

Go to college in New York City and avoid the crowds.

Location. Size. Program. Only Wagner has all three.

Wagner College is 86 beautiful, wooded acres on Staten Island—located just a few miles from midtown Manhattan. We offer small, intimate classes minutes from a bustling city of 7 million. And our liberal arts curriculum is designed to educate students while preparing them for the world of opportunity that's a ferry ride away.

60% of Fortune 500 CEOs graduated from colleges like Wagner. That's why we've held on to our small, private status. Wagner knows small classes where professors know their students as well as their subjects is the best way to learn.

High atop a hill on Staten Island, Wagner College has a unique view of the cultural and professional opportunities of Manhattan. With programs in liberal arts, business, education, the sciences, nursing and the performing and visual arts, Wagner's the natural place to learn in New York—or anywhere.

Call for a viewbook and application. 718-390-3411

WAGNER COLLEGE
STATEN ISLAND, NEW YORK

The only copy that I could find of this first ad was from an annual report that included a paper-clipped explanation. The ad ran without that tab.

Year TWO 1989–1990

Chapter 12
Trying to Turn a Pumpkin Into a Coach

Susan's concerns about all the missing or substandard resources throughout the college haunted me. Facing great austerity if Wagner was going to maintain fiscal balance, there was no money to spend on the needed improvements. Cleaning up the grounds, along with the investments we were making in admissions recruiting materials, were about the only such expenditures incurred, both of which were essential to generating enrollment revenues. Everything else Susan was citing would also contribute to future revenues. If it wasn't already clear to me, additional improvements were necessary before new enrollment revenues would be realized. The 1989–1990 year had to be a busier time of undertaking meaningful upgrades that would help sell Wagner to paying customers. Those improvements would be possible only from donations, not from greater tuition revenues, which were still several years away.

David Long was very aware of the need and aggressively went after all the foundations and corporations that had supported Skidmore throughout his tenure there. Many turned him down, but the ones that came through were a shot in the arm. In addition to the Calder Foundation's $250,000 grant, David also persuaded the Booth Ferris Foundation to give $100,000 for science center improvements, and the Clark Foundation gave $100,000 for computers. These projects were all important improvements since the science labs were a disgrace and there were no computers whatsoever — a void that virtually every prospective student noticed.

Martha Megerle's son, George, had joined the trustees and had become very interested in the condition of the science labs since the building was named in honor of his father. The current state of the labs didn't make the naming that much of an honor. George and his wife Judy wanted the problem corrected and contributed $175,000 to upgrade some of the labs that we put on the to-do list for the coming summer.

Wagner gets $175,000 for science center

By GLENN GOLZ
ADVANCE STAFF WRITER

Wagner College received a $175,000 grant to improve its science teaching resources, the college's chief fund-raiser David E. Long announced yesterday.

The gift comes from Wagner trustees Dr. George Megerle and his wife Judith and will go to renovate the Megerle Science Center, where "it has probably been 20 years since the last improvements were made," said College President Dr. Norman R. Smith.

"I hope it's a first step in what will ultimately be a renovation of the science center," Smith said. One third of Wagner College's faculty works in the Science Department, he said.

Renovations will begin later this spring and continue throughout the summer so that "we'll have this ready for the fall," Smith said.

"I hope it's a first step in what will ultimately be a renovation of the science center."

According to Smith, renovation of the center will make "significant contributions to improving resources and (will) certainly put us in a better position to recruit top science students."

Megerle, a retired chemist, is the son of Eugen Megerle, founder of the Wella Corp. for whom the science center is named.

After the Megerles attended the opening of the college's communications center last spring, Smith said, they were so impressed with the renovation that they decided to do the same thing for the science building.

"It came out of George's initiative," Smith said. "George is a scientist, and he wants to see us able to compete in the sciences."

Smith expressed gratitude to Megerle for getting "the ball rolling" but said more funding will be needed for the science center.

"This won't do the whole building," he said. "We are not sure how far this will get us."

The development office of Wagner College is looking for matching funds to supplement the funding for the science department, Long said. The amount of money needed will depend on the scope of renovations, he said, which has yet to be determined.

The Megerle family has been a long-time supporter of the college ever since Eugen Megerle and his wife moved to Staten Island from Europe, Smith said. "The Megerles have always been very close to the college," he said.

The renovation of the science building is just part of the renewed enthusiasm Wagner College has experienced recently. "All the numbers are pointing in the right direction, school spirit is up and our reputation is broader" said Smith, who also said more students are applying to the school from a wider geographical boundary.

According to Smith, much of the school's recent success has to do with Long, who he says is "one of the national stars of fund raising."

"All the numbers are pointing in the right direction, school spirit is up and our reputation is broader."

Previosuly Long worked at Skidmore College in Saratoga Springs, N.Y., where he played a key role in building the campus and endowment. "Wagner was very lucky to get him," Smith said.

Staten Island Advance circa 1989

A big boost was Don and Evelyn Spiro's $250,000 gift to build an expansive student personal computer lab. That was enough money, back in the late 80s, to do something impressive in a building called the communications center, which was in a state of terrible disrepair.

Computer center opens at Wagner

"It doesn't matter what field you go into, whether it's business or nursing or art, you are going to have to know how to use a computer to meet the competition."

The new Donald and Evelyn Spiro Computer Center at Wagner College

Staten Island Advance circa 1989

Another problem area was the Student Union. It really wasn't much of a student center at all, except for providing a place to eat. The only student recreational area, which appalled me, was a seedy-looking billiards parlor that sent out all the wrong messages about Wagner College. The Union needed to look better as it was also the building we used when gathering prospective students and their parents during campus visit days.

Don and Evelyn Spiro came to the rescue again. They agreed that the pool hall had to go and were drawn to the idea of a fitness center I sought for the primary use of non-athletes. The college's only sports facility was dominated by an expansive NCAA Division I athletic program, making it almost inaccessible to non-athletes. Colleges had been experiencing a generational shift that brought a new popularity to fitness centers with treadmills, stationary bicycles, and rowing machines. Such facilities had become a gathering place not only to exercise but also to meet new friends. Turning the pool hall into a modest version of a fitness center could make the entire building more student friendly. In reality, a fitness center in the Union would have its limitations since there were no locker rooms or showers — but it would be better than a pool hall.

At Don and Evelyn's request, the fitness center was named for a classmate and friend, Captain Joseph Parise, class of 1948. Parise was a World War II hero who had died in 1969. To open the center, Susan and I challenged the head basketball coach, Tim Capstraw, and a student, Brette Grae, to a one-mile race on the new treadmills. Athletic director Walt Hameline oversaw the race. I decided to start off at an easy pace of about five miles an hour and close with a sprint. Susan started at over six miles an hour, but I thought she would burn out and I would surpass her. In the final quarter mile, I pushed the treadmill to full speed, discovering, to my horror, that full speed was seven miles an hour, not fast enough for me to pass her in the final stretch. Susan won, I came in second, Brette third, and Coach Capstraw looked like he was ready to pass out.

Wagner unveils new fitness center

"Dr. Norman Smith, the school's president, finally broke into a sweat yesterday."

"I feel physical fitness is a prerequisite for mental fitness."

"By the way, he lost the race to his wife."

Fall 1989 Staten Island Advance

Excerpt from above media account

"After turning in a balanced budget for the first time since 1982 and bringing back to life a college facing hard times only a year ago, Dr. Norman Smith, the school's president, finally broke into a sweat yesterday. But the beads of perspiration on his brow did not come from the stress of running the Grymes Hill school. Rather, he was breaking in a treadmill at the school's new Capt. Joseph Parise Fitness Center."

Making a statement about the arts also seemed important. David responded by finding foundation support to upgrade the gallery.

Additionally, Stan Shilling approached a local plate-glass company to install a glass wall entry. The company, headed by the Steinman family, enthusiastically contributed materials and labor. The Steinmans became good friends and advocates throughout our years at Wagner.

In addition to the art gallery, we upgraded a space in Campus Hall that was originally a student lounge when the building was a dormitory. Although not ideal, the space at least gave the music department a place for their orchestras, bands, and choirs to rehearse and, occasionally, to perform.

My longer-term aspiration was to build a performing arts center that would serve these groups, not to mention the college's truly extraordinary theatre department.

Wagner students enjoying 'new' arts spaces

Staten Island Advance circa 1989

Chapter 13
Diamonds in the Rough

Two Wagner programs managed to be their very best with little support and even less in the way of resources. My first Wagner theatre experience was in the fall of 1988. *My Fair Lady* would be the first of four fully staged performances that year.

The theatre department had been cited as something special, but my earlier visit to their facilities left me underwhelmed. They operated out of what most would consider a poor excuse for even a high school multiuse auditorium. Nothing suggested college-level performing arts.

I attended opening night, pleased to see that the auditorium was full. What I didn't realize, but what all the other attendees already knew, was that these performances were well worth attending. In fact, the theatre department ran each of their shows for up to two continuous weeks filling their albeit-small 350-capacity venue every night—and with *paying* customers.

From this first performance, I was swept off my feet by how well every detail was presented, and I wondered how they did it. Wagner's theatre program had been a longstanding center of excellence well known to students aspiring to careers in theatre. And why not? Here was a college near Broadway. What better place to study theatre, except, of course, in Manhattan? This was exactly the message that made the case for Wagner College.

Throughout my fourteen years as president, I never missed one of the fifty-six Broadway-class shows they performed. In fact, I usually attended multiple performances, using them as opportunities to bring friends, guests, and prospective patrons. I was never disappointed.

Once, during a run of *Damn Yankees,* we invited the show's librettist, Richard Adler, to attend. Adler, who had also written *The Pajama Game,* reacted passively to the invitation. He said he rarely attended performances of his works anymore.

Nevertheless, with the promise of a stretch limo and Veuve Clicquot champagne (his favorite expensive brand), he somewhat reluctantly agreed to attend.

Upon seeing the performance, Adler declared it as good as the original Broadway version and better than any revival he ever attended. Not having seen the original, I couldn't say, but Wagner's interpretation ranks among my fondest memories.

I think I attended at least a dozen performances of that one show, each time taking a Trustee or prospective major donor.

These wonderful theatre performances were perhaps my most effective fundraising catalyst. Night after night, we would invite potential benefactors.

Never did anyone walk away from one of these performances unconvinced that Wagner had something special going for it.

And—they were right.

Wagner: 'Act-centuate' the positive

School's theatrical program has nationwide reputation

The cast of "Our Town" featured students from 13 different states.

By RICHARD T. RYAN
ADVANCE STAFF WRITER

They come from all over — Houston, St. Louis, Louisville, Miami and Brooklyn — with differing degrees of talent, but a common dream. All they want is a chance to sing the song, to read the lines — to show the director what they really can do.

These are not, however, chorines and chorus boys auditioning for parts in a Broadway musical, but rather students at Wagner College. In the world of college theater, Wagner has been quietly making a national name for itself as a school with a top-flight program that deserves due consideration from anyone interested in pursuing a career on the stage.

"In theater circles, we have become one of the schools that students who are serious about theater hope they can get into," said Gary Sullivan, chairman of the theater and speech department.

Couple Wagner's location, just a ferry-ride from Broadway, with its attractive, idyllic campus, and you can offer students the best of both worlds. As an added incentive, Wagner can point to graduates such as Betsy Joslyn and Randy Graff — both of whom have appeared on Broadway — which makes recruiting that much easier.

"Our students come from Maine to Florida and from California to the Carolinas," Sullivan laughed. He's not exaggerating.

"In the world of college theater, Wagner has been quietly making a national name for itself as a school with a top-flight program that deserves due consideration from anyone interested in pursuing a career on the stage."

Among the cast members of "Our Town," the most recent Wagner production, were representatives from 13 different states. Their reasons for studying at Wagner are as varied as the parts they play, yet there are certain threads they all share in common.

Dori Rosenthal, a junior from Louisville, Ky., was recruited by Wagner at the annual Southeastern Theater Conference. A graduate of Performing Arts School in Louisville, Miss Rosenthal said, "I never wanted to go to college, and now I want to go to graduate school."

With several featured roles to her credit including Audrey, the female lead in "Little Shop of Horrors," Miss Rosenthal said that she received "a lot of offers" from different colleges but selected Wagner primarily because of its location.

Although she has yet to land her first professional job, the exposure gained from "Little Shop" has gotten her a manager. "I'm so glad I came here," she said.

In addition to her acting experience, she has also served as assistant director for "Our Town," a position that earned her intern credits.

A junior from St. Petersburg, Fla., Amy Bender, like Rosenthal, was recruited at the Southeastern Theater Conference. "I had heard about Wagner prior to the conference. It's one of the few schools that do a lot of musicals.

"I didn't feel that I was ready for a heavily dramatic program, so this was perfect for me."

Although she confesses to approaching Wagner somewhat unrealistically — "It's in New York, so you think you'll be on Broadway by the time you're a sophomore" — she now looks at things differently.

"We learn so much. I'm seeing others do it (professionally) and reading the trade papers, and learning how to do it myself."

Although it's been a bit different from what she expected, Miss Bender said, "I could never say that I wasn't pleased."

James Tambini, a sophomore from Portland, Maine, found Wagner because of an alumnus who lived near him. "I had never heard of Wagner, but James Fontaine, a graduate, told me to take a look at the school." Obviously, Tambini liked what he found.

"I'm here for the theater — to do the shows. Also, it's great to be near the city," he said. Although he had looked at other schools, the universities of Maine and Maryland, with the help of Fontaine, Tambini ultimately decided to try life on Grymes Hill.

"When someone graduates from Wagner, even if they haven't played a lot of roles, they have confidence because they know so much."

Despite only being in his second year, Tambini was recently seen as Seymour, the male lead in "Little Shop of Horrors." He will also be seen as Anselmo in the upcoming production of "Man of La Mancha."

Mike Walsh is another transplanted Floridian. He attended the same high school as Miss Bender, and was also recruited at the Southeastern Theater Conference. "I was considering schools like Emerson in Boston and the Florida schools, but since Wagner was in New York, it seemed like the right place to be."

learn about the business. A lot of people who graduate from other schools don't know where to go to look for a job, who to see, what papers to read or how important a good head shot is. I chose a roommate from here who could show me around. A lot of kids from out of state appreciate that fact.

"When someone graduates from Wagner, even if they haven't played a lot of roles, they have confidence because they know so much," Dell'Armo added.

Anne DeFazio, a junior from Niagara Falls, said that her mother "had friends who graduated from Wagner." In addition to acting, Miss DeFazio plays the piano and sings. She's also carrying a double major — theater and education — "just in case."

"I can see myself as a 40-year-old teacher but not as a 40-year-old unemployed actress. I'm a realist," she said.

Staten Island Advance circa 1990's excerpt:

They come from all over --- Houston, St. Louis, Louisville, Miami and Brooklyn – with differing degrees of talent, but a common dream. All they want is a chance to sing the song, to read the lines – to show the director what they can do. These are not, however, chorines and chorus boys auditioning for parts in a Broadway musical, but rather students at Wagner College. In the world of college theater, Wagner has been quietly making a national name for itself as a school with a top-flight program that deserves due consideration from anyone interested in pursuing a career on the stage. "In theater circles, we have become one of the schools that students who are serious about theater hope they can get into," said Gary Sullivan, chairman of the theater and speech department. Couple Wagner's location, just a ferry-ride from Broadway, with its attractive, idyllic campus, and you can offer students the best of both worlds.

The theatre's tradition of excellence had nothing to do with me. The great character actor, Robert Loggia (*Scarface, The Sopranos, etc.,*) was part of the theatre department in the late 1940s when he was a classmate of Don Spiro. Randy Graff,'76, who won the Tony Award for *City of Angels* and introduced the Broadway role of Fantine in *Les Miserables* (*I Dreamed a Dream*) was also a graduate before my time. And there are many others who ended up on the Broadway stage.

Norman Smith

I saw* Damn Yankees *at least a dozen times

Another diamond in the rough was Wagner's athletic program. All the accolades of his spinning gold from straw rightfully go to Walt Hameline, athletic director and football coach, who made miracles happen while working in the worst possible conditions that any athletic director in NCAA Division I faced. Today, the football field is named for him and he is a Wagner Vice President.

Like me, Walt was then what many would typically characterize as a Young Turk ... and, like me, he may have seen the same opportunity that Wagner represented. A graduate of the University of Albany who then went on to a junior coaching job at Brown University, Walt was offered the position of athletic director and head football coach at a very early stage in his career, when only a college like Wagner would make the offer to someone so young.

September 1988 *Sports Illustrated* article is available in full at www.sivault.com

The year before I arrived at Wagner, Walt's football team had won the coveted NCAA national championship (Division III) and *Sports Illustrated* magazine had already heralded the achievement, albeit in a backhanded kind of way. In a four-page feature, the article had essentially lauded Walt for managing to turn a sow's ear into a silk purse. Although the magazine may not have been wrong about that, there didn't seem much promise in that sow's ear drawing students, other than football players, to such a characterization.

Archival

Coach Hameline with his grasp on the situation, as always

Walt was, and continues to be, special. Even though he had already established himself as a winner, he didn't behave as someone with expectations of reward—at least, not at any time soon. Most remarkable were the conditions and resources with which he was trying to run an NCAA Division I program. Being in Division I lines up an institution with the Notre Dames, USCs, and Ohio States, not to mention Harvard,

Princeton, and Yale. Wagner was so far away from that classification that it was reminiscent of the Peter Sellers' movie, *The Mouse That Roared,* in which a tiny European duchy declared war on the USA to be eligible for the aid typically granted to the defeated country. The David-and-Goliath comparisons defied most onlookers' sense of logic.

To say that Walt had facilities comparable to a run-down urban high school might be an overstatement. He was running a full college program of about twenty different sports, male and female, out of what would be compared to a low-class high school basketball gymnasium. A small row of offices ran the length of the basketball court on one side. Additionally, there was a basement with a few locker rooms, showers, and a couple of squash courts. That was it. Out of doors, Walt had a football field, but no seating for fans. Every fall, the college rented some makeshift, circus-type wooden bleachers for the home games. There was also a baseball field without bleachers. Additionally, there were six tennis courts on the far side of the campus, all of which needed to be resurfaced.

Yet Walt had assembled an enthusiastic group of young assistant coaches who were happy to be in a Division I program early in their careers. The downside, though, was that all these young coaches moved on quickly as soon as another Division I job materialized at a college or university that had the resources to support such a program. Walt was faced annually with recruiting a new cadre of short-term coaches. Yet there was nothing beleaguered about Walt. He was everything a motivational coach needed to be. His enthusiasm was infectious, and the quality of his athletic program defied the circumstances under which he was operating.

It didn't take long for me to realize that Wagner's strongest enrollment magnets were these two programs: theatre and athletics. On the merits of exceptional leadership (Gary Sullivan, Lewis Hardee, and Randy Alderson in theatre, and Walter Hameline in athletics), these two programs were the only ones drawing students from other parts of the country, and both were receiving media attention from sources other than the *Staten Island Advance.*

Both programs had earned the College's commitment to their future and deserved to eventually have suitable facilities and resources. That might not happen for years to come, but a sports center and performing arts center were needed at Wagner College. I started making that case every chance I could get, at least to the trustees, to hopefully plant some acorns that would someday become oak trees.

The enrollment solution, though, was not going to be found in theatre and athletics. As a Division I program, Wagner was spending a great deal of money (or forgoing it) by offering sports scholarships, a requirement of Division I. As a result, unless additional sports were added, the athletic program was enrolled to capacity. Significant enrollment growth wasn't going to come from finding more athletes.

The same capacity issue existed in theatre. With only one stage showing four fully staged plays, the program couldn't handle additional students. The theatre faculty was turning away good applicants because there were only so many students who could be cast or otherwise engaged in the productions. To their credit, the theatre faculty always selected shows that had large casts but even then they had more students than they needed and certainly didn't want to take on more.

Enrollment growth was going to have to be in the other academic areas of the college. That didn't mean, however, that theatre and athletics couldn't be used to establish a standard of excellence at Wagner. Both were crown jewels, and the college could sparkle that much more by their example.

The athletic program did strike me as a magnet that could attract other students. Since Walt had the luxury of awarding Division I sports scholarships that didn't have to be financial need based, I asked him to increase his efforts to recruit students from schools in economically stronger communities, where most students come from families that have the financial wherewithal to send their kids to a private college.

Most small, private colleges like Wagner participate in Division II and III athletic programs where only need-based scholarships are permitted. As a result, Division II and III coaches too often recruit their top athletes from economically depressed areas, thereby optimizing the recruits' eligibility for need-based aid. The student and his or her family tend to perceive the need-based scholarship as an athletic one, even though it really isn't. Division II and III programs cannot offer financial grants to a good athlete from a more affluent area where financial need cannot be justified.

Wagner, however, was among the few small, private, residential colleges that could recruit an athlete from these more affluent suburbs and raise the visibility of the college at that high school, which might, in turn, draw applications from non-athletic students at that same high school. If a star baseball or basketball player is recruited to Wagner, some of his or her friends and admirers might want to come along too. If, on the other hand, Wagner recruited too heavily at high-need schools, the scholarship athlete will not be a magnet for other students. Walt understood the concept and redirected his recruiting efforts in ways that, over time, worked to Wagner's benefit.

In 2022, the Wagner football team took on Temple University in the Philadelphia Eagles stadium. We once "Young Turks" with spouses Susan and Debi watched Wagner lose but otherwise enjoyed every moment. While the Wagner football players are often outscored by teams like the Naval Academy and Rutgers, Walt says they love the big-time aura of such games and wouldn't avoid them at any cost.

Chapter 14
The Financial Time Bomb Ticks Loudly

Although the priorities of the first year, 1988-1989, had been pretty straightforward, everything wasn't going to get done in one year. The top items that did need to happen were, first and foremost, staying within budget, and closing with an operating balance for the first time in six years. That outcome was necessary to satisfy the minimum expectations of the local banks that had provided a short-term loan. The New York State Department of Higher Education similarly required that result if they were going to let the college stay in business. And the Middle States Commission on Higher Education was going to rescind accreditation if the deficits had not been reversed.

The next priority was to raise the visibility of the college among prospective applicants from a wider geographic parameter to start filling more dorm rooms before yet more overtures to sell the Harborview residence tower re-emerged. And, of course, improved enrollment revenues were expected and very much needed. These additional students had to pay a larger portion of their tuition. The 50+% average discount that had been in place to attract students away from CUNY had to be reduced by finding students whose families had greater wherewithal to afford the cost of a private college.

Another pressing priority was the need to find a long-term debt model that would replace the two-year mortgage provided reluctantly by the local banks. This was turning out to be harder than should have been the case. The local bankers made it clear that they wanted out *yesterday*, and they had no interest in giving the college a conventional twenty- or thirty-year mortgage.

One of the participating bank presidents expressed serious regret for having participated in the short-term loan, fearing that foreclosure might be necessary if I couldn't find a long-term solution. None of the bankers wanted to foreclose because Wagner was too important to Staten Island. Too many of their depositors were Wagner alumni. It wouldn't be pretty for them. Off-island, no one seemed interested in financing the college's debt.

When your audited books for the past six years were in annual multimillion dollar deficit, there isn't much there to justify a loan. Most bankers told me that I would have to show an audited outcome of fiscal balance for at least two years combined with a meaningful upswing in enrollment revenues. Neither of these outcomes could happen within the two-year deadline set by the local banks. Throughout the first year, we were staying in fiscal balance, but it would take time to end the fiscal year and then be audited before there were verifiable results for the banks. Similarly, the earliest enrollment upswing would be in the fall of 1989.

All we could do was focus on fiscal restraint and admissions marketing in hopes that the vital signs would look better next year. If they did, little time would remain to refinance before the short-term debt came due. Like Gary Cooper in the classic western *High Noon*, I could hear the clock ticking loudly throughout every day.

Chapter 15
Is That a Light at the End of the Tunnel?

The fall of 1989, the beginning of my second full academic year, was highlighted by what looked like a bona fide successful fiscal balance that had been achieved for the prior year. The books still had to be audited, as the fiscal year ended August 31, but we had been carefully monitoring virtually every expense throughout the year and were pretty sure we had achieved the first year of fiscal balance in years, although not without considerable restraint that had prevented making a lot of progress that would have helped enormously.

We were looking forward to soon being able to report to our bankers, our accreditors at Middle States, and to the New York State Department of Education, that the six years of multimillion deficits were now under control and that we had accomplished that quite remarkable turnaround in the first year. That outcome had to count for something and would hopefully lend credibility to the ambitious plans that had been laid out for Wagner's future.

Enrollments had not been turned around as quickly and were going to be harder to sell to the nonbelievers. As Jack Kerouac declared, "*Walking on water wasn't built in a day.*"

The fall enrollment was pretty much the same as it had been the year before, just under 1,200 total students, although academic quality had improved, as had out-of-state enrollments and net revenues as the result of lower discount rates. There just hadn't been enough time to get a viable admissions machine running since the fall before. In fact, most prospective applicants start making decisions about college choice in their junior year. If you don't have them as juniors, you are unlikely to get them as seniors. By the time Susan took over admissions, most of the annual admissions cycle was past, and the die was largely cast. It is almost impossible to generate new applications for the coming year after the fall of the existing year except among those students who were turned down elsewhere and were now looking for a fallback.

This ship wasn't going to be turned around as quickly as needed. It was going to take years.

There was a silver lining in the enrollment data. One of the reasons Wagner had been in multimillion dollar deficit for six straight years was that no one seemed to understand Wagner was selling the product for less than it cost. Wagner had been discounting its tuition at a rate exceeding 50%. Having a Division I program didn't help because of the full-scholarship athletes mandated by the NCAA. Additionally, Wagner was "buying" local students who would cite the low cost of attending the City University of Staten Island campus that, along with St. John's, had been key to Wagner's decline fifteen years earlier.

When 1,200 students are discounted an average of 50+%, the net enrollment is half the headcount. That is, Wagner needed to recognize it was only enrolling fewer than 600 net students and needed to build budgets based on 600 instead of 1,200 students — even though 1,200 heads were attending.

Throughout the first year, Bea Snyder, the new financial aid director, had been going through all upper-class financial aid packages attempting to re-craft each to reflect financial reality. Many of the students enrolled had been given college grant aid unconditionally, without having to submit the financial reports that might have made them eligible for state or federal aid that would represent additional actual dollars for Wagner. If the discounting could be replaced by the state and federal aid, Wagner could get money that was needed.

Bea also checked all students for financial wherewithal and for bill payment delinquency. Any student receiving grant aid and posting failing grades, along with those who were not paying their portion of the outstanding tuition bill, lost renewal of their grant for the coming year.

All these policies, along with similar guidelines being adopted in admissions, resulted in the fall 1989 enrollment of 1,200 averaging a 42% average grant aid offering, down from 50% the year before. At a 42% discount instead of over 50%, the net enrollment was growing even though the headcount itself remained unchanged. So, there were two quite different ways to look at the enrollment outcome. Those who counted heads, as most of the Wagner community, including trustees, had done for years, saw no progress: 1,200 versus 1,200.

Those who were counting net heads saw an increase of 100 students, from 600 full-paying customers to 700 full-paying customers. This translated into one million dollars more revenue without one additional actual student.

Don Spiro had now assumed the chairmanship of the board for this second year. Al Corbin moved from treasurer to vice chair. Kevin Sheehy took over the secretary's position. Richard Herburger, '66, who was Chief Financial Officer of Citicorp Credit Services, had been recruited by Al Corbin to join the trustees and take over as treasurer. The composition of the trustee leadership had changed dramatically in just one year, and not a moment too soon.

Unfortunately, the local bankers weren't happy to hear that the enrollment 'headcount' hadn't increased. One bank president declared to my face that I had failed to live up to my promises. All the local bankers once again reiterated their disinterest in extending the debt while concurrently reminding me that Wagner had less than a year remaining to pay them back. In fairness, some of the bankers, most notably John Amodio, were at least somewhat complimentary of the changes that had been occurring. To my gratification, both the State Department of Education and the Middle States Commission on Higher Education reacted positively to the outcomes, declaring that a great deal of improvement had taken place in a very short period.

We had pushed our auditors to get to work quickly so that we could confirm a first balanced year in nearly a decade, and they did come to that conclusion. It wasn't much of a surplus: $20,000, to be exact. But after spending millions more annually than it had been making, Wagner had shown the world that it could live within its means—a giant step toward securing a future for the college.

Most important, this was the first good fiscal news that could be quantified. Something had turned for the better. There was hope. I assembled the faculty and staff to show them the budget and how we had turned one million in overspending into a balance. The faculty and staff had never previously seen an operating budget and had no idea how revenues were realized or how they were spent. That wouldn't happen again.

Wagner's $$ surplus a big plus

By DON GROSS
ADVANCE STAFF WRITER

An audit of Wagner College gives the school some very good news after several years of financial strain.

The audit by the accounting firm of Peat Marwick Mitchell delivered late Tuesday shows the Grymes Hill school closed the 1988-89 fiscal year with a $20,779 surplus. It is the first time Wagner has closed its books without a deficit since 1982.

"A $20,000 surplus out of a $20 million budget isn't very much," said Dr. Norman Smith, president of Wagner. "But it is a surplus."

In 1988, the school ended the year with $1.4 million in red ink.

The fact the college ended the year in the black he said, was the important thing. "It means we're not going to have a problem anymore," he said.

Smith said bringing the budget under control was a major demand of the banks that lent the school $6.5 million a year ago.

"We can now go to them and try and convert this very expensive short-term debt into a long-term loan," he said.

Although the school has been paying only interest on the two-year note since July 1988, Smith said the interest rates were high and that extending the terms of the loan would mean a reduction in the amount of the school's payments, actually allowing the school to spend more.

"This school's problem wasn't that it was spending too much, but that it wasn't making enough," he said.

Among Smith's first acts on taking over as president in July 1988, was ending a longstanding policy of giving scholarships that weren't supported by endowment. Smith referred to these scholarships as "discounts" on tuition.

Smith is one of a new breed of college administrators with degrees in higher education administration. He received his doctorate in this area from Harvard University's Graduate School of Education.

Smith, however, credited the Wagner staff, particularly its grounds crew, with improving conditions at the college while spending less money. "The conditions of the surroundings has a lot to do with our recruitment and retention efforts," he said.

"Smith, credited the Wagner staff, particularly its grounds crew, with improving conditions at the college while spending less money."

But with the improvements of the college grounds and buildings under way, Smith said he now intends to turn his attention to the faculty.

"We need to add about 10 faculty positions," he said. He would particularly like to beef up the humanities teaching staff and the school's business department.

"We just don't have the kind of expertise we need to run both an undergraduate and a graduate business school," he said.

Smith also said that bringing in a balanced budget would help the school raise endowment money it needs to permanently end its financial problems.

"We now have a strong budget we can show corporate givers who might have been put off by our past problems," he said. "We can now go to them and tell them we are as strong as any small college in the country."

Staten Island Advance Fall 1989 excerpt:

An audit of Wagner College gives the school some very good news after several years of financial strain. The audit by Peat Marwick Mitchell delivered late Tuesday shows the Grymes Hill school closed the 1988-89 years with a $20,779 surplus. It is the first time Wagner has closed its books without a deficit since 1982. "A $20,000 surplus isn't very much," said Dr. Norman Smith, president of Wagner. "But it is a surplus." In 1988, the school ended the year with $1.4 million in red ink.

Faculty and staff also needed to understand the enrollment outcome. By my accounting, we opened the second year with one hundred more students than the previous year. At a net level, going from 600 to 700 full-paying equivalents was a 15% improvement. The faculty and staff did understand. A sense that things were getting better was beginning to prevail.

Enrollment on rise at Wagner

Many institutions witnessing declines

By TOM BERMAN
Advance STAFF WRITER

While many colleges throughout the country are facing declining enrollments, Wagner College is anticipating a 15 percent increase in its freshman class for the coming academic year, officials at the Grymes Hill institution announced yesterday.

"Things have been looking good all year" said Dr. Susan Robinson, the college's dean of admissions. "Now that we're only a few weeks away from the fall opening, it appears that we are indeed ahead in our freshman enrollment."

Dr. Robinson attributed Wagner's growing enrollment to the college's burgeoning academic reputation. Last month, for example, the prestigious Middle States Commission of Colleges affirmed Wagner's full, unqualified re-accreditation.

Another factor contributing to Wagner's increasing attractiveness to prospective students, Dr. Robinson said, is the administration's ongoing effort to refurbish the campus and improve its aesthetic appeal.

"Most of our applications come from students and their parents after they visit the college," Dr. Robinson said. "As they walk around the campus, out-of-state visitors remark that they can't believe they're actually in New York City."

I'm very gratified that everything we've been doing to improve Wagner's quality is being acknowledged by our admissions results," Smith said. "We've been receiving a lot of unofficial reports from neighboring private colleges that are facing enormous enrollment declines this fall."

Citing a national decline in college-age students that will last through the mid-199Os, Smith said: "A lot of colleges may not make it through the enrollment drought, but it appears Wagner College has the traits and quality that parents and students seek."

Staten Island Advance Winter 1990

However, we still needed someone who would give us a loan to replace the one the local bankers wouldn't extend. No one on Staten Island seemed interested and everyone off Staten Island was even less interested. Then along came a mass mailed promotional postcard from David Czyganowski at First Boston. The mailing was a boilerplate solicitation not dissimilar to what homeowners get from real estate agents wanting to sell their houses. David was a young hot-to-trot investment banker at First Boston whose territory was nonprofits like colleges and universities. His postcard read like it had been custom made for Wagner's needs, asking if we were having trouble financing debt through traditional banks because of our nonprofit status.

David offered a First Boston solution that, in retrospect, sounded much like ads today that give credit card debtors a hope that they can dig themselves out of the financial hole they are in. Dave proposed that we issue our own bonds to investors who might be willing to take more risk than a bank, but, of course, for a heftier premium.

Paying an excessive premium in what was already a high-interest rate environment didn't thrill any of us, but beggars can't be choosers. The loan repayment deadline was closing in on the college, and no good deals were coming our way. So, I decided to at least invite Dave to tell us more. Dave visited the college within a day or two of my follow-up. He was high-energy and gregarious, very much like a Hollywood casting Wall Street "Master of the Universe."

At this point, Wagner had an impressive chief financial officer, Dr. Sebastian Persico, who was recruited a few months earlier. Sebastian earned his doctorate at Harvard Graduate School of Education during the time I was an assistant dean there. Like Dave Czyganowski, Sebastian had a gregarious personality. They got along well.

Sebastian, David Long, and I took Dave on a tour of the college. By now the campus was starting to look very presentable, and Dave immediately picked up on that. He also said he was impressed with the kinds of people who were coming on to the management team if David and Sebastian were typical. The big hurdle in issuing bonds, he advised us, was whether we could successfully obtain an investment grade bond rating from a rating agency like Standard and Poor's or Moody's. The farther away from junk bond status we could get, the better interest rates we could obtain in the sale of the bonds.

Czyganowski said he very much liked our vision and was impressed with the way we presented the future of the college. He also believed that what had been accomplished in the first year was extraordinary and a demonstration of what could happen going forward. He said he wanted to help us prepare for some bond rating agency meetings if we were game. As a management team, he thought we would make a good impression with the rating agencies, and he encouraged us to proceed. He also, of course, wanted the business.

I contacted Don Spiro, who gave the green light to proceed. We didn't have any other irons in the fire, and the bank mortgage deadline was closing in. No alternative ideas were emerging from any of the trustees. I had most wanted a long-term mortgage with a more conventional interest rate, but there were no offers. I had hoped some of our newer trustees could open doors that were closed to us, but it wasn't happening.

The bond rating process turned out to be more time consuming than I had thought it would be. There were lots of rehearsals. Czyganowski was a taskmaster who seemed to know what needed to be done to win over the rating agencies. We went to Standard and Poor's, Moody's, and a couple of other rating agencies. The smaller agencies turned us down. We were too much of a risk, having only had one year under our belts.

Standard and Poor's, however, responded favorably. The rating team specialized in nonprofits and seemed to understand what we were trying to accomplish. Further, they were persuaded by our vision.

The presentation team for the rating reviews included Susan Robinson, who was especially effective in making the case for improved future admissions outcomes. As ratings are largely dependent on financial outcomes, and Wagner was over 90% dependent on enrollment revenues, admissions prospects were most important.

Susan made a notably favorable impression with the Standard and Poor's people. Her doctorate from Harvard and prior success in admissions at Moore College of Art in Philadelphia were strong factors, as was her overall intelligence in being able to respond with authority and without hesitation to the aggressive questioning coming from the credit rating team. Sebastian was also effective in being able to present a financial story that assured continued fiscal stability. David Long made a very strong impression when comparing Wagner to what Skidmore had been when he and venerable president Joe Palamountain started there together decades earlier. One couldn't have asked for more gravitas and credibility for these rating agencies than what David brought to the table.

My presentation, Dave volunteered, laid out an ambitious future for Wagner that sounded plausible and generated enough credibility to win a Standard and Poor's investment grade credit rating — exactly what we needed to launch a successful bond sale in time to pay back the local banks that continued to want out.

Our S&P rating ranked Wagner with Pratt, Pace, Hofstra, Rider, and Seton Hall, giving a new level of stature that we included in admissions recruiting marketing campaigns.

At about the same time, Barron's upgraded their rating of Wagner to *competitive*— another welcome surprise. St. John's University, routinely considered superior among locals, had been ranked *less competitive*, and CUNY-Staten Island was declared to be *non-competitive*. We were on our way up the ladder. On Staten Island, where just two years ago we were the third of three, we were now the top dog in at least one rating source.

The *Staten Island Advance* ran a headline story that heralded Wagner's *top financial rating*. While we knew that "investment grade" wasn't the top rating that Standard and Poor's awarded, we were happy with the way in which the story reinforced a spirit of progress and optimism to Wagner onlookers.

With an investment grade rating, we were able to consider an amount of debt more than the short-term bank loan, which would provide the college with some up-front capital to repair and upgrade the most pressing physical problems that were deterring paying customers from enrolling.

The dorms were in terrible shape. Bathrooms needed repair. New mattresses were needed throughout, along with the replacement of missing furniture. The Student Union had no furniture. The dining hall needed a new ceiling, new lighting, and new furniture. The campus was pitch black at night. Students needed flashlights to walk from the classrooms to the dorms. All the classrooms needed work. In some cases, the blackboards were completely worn out and wouldn't even take chalk.

Al Corbin, John Lehmann, Don Spiro, Bob Evans, Kevin Sheehy, and Richard Herburger all took the lead in making the case for a seventeen-million-dollar bond issue that would provide repaying the local banks, while also providing ten million dollars for improvements, endowment reimbursement, and contingency reserves.

The spring of 1990 was spent formulating the bond issue, including more meetings to sell prospective investors. These gatherings were like the credit rating agency presentations and consumed an enormous amount of time, especially from David Long, Sebastian Persico, Susan Robinson, and me.

I worried that David and Susan were being taken away from their important revenue-generating jobs too frequently, thereby making it even more impossible to fulfill the promises we were trying to sell to these investors.

Our most promising investor, it would turn out, was the Harvard University endowment. David Czyganowski went to them noting that Wagner's president, dean of admissions, and chief financial officer all had Harvard doctorates, and the president, me, was a former Harvard graduate school dean. It worked.

The Harvard investors came to Wagner, expressed great enthusiasm about what they saw, and appeared to be ready to buy up the entire issue of seventeen million on the spot. As it turned out, they did take the largest portion but not all of it.

At this point, we were also getting good indicators that Susan's admissions efforts were starting to pay off. Applications were up for the fall by over 30% and most, 27%, were residential students, comprising a breakthrough in new applicant markets. All this added to the appeal of the bond issue at a very timely moment in the process

The actual bond transaction date, the one that set the interest rate, was August 2, 1990, the exact same day that the United States launched the Desert Shield defense of Kuwait. On that day, Treasury Bond interest rates were set at a gruesome 8.5% that within days rose to 9%.

If only the local banks had given us a mortgage, we would have saved massive amounts of interest payments in the years ahead.

But even with a new board of trustees that featured myriad Wall Street investment bankers, this was the only refinancing opportunity that came our way. The board agreed that we were without alternatives, given the state of the economy, and that we should take it with the hope that we could refinance at better rates when both the economy and the college were better positioned.

After my departure in 2002, I was told that some have characterized this financial transaction as unwise and even worse. While I don't claim the solution was ideal, it was the only solution at that time and I don't know what could have been done that was wiser, given the cards we were dealt.

Sometimes we are victims of the circumstances of the moment, which greatly reduces options. That Wagner had so little going for it two decades ago may be hard to fathom for those who arrived later and found a college that seemed generations away from the troubles that nearly closed it down. Monday morning quarterbacks often shoot from the knee without knowing or appreciating history.

The bond transaction date was halfway through the summer of 1990. We had known months earlier that the bond sale was going to happen with Harvard University being the largest investor. Not only would we realize the monies needed to reimburse the reluctant Staten Island banks, but we would also have the money needed to improve facilities that were a deterrent to recruiting students.

Bond sale a big plus for Wagner

BY ADVANCE STAFF WRITER

Portraying it as the "final step" in the restructuring of finances at Wagner College, the college's president, Dr. Norman Smith, announced today that the First Boston Corporation has successfully sold a bond issue of $17 million that gives the college the long-term financing it has been seeking since Smith's arrival more than two years ago.

The bond proceeds were sought to refinance accumulated debt incurred prior to Smith's arrival that was currently being paid through a short-term, high-interest mortgage. "That mortgage is now paid in full," said Smith, noting that the bond issue does not require land as collateral.

"What is most exciting about this refinancing is that the proceeds will provide us with several million dollars for campus improvements that will permit us to renovate student housing, dining facilities and classrooms," said Smith. He confirmed that the improvements are already under way. "Before the end of the academic year, most of the work will be complete."

Smith emphasized the importance of the improvements in recruiting and retaining students. "It has been my belief that Wagner's future is based on its success in recruiting students from a wider geographic distance. After college in the area and therefore the only one capable of a diverse student body," said Smith. "One of the real advantages in attending a private residential college is the opportunity to meet students from other parts of the country and build personal and professional networks that last a lifetime."

He said that the campus improvements would make the college more attractive to students from other areas who may be visiting a variety of colleges as they consider which one to attend. "The appeal of a well cared-for campus is fundamental to recruiting success," he said.

Smith expressed relief that the bond financing was successfully completed.

"Our bonds were sold on the day that Iraq invaded Kuwait," he reported. "Interest rates started going up the next day and have been increasing steadily ever since. To date, we have saved over $2 million in potential debt service by closing when we did."

Sources close to the college indicated that the major investor in the Wagner bonds was the Harvard University endowment, which reportedly found interest in Wagner because of Smith's background at Harvard. Prior to coming to Wagner, Smith received his doctorate from Harvard and was a dean at two of the university's

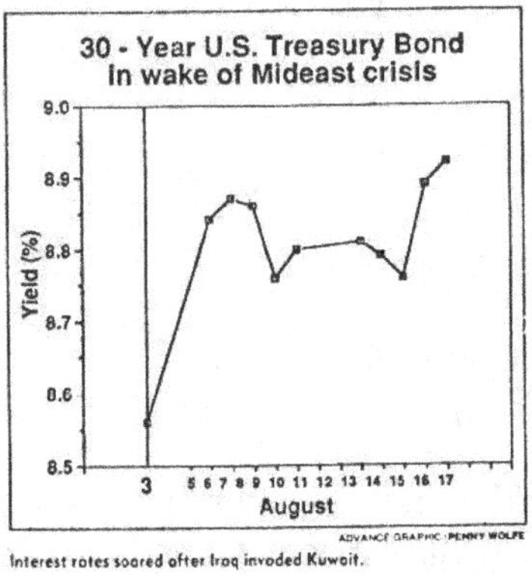

Interest rates soared after Iraq invaded Kuwait.

"It's now on to other issues," said Smith, "with the confidence that the college is well into a position for a strong future."

Smith would not confirm the Harvard investment. "Our investors wish to remain anonymous as a standard practice associated with keeping their investment strategies confidential," said Smith.

"While I'm grateful that our financial position is now secured, I do want to thank the community bankers on Staten Island for giving me the time to pursue this long-term solution," said Smith. He acknowledged Gateway Bank, Community National Bank and Northfield Savings Bank as the three local financial institutions that provided the short-term financing two years ago that permitted Wagner to reorganize financially.

"Two years ago, Wagner was a potential risk that only institutions with local civic responsibility and pride might be willing to stand behind," acknowledged Smith. "Their desire to give Wagner a future was commendable and I'm pleased we've been able to make the progress necessary to prove that they had made a good investment."

With the bond issue completed, Smith declared that Wagner's finances are in order and comparable to successful private colleges elsewhere. "It's now on to other issues," said Smith, "with the confidence that the college is well into a position for a strong future."

Staten Island Advance

We wanted to make the most of the summer and accomplish as many improvements as we could. So even before the actual bond transaction, we were underway with a wide range of improvement projects that topped the list of the most damaging when it came to recruiting and retaining paying customers.

All the residence halls were going to be more livable in time for the fall of 1990, now just a month away. The dining hall was going to be transformed into one of the showpieces of the college. The stalactites were going to be removed, and a new ceiling would be installed that would guarantee an end to ruined silk blouses.

The main level of the Student Union was now going to actually have furniture. The Hawk's Nest eatery (for non-dining hall patrons) was being upgraded, including hand-me-down furniture donated by trustee and class of 1966 alumnus Richard Herburger's Citigroup executive dining room.

One of the most exciting improvements was campus lighting. We installed over one hundred Victorian cast-iron lampposts throughout the walkways. All the amber light towers that gave out an aura of being in a prison yard were removed. The front of Main Hall was illuminated. Wagner had come to life, and the lighting symbolized that awakening.

Improvements shed new light on Wagner campus

By VIVIAN SCHLESINGER
ADVANCE STAFF WRITER

Staten Islanders who travel over Grymes Hill by night and admire the view of the Narrows may also notice that another familiar sight has a new nocturnal look.

As part of a plan to heighten safety and aesthetics on the Wagner College campus, new lights have been placed strategically around the Sutter Oval, which faces Howard Avenue. Shining upward, the beams bounce off the large birch trees lining the walkway leading to the college's flagship building, Main Hall.

The new floodlights portray Main Hall in a favorable light.

Two ground-level floodlights have also been positioned at either end of the building's facade.

In addition, approximately 75 wrought-iron street lamps with textured glass have replaced industrial floodlights along walkways.

The industrial lights are being relocated to the college's parking lots, according to Dr. Norman R. Smith, Wagner president.

"It's gorgeous, isn't it?" beamed Smith about the new lighting system.

Built in 1929, Main Hall resembles a medieval castle with its twin towers, cross motifs, high relief sculptures and gargoyles. The new lighting system seems to emphasize its majestic lines.

"We were just remarking on the dramatic improvement in the beauty of the campus," said Werner Johnson, a 1941 Wagner alumnus who was out for a stroll last night with his Grymes Hill neighbor, Winfield Winter, also a graduate of the school.

Pausing to look at the building last night, Sophia Baker, a junior, pointed out the detailed architecture.

Standing beside her, Takulu Poto, a graduate student majoring in business, agreed that the building "looks much better."

Cathy Guerriero, a junior majoring in English, said the efforts to beautify the school and increase visibility on campus have been much appreciated by students.

Other recent security measures include construction of a main entrance gate which will, when completed, be controlled by identification cards. Those without a card will not be able to drive cars off the campus unless a security guard opens the gate. This will prevent car thefts, Smith explained.

The cards will also control entrance to the school's dormitories, he added.

Work on the gate system began in January and is expected to be completed next week, Smith said.

"Cathy Guerriero, a junior majoring in English, said the efforts to beautify the school and increase visibility on campus have been much appreciated by students."

Excerpted from "Improvements..."

Staten Islanders who travel over Grymes Hill by night and admire the view of the Narrows may also notice that another familiar sight has a new nocturnal look. As part of a plan to heighten safety and aesthetics on the Wagner College campus, new lights have been placed strategically around the Sutter Oval. "We were just remarking on the dramatic improvement in the beauty of the campus," said Werner Johnson, a 1941 Wagner alumnus who was out for a stroll last night with his Grymes Hill neighbor, Winfield Winter, also a graduate of the school. Takulu Poto, a graduate student majoring in business agreed that the building "looks much better." Cathy Guerriero, a junior majoring in English, said the efforts to beautify the school and increase visibility on campus have been much appreciated by students."

Wagner College campus looking better than ever

Cleanup crews go above and beyond

By STEPHANNIA CLEATON
ADVANCE STAFF WRITER

Unlike many other college presidents, Wagner College's Dr. Norman Smith isn't territorial when it comes to picking up trash. Often, his grounds crew can be found a few miles from the Grymes Hill campus picking up litter and planting flowers and shrubs.

One day last month, the five-man crew walked from the college campus on Howard Avenue to Clove Road and then to the nearby Staten Island Expressway exits picking up trash along the way. They filled 130 40-gallon heavy duty trash bags.

It is easy to see why he would want to beautify the neighborhood. Wagner, a small, private liberal arts college, has a high reputation for quality and, with its beautiful wooded 86-acre campus on Staten Island, Wagner has attracted some of the brightest and most talented young people from across the country. It has also turned out many successful graduates.

In his three years as Wagner College president, Dr. Smith has transformed areas that were eyesores to botanical gardens. Along Howard Avenue, on property that doesn't even belong to the college, his crew has raked leaves, trimmed tree limbs, and removed all types of trash — even a discarded refrigerator.

On campus, the student and visitors parking lot, which was simply a parking area surrounded by tall weeds has been transformed into picturesque area with green rolling hills.

All over the campus, the grass is mowed at least twice a week, trees limbs and bushes are trimmed, and flower beds are changed seasonally, said Walter Earl, grounds superintendent.

Most important, there's no litter.

"I am a big believer that one's environment has an effect on one's achievement. Since we are a college, I think that our environment should be one that inspires," explained Smith. He pointed out that a well-known psychologist who studied human behavior concluded that people's motivation to work and their self-esteem are directly connected to the quality of their environment.

"If you are in a dirty, crummy, unkempt environment, your spirit drops, your attitude drops, your motivation to achieve drops. On the other hand, if you are in a beautiful environment, a wellkept environment, your spirit is exactly the opposite and you have a desire to achieve," he said, noting a positive change in the attitudes of both faculty and students since the renewed effort to keep the campus neat and clean was initiated.

While planting flowers near the library, Walter Earl, chats with Dr. Norman Smith, president of Wagner.

Staten Island Advance March 1990

The above* Advance *feature also captures the only picture I could locate of Walter Earl, Wagner's green thumb who played an incalculable role in bringing the college back to life. He should never be forgotten for the magic his hard work and dedication contributed to the College's turnaround.

Dr. Norman Smith, Wagner College president, stands in front of a new granite sign bearing the school's name. The area is landscaped and lit at night.

Wagner restoration: 'It's a showpiece'

By CRAIG SCHNEIDER
ADVANCE STAFF WRITER

In his three years as Wagner College president, Dr. Norman Smith has worked hard to improve what was the declining appearance of the 108-year-old college.

"The campus was indeed in disrepair," Smith wrote in his annual review for 1989-1990. But the college has undergone a restoration, he said, "that has turned it into a showpiece."

More than renovating dorms and replacing cafeteria furniture, Smith is overhauling the college's image.

Known mostly as a local college, Wagner has initiated a marketing campaign to attract students from as far away as Pennsylvania and Boston.

Applicants who make Wagner their first choice is up 25 percent

"We want to become more competitive among small, private colleges in the Northeast," said Smith during a campus tour with an Advance reporter.

From new lighting along its tree-lined walks to a new fitness center, the Grymes Hill campus is decked out like a young buck ready to woo.

And that is exactly the plan.

Next year, colleges are expecting the fewest college-bound graduates in the last 30 years. Faced with a shrinking market of students headed for college and stiff competition from other local colleges, Wagner has had to rethink its recruitment strategy.

While concerns about campus aesthetics may seem minor in the world of higher learning, they make a difference in attracting students.

Since he took the helm, Smith has promoted a full-steam-ahead program of campus renovation. And last year, after a decade of declining enrollment, the school saw a 30 percent increase in applications.

"When a student is considering a college, a paramount consideration when visiting the college is the condition of the campus," Smith said.

The dining hall has been refurbished, including a new acoustic ceiling and new dining chairs that are the same ones that were made for the Eisenhower Library in Gettysburg, Pa.

Standing in the cafeteria, Smith commented on the new acoustics. "This place used to ring with echoes," he said. "You have to remember, students eat here seven days a week. They want a nice atmosphere."

Around the bend in the Student Union building, the terrace by the large windows has received new tiling, plants and wrought iron furniture.

"This place used to be called 'The Pit,'" said senior Robin Fago, studying in the area. "Now it's nice and relaxing."

About 100 black lamp posts have been added to the campus, improving its appearance at night and adding to general security. Dorms now have computerized card-access locks. A current card, with a valid identification number, is required. When a student leaves, the number is removed from the computer.

ADVANCE PHOTOS/FRANK J. JOHNS

A panoramic view of the Wagner College cafeteria shows a spacious, comfortable setting embellished by plenty of foliage.

The dorm furniture had not been replaced in 20 years, and Smith himself described it as shabby. Beds, desks and chairs have been replaced.

Senior Jennifer Norton appreciates the difference. "Before, the bedrooms looked kind of dismal," she said. The veneer was chipping, chair legs were weak.

"The new furniture — I love it," she said.

The college is doing more than simply replacing furniture to improve living conditions. One dorm has been reconstructed into two-bedroom suites with a living room. "It creates a more adult atmosphere," Smith said. "More privacy."

This all comes in addition to a new fitness center, a computer center and renovated classrooms.

The difference is showing. The average SAT score of applicants has gone up 100 points in the past two years. Student retention is up 20 percent. The number of applicants who made Wagner their first college choice is up 25 percent, Smith said.

Smith believes that attracting students from a broader geographic area will elevate the campus atmosphere, introducing students from different parts of the country.

School officials are not, however, looking for a great increase in enrollment. Smith wants to keep Wagner a small, liberal arts college, where students don't feel lost in the crowd. Sixty percent of Fortune 500 executives graduated from small colleges, he said.

"The campus is park-like, but is near top employment opportunities in Manhattan," he said.

He showed with pride an article from the Chronicle of Higher Education, which indicated that students at large universities often feel ignored by professors and crowded into large classrooms.

At Wagner, an amphitheater classroom used for large lectures will be converted into a video room in which movies and video lessons will be shown.

Other plans include a television production studio where students can film their own projects, renovating the music recital hall, and a high-tech language lab that moves away from earphones and cassettes to interactive projects involving computer and video.

"We are reshaping the reputation of this college, adding to its stature," Smith said, standing beside a new granite sign bearing the school name. The area is landscaped and lit at night.

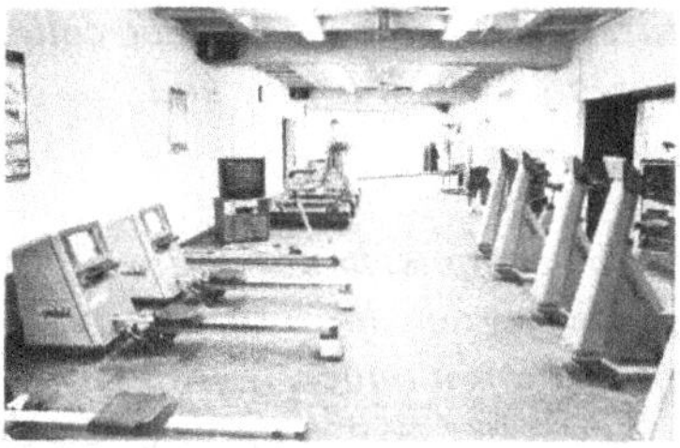

The school's new fitness center features a variety of equipment for the health-conscious student.

Wagner College students Margaret Areno, left, and Jennifer Norton relax in their dormitory room, which sports new furniture.

Staten Island Advance May 1991 excerpts:

In his three years as Wagner College president, Dr. Norman Smith has worked hard to improve what was the declining appearance of the 108-year-old college. "The campus was indeed in disrepair," Smith wrote in his annual review for 1989-90.

But the college has undergone a restoration, he said, "that has turned it into a showpiece." More than renovating dorms and replacing cafeteria furniture, Smith is overhauling the college's image. Known mostly as a local college, Wagner has initiated a marketing campaign to attract students from as far away as Pennsylvania and Boston.

NORMAN R. SMITH

"We want to become more competitive among small private colleges in the Northeast," said Smith during a campus tour with an Advance reporter. From new lighting along its tree-lined walks to a new fitness center, the Grymes Hill campus is decked out like a young buck ready to woo. And that is exactly the plan.

Next year, colleges are expecting the fewest college-bound students in the last 90 years. Faced with a shrinking market of students headed for college and stiff competition from other local colleges, Wagner has had to rethink its recruitment strategy.

While the concerns about campus aesthetics may seem minor in the world of higher learning, they make a difference in attracting students.

Since he took the helm, Smith has promoted a full-steam ahead program of campus renovation. And last year, after a decade of declining enrollment, the school saw a 30 percent increase in applications. "When a student is considering a college, a paramount consideration when visiting the college is the condition of the campus," Smith said.

The dining hall has been refurbished including a new acoustic ceiling and new dining chairs that are the same ones that were made for the Eisenhower Library in Gettysburg, Pa. Standing in the cafeteria, Smith commented on the new acoustics. "This place used to ring with echoes", he said. "You must remember that students eat here seven days a week. They want a nice atmosphere."

Around the bend in the Student Union, the main terrace by the large windows has received new tiling, plants and wrought iron furniture. "This place used to be called "The Pit," said senior Robin Fago, studying in the area. "Now it is nice and relaxing."

About 100 black iron lamp posts have been added to the campus, improving appearance at night and adding to general security. Dorms now have computerized card access locks. A current card, with a valid identification number, is required.

The dorm furniture had not been replaced in 20 years and Smith himself described it as shabby. Beds, desks and chairs have all been replaced. Senior Jennifer Norton appreciates the difference. "Before, the bedrooms looked kind of dismal," she said. "The veneer was chipping and chair legs were weak. "The new furniture – I love it," she said.

The college is doing more than simply replacing furniture to improve living conditions. One dorm has been reconstructed into two-bedroom suites with a living room. "It creates a more adult atmosphere," Smith said.

This all comes in addition to a new fitness center, a computer center, and renovated classrooms.

The difference is showing. The average SAT score of applicants has gone up 140 points in the past two years. Student retention is up 20 percent. The number of applicants who made Wagner their first college choice is up 25 percent, Smith said.

Smith believes that attracting students from a broader geographic area will elevate the campus atmosphere, introducing students from different parts of the country. "We are reshaping the reputation of this college adding to its stature," Smith said, standing beside a new granite sign bearing the school's name.

The *Wagner restoration: It's a showpiece* article featured a photograph of me standing in front of a new entry sign, an improvement that was important to me. I was troubled that first-time visitors saw a sign at the entrance to the campus that looked like a *FOR SALE* sign. Two wood posts held up a small plywood board on which WAGNER COLLEGE was painted.

I envisioned a stone and granite sign engraved with WAGNER COLLEGE, sending a message that Wagner was here to stay. To establish Wagner's gravitas, I sketched out what I wanted and passed it along to Stan Shilling and Dom Fontano who together went to some of their building subcontractor colleagues. Stan and Dom pressed the contractors to keep their labor costs low, on the prospect that as Wagner grew and prospered, they would also benefit. We ended up with exactly the sign I had wanted. The materials had been donated, so the total cost of the construction, including lighting, was about $10,000. I don't recall one comment, firsthand or otherwise, from anyone who didn't think it would have been worth five times that amount.

Someone once declared *excellence is in the details*. Amen.

The restoration also included improvements throughout the college. The dining hall transformation was particularly striking. We used the large gathering space for other public events because of its size and its dramatic glass wall with views of the New York harbor. Wagner was now in the forefront of a dining model that had become commonplace at colleges and universities. We eliminated the cafeteria line and set up serving stations throughout the dining area, thereby eliminating long lines. In more recent years, the dining hall has been used as a setting for major motion pictures.

Wagner's turnaround elicits accolades

It's good news!

By DON GROSS
ADVANCE STAFF WRITER

Wagner College has accomplished a turnaround that appears to be nothing short of miraculous by putting the problems it faced just two years ago in its past, according to faculty and staff at the 107-year-old college.

Interviews with almost a dozen members of the college community reveal a new spirit on the Grymes Hill campus that matches a new look.

This contrasts sharply with both the mood and appearance of the college at the close of the 1987-88 academic year.

"Wagner College has accomplished a turnaround that appears to be nothing short of miraculous."

ADVANCE PHOTO FRANK J. JOHNS

Wagner College president Dr. Norman Smith speaks during a board of trustees meeting last Tuesday in the Student Union. Dr. Donald Spiro, left, and Kevin Sheehy also are pictured.

"I've been here for almost 20 years and I've never seen so many changes take place in so short a period of time," said Dr. Walter Kaelber, chairman of the Humanities Department.

All those interviewed cited the appointment of Dr. Norman Smith as president of the college in May 1988 as the moving force behind the changes.

The most visible change to people passing by Wagner at night is the architectural lighting that enhances the campus's picturesque qualities. Main Hall is bathed in white light and so are the trees surrounding it.

"People come up here to the theater (in Main Hall) and actually come early so they have time to walk around the campus," Kaelber said.

Two years ago, he said, that didn't happen. While crowds have always been drawn to plays put on by the college's renowned theater department, conditions at the school two years ago reflected almost a decade of financial strain and poor morale.

"I was ready to leave," said Richard DiRuzza, vice president for academic affairs. What was driving him away, he said, was the factional infighting among supporters of the previous administration and those who wanted immediate change.

He wasn't alone. Others said they, too, were ready to walk away from Wagner — enough to have decimated the faculty and perhaps crippled the school.

"I've been here for almost 20 years and I've never seen so many changes take place in so short a period of time," said Dr. Walter Kaelber, chairman of the Humanities Department.

Gary Sullivan, chairman of the theater department, said Smith's appointment changed many minds.

"He has an open style of leadership," he said. "If you have an idea you can go and talk to him."

Smith also came to the school with an amount of energy never before seen on the campus.

"No president ever paid attention to the maintenance staff before and I've been here 22 years," supervisor Dominick Fontano said.

But at the same time, he said Smith conveyed an enthusiasm that drove the men to take pride in the college themselves.

Student furniture in the dorms, including beds, would fall apart before it was replaced, he said. "We'd look at it and figure it can go another two or three years. Now it goes when it starts to look worn."

Everything, according to the interview subjects, has been done with the convenience of the students in mind.

Registrar Mildred Nelson said a new computer system has put an end to the process that kept students shuffling from room to room and spending hours in line in order to register for classes and pay their tuition.

"Now they can get it done without standing on any lines," she said.

Also in the works is an expansion of the faculty. Eight new professors were hired last year and a search is being conducted for 10 more.

The aim, according to Dr. Anne Schotter, an English professor, is to add new courses and new material.

The combined effect has already had an impact. While most small, private colleges suffered a nearly 20 percent decline in the number of applications in the last few years, Wagner recently reported applications are up 30 percent. More significantly, the Scholastic Aptitude Test (SAT) scores of the applicants were up by an average of 100 points, according to Dr. Ronald Lee, the school's director of corporate and foundation grants.

Lee uses figures like this to help obtain corporate and private foundation grants needed to move the school forward. Just the physical changes were enough to impress foundation representatives.

"Nobody is talking about the past anymore," Kaelber said. "Only the future."

More important, he said, has been the school's improved financial health. Wagner went from a massive deficit to a small surplus within a year. Where once organizations such as the Clark and Calder foundations had put Wagner on a list of schools to avoid, the Grymes Hill school was again acceptable and receiving some of the largest grants given — $250,000 from the Calder and $100,000 from the Clark.

The progress has given the college community hope it never thought it would have about the school, faculty and staff members said.

"Nobody is talking about the past anymore," Kaelber said. "Only the future."

DiRuzza agreed. "It's nice to be on a winning team," he said.

Transcript from spring 1990* Staten Island Advance *article above.

Wagner College has accomplished a turnaround that appears to be nothing short of miraculous by putting the problems it faced just two years ago in its past, according to faculty and staff at the 107-year-old college.

Interviews with almost a dozen members of the college community reveal a new spirit on the Grymes Hill campus that matches a new look. This contrasts sharply with both the mood and appearance of the college at the close of the 1987-88 academic year. I've been here for almost 20 years, and I've never seen so many changes take place in so short a period of time," said Dr. Walter Kaelber, chairman of the Humanities Department.

All those interviewed cited the appointment of Dr. Norman Smith as president of the college in May 1988 as the moving force behind the changes.

The most visible change to people passing by Wagner at night is the architectural lighting that enhances the campus's picturesque qualities. Main Hall is bathed in white light and so are the trees surrounding it. People come up here to the theater in Main Hall and actually come early so they have time to walk around the campus," Kaelber said. Two years ago, he said, that didn't happen. While crowds have always been drawn to plays put on by the College's renowned theater department, conditions at the school two years ago reflected almost a decade of financial strain and poor morale.

"I was ready to leave," said Richard DiRuzza, Vice President for Student Affairs. What was driving him away, he said, was the factional infighting among supporters of the previous administration and those who wanted immediate change. He wasn't alone. Others said they, too, were ready to walk away from Wagner -- enough to have decimated the faculty and perhaps crippled the school.

Gary Sullivan, chairman of the Theater Department, said Smith's appointment changed many minds. "He has an open style of leadership," he said. "If you have an idea, you can go and talk to him.

Smith also came to the school with an amount of energy never before seen on the campus. "No president ever paid attention to the maintenance staff before and I've been here 22 years," supervisor Dominick Fontano said. But at the same time, he said Smith conveyed an enthusiasm that drove the men to take pride in the College themselves. Student furniture in the dorms, including beds, would fall apart before they were replaced, he said. "We'd look at it and figure it can go another two or three years. Now it goes when it starts to look worn." Everything, according to the interview subjects, has been done with the convenience of the students in mind.

Registrar Mildred Nelson said a new computer system has put an end to the process that kept students shuffling from room to room and spending hours in line in order to register for classes and pay their tuition. "Now they can get it done without standing on any lines," she said.

Also in the works is an expansion of the faculty. Eight new professors were hired last year and a search is being conducted for 10 more. The aim, according to Dr. Anne Schotter, an English professor, is to add new courses and new material.

The combined effect has already had an impact. While most small, private colleges suffered a nearly 20 per cent decline in the number of applications in the last few years, Wagner recently reported applications are up 30 percent. More significantly, the Scholastic Aptitude Test (SAT) scores of the applicants were up by an average of 100 points, according to Dr. Ronald Lee, the school's director of corporate and foundation grants. Lee uses figures like this to help obtain corporate and private

foundation grants needed to move the school forward. Just the physical changes were enough to impress foundation representatives.

More important, he said, has been the school's improved financial health. Wagner went from a massive deficit to a small surplus within a year. Where once organizations such as the Clark and Calder Foundations had put Wagner on a list to avoid, the Grymes Hill school was again acceptable and received some of the largest grants given. -- $250,000 from the Calder and $100,000 from the Clark. The progress has given the College community hope it never thought it would have about the school, faculty and staff members said. "Nobody is talking about the past anymore," Kaelber said. "Only the future."

DiRuzza agreed. "It's nice to be on a winning team," he said.

Applications at Wagner up by 30 percent

BY ADVANCE STAFF WRITER

After struggling with declining enrollment throughout the 1980s, Wagner College announced a 30 percent increase in freshman applications this year for September 1990.

While a modest increase in applications was experienced last year also, "The big result is this year," said an elated Dr. Norman Smith, president of Wagner College.

Smith claims the increase in applications is even more significant when compared to the trend in other private schools where numbers have been decreasing in recent years.

Skidmore College, Saratoga Springs, a highly competitive private school in upstate New York, experienced a 5 percent decrease in applications this year, according to Smith.

"Over the last two years, Wagner has widened its recruiting market to include other urban areas such as Boston, Washington D.C. and Philadelphia."

The college president credits a more aggressive recruitment campaign aimed at markets outside the New York City area for the application boost at Wagner.

"For decades this school relied on the density of the population in the local area, it didn't have to work too hard at recruiting outside," Smith said.

But faced with a shrinking market of college-age students and stiff competition from City University of New York (CUNY) schools like the College of Staten Island, and State University of New York (SUNY) schools offering lower tuition, Wagner College has had to rethink its strategy.

Over the last two years, Wagner has widened its recruiting market to include other urban areas such as Boston, Washington D.C. and Philadelphia.

Recruiters have been selling students on Wagner's unique location, the only private college in the New York area that can offer students the "best of both worlds" -- a location close to Manhattan and a 100-acre "New England-like" campus.

Smith also credits Phil Dusenberry, chairman of BBDO, one of the nation's most prominent advertising agencies, with helping to raise the college's profile.

Dusenberry, the man behind the commercials for Diet Pepsi and Apple computers, was recruited last year to serve on the Wagner College Board of Trustees.

The ad executive developed a multi-media advertising campaign for the college last January.

The recruiting strategy appears to have paid off. Not only is Smith enthusiastic about the number of applications he is receiving, but the college president is pleased with the quality of students applying as well.

Wagner College has increased its recruitment budget in recent years to allow its representatives to travel farther distances to do their recruiting. Recently, the college has ventured into northern Virginia, Washington, D.C., New Hampshire and Connecticut -- all previously unexplored territory.

Dr. Susan Robinson, director of admissions at Wagner, said the move has paid off.

"I'm delighted with the results," Dr. Robinson said. Freshman applications for the fall are up 30 percent over last year, and resident applications are up 27 percent from last year.

Wagner is selling students on the "best of both worlds," a beautiful suburban campus only minutes from Manhattan.

Staten Island Advance Fall 1990 excerpted from above:

After struggling with declining enrollments throughout the 1980s, Wagner College announced a 30 percent increase in freshman applications this year for September 1990. While a modest increase in applications was experienced last year also, "The big result is this year," said an elated Dr. Norman Smith, president of Wagner College.

Smith claims the increase in applications is even more significant when compared to the trend in other private schools where numbers have been decreasing in recent years. The college president credits a more aggressive recruitment campaign aimed at markets outside the New York City area for the application boost at Wagner. "For decades Wagner relied on the density of the population in the local area." Smith said. But faced with a shrinking market of college-age students and stiff competition from City University of New York (CUNY), schools like the College of Staten Island, and State University of New York (SUNY), schools offering lower tuition, Wagner College has had to rethink its strategy.

Over the last two years, Wagner has widened its recruiting marketing to include other urban areas such as Boston, Washington, D.C. and Philadelphia. Recruiters have been selling students on Wagner's unique location, the only private college in the New York area that can offer students the "Best of both worlds" – a location close to Manhattan and a 100-acre New England like campus. The recruiting strategy appears to have paid off.

Not only is Smith enthusiastic about the number of applications he is receiving, but the college president is pleased with the quality of students applying as well. Wagner College has increased its recruitment budget in recent years to allow its representatives to travel farther distances to do their recruiting. Recently the college has ventured into northern Virginia, Washington, DC, New Hampshire and Connecticut --- all previously unexplored territory.

Dr. Susan Robinson, Dean of Admissions, said freshman applications for the fall are up 30 percent over last year and resident applications are up 27 percent from last year. Wagner is selling students on the "best of both worlds": a beautiful suburban campus only minutes from Manhattan.

Missing from the media credits for enrollment growth at Wagner is the enormous contribution of the STAMATS company (headquartered in Iowa) and its Senior Vice President Marilyn Osweiler *(above photo by Jason Jones).* Marilyn and her staff, notably photographer Jason Jones, created marketing materials that were stunning and captured the 'best foot forward' aspects of the College.

I involved Marilyn in several of the colleges and universities I went on to after departing Wagner and she consistently hit grand slam home runs that turbo-charged admissions recruiting outcomes.

Year THREE 1990–1991

Chapter 16
A+ for Wagner College!

While only four or five weeks had passed since the seventeen million dollar bond issue, a milestone that marked the single-most significant breakthrough to date, the reaction of returning faculty and upper class students for the beginning of my third academic year at Wagner was the most gratifying moment since my arrival a little more than two years ago. The transformation of Wagner College could now be seen everywhere, and everyone was noticing. Returnees felt like they were arriving at a completely different institution.

Enrollments were improving, but not at the blinding pace we ideally wanted. Applications had been up 30%, but we were trying to improve academic standards to hold on to Barron's newly established ranking declaring Wagner College to be a *competitive* institution. And the college continued to be vexed by the *US News and World Report* bottom-tier ranking. We needed to get out of that hole as quickly as possible.

After some persistence, I was granted an audience with Mel Elfin, the managing editor of the *US News* rankings, and I traveled to their Washington DC headquarters to make a case for a better grade for Wagner. Elfin reminded me of *60 Minutes*' Andy Rooney or Ed Asner as Mr. Grant on *The Mary Tyler Moore Show*. Nonetheless, he was gracious and welcoming.

Mel indicated that he had been keeping an eye on Wagner since receiving my requests for an audience and he was impressed about the rapid way in which Wagner had been changing for the better.

The problem, though, was that *US News* was averaging five prior years of data, so it takes at least that long for the rankings to change in any meaningful way. Additionally, *US News* was relying heavily upon the peer votes from the senior officers of similar colleges and universities. It can take years for long-established negative perceptions to be reversed in the minds of voters at other colleges.

I challenged Mel to rethink the ground rules for the ratings, contending that *US News* risked sending inaccurate portrayals to their readers by not having a way of accounting for significant changes that occur. It was like Zagat not re-rating a restaurant that had a new cooking staff. Should new management be subject to the ratings lost by now-departed management?

Mel didn't offer to change our ranking, but promised he would think of ways in which my concerns could perhaps someday be incorporated into the process. From that point forward, I sent him a note every time something good happened at Wagner, including all of the *Staten Island Advance* newspaper clippings that lauded the Wagner turnaround.

The fall 1990 opening, along with the August bond issue, had taken a lot of pressure off the most serious problems burdening the college. The NYS Department of Education was now cheerleading for Wagner, having removed us from its endangered species list and no longer requiring the submission of monthly financial statements. Any talk of closing Wagner was in the past.

The next big hurdle would be the on-site once-a-decade reaccreditation visit from the Middle States Commission on Higher Education, which had been successfully delayed from 1990 to 1991 allowing some additional time to make corrections. Middle States had had Wagner on deathwatch for a number of years but acknowledged that new leadership was in its infancy and deserved an additional year before being intensely evaluated. This visit would be crucial. The accreditation visit is preceded by a mandated self-study that must be conducted by the institution — and that undertaking was premature in only the second year of new leadership.

In the late spring of 1990, the time had come for a chief academic officer comparable to David Long, Sebastian Persico, and Susan Robinson. The chief academic officer is really the number two-ranking position at most colleges, and Wagner now needed an experienced academic leader if it was going to rise in stature.

I did feel badly about returning Eleanor Rogg to the faculty. She had worked hard to maintain a positive spirit throughout the faculty. But most faculty members had been calling for someone overseeing academics who had experience and stature comparable to what David Long brought in fund raising. Wagner needed an academic leader from an institution that we would want to emulate in the same way David's Skidmore past turned heads. Ellie was not to blame for lacking broader experiences that someone else could bring to Wagner.

By good fortune, an exactly right academic leader was available. Mort Rozanski was vice president for academic affairs of Fairleigh Dickinson University in New Jersey and formerly associate provost of Adelphi University on Long Island. Mort was seeking to leave Fairleigh Dickinson, which was in upheaval due to a controversial president who was under fire for major fiscal deficits and who was not being supported by the faculty or the media.

Mort turned heads. He would bring a lot of academic credibility to Wagner. The faculty was elated with his candidacy, not only because of his experience to date, but also because he was a PhD from the University of Pennsylvania. A Chinese and political science scholar, he spoke Mandarin. He would be the kind of chief academic officer who could get us through the imminent Middle States evaluation — and he was available to move over in mid-semester.

Mort agreed to assume the vice presidency, which we renamed provost, in January 1991. This gave us several months to get the Middle States accreditation visit organized, including the complicated self-study, which needed a lot of work.

In addition to having an impressive academic scholar and administrator coming on board to round out the executive team of the College, Mort's Jewish heritage was a bonus, although it was not a factor in the decision. He would be a first for Wagner, which, having been founded by the Germanic Lutheran church, had historically been viewed as anti-Semitic according to members of the Jewish community on Staten Island.

There were very few Jewish students enrolled at Wagner. Although Staten Island wasn't heavily Jewish, New York City was. And many of the most generous patrons to New York arts, cultural, and education came from within the Jewish community. While there were no immediate surges in Jewish student enrollments, Mort's appointment laid a foundation for a more inclusive future.

From the day Mort arrived at Wagner in January 1991, he was operating on all cylinders. He proved to be the right person for the right job at the right time. Mort knew exactly what he was doing every step of the way.

As for the Middle States preparation process, we couldn't have been better positioned for the team's arrival. Mort had done a great job preparing for the accreditation, which included the comprehensive self-study report submitted prior to the visit.

The Middle States team was headed by the high-energy president of Mount St. Mary's College of Maryland, Robert Wickenheiser. Bob and his team of fellow higher education faculty and officers couldn't have been more enthusiastic about what they discovered had been accomplished at Wagner in less than three years.

They were also very impressed with the new management team, and they said so.

Their evaluation was glowing. Just a few excerpts include:

"Wagner College has experienced dramatic changes in the past three years since the appointment of a dynamic and talented new president, who, together with a very supportive Board of Trustees made the necessary and gutsy decisions which have resulted in the vibrant institution we find Wagner College to be"

"For all these successes and more, Wanger College, and particularly the President and Board of Trustees are to be highly commended."

"We applaud, as loudly as we possibly can, the great successes achieved by President Norman Smith in just three short years. Words cannot adequately capture all that he has done."

"Suffice it to say that the evaluation team endorses the monumental achievements of the President and the College in the past three years."

"We have no real recommendations for the President except to urge him to keep on doing what he has been doing."

Shortly after the Middle States team submitted their report, which we made public, the *Staten Island Advance* ran a front-page story with a headline that was worth its weight in gold: ***A+ for Wagner College.***

In fact, Middle States doesn't give a grade. An institution is either reaccredited or not. But the *Advance's* assessment of the evaluation report's content did accurately capture the spirit of the commentary, which certainly felt like an A+ to all of us.

A+ for Wagner College

A glowing evaluation from accreditation agency

By DIANE C. LORE
ADVANCE STAFF WRITER

A team of educators representing the prestigious Middle States Association of Colleges and Schools has given Wagner College a glowing evaluation, a prelude to renewal of the school's accreditation.

The report, based in part on a three day visit to the Grymes Hill campus earlier this month, gives the college the highest marks in the areas of governance, organization and administration, and the quality of its faculty, students and curriculum.

The committee credits the leadership of Wagner President Dr. Norman Smith for turning the college around, financially and academically, over a three year period.

Although the results of Middle States evaluations are not generally released, a copy of the report was obtained by the Advance, and copies were reportedly being circulated among Wagner faculty and staff on Friday.

The eight-member evaluation team was chaired by Robert J. Wickenheiser, president of Mount Saint Mary's College, Emmitsburg, Md.

In its introduction, the Middle States report notes that Wagner "has experienced dramatic changes in the past three years which have affected most areas of campus life."

The report identifies as "first and foremost," the appointment three years ago "of a dynamic and talented new president, who, together with a very supportive board of trustees, made strong, necessary, and extremely gutsy decisions, which have resulted not only in Wagner College being alive today, but in the college being the vibrant institution we find it be, and one positioned for a very promising future."

The committee lauded the college for undertaking a comprehensive and balanced self-study, and concurred with many of the study's findings. It also praised the college for defining the role of the faculty in a newly written and unanimously approved faculty handbook, and favorably noted the appointment of Dr. Mordechai Rozanski as college vice president for academic affairs.

It commended the commitment of the board of trustees in appointing and standing behind the president and administration, and for "improving communication between the board and the faculty between the faculty and administration, between students and the administration, and between students and the board."

It also lauded the trustees for "avoiding overinvolvement in the management of the college during its crisis" and recommended the board stick to its role of setting policy.

Among the strengths of the college pinpointed in the report are "the faculty, administration and staff who are not only by and large a talented and very dedicated group of individuals, but who exhibit unusual and very strong commitment to the college and its mission."

The committee also made two key recommendations concerning future finances and faculty.

It recommended the college become less dependent upon tuition and focus its attention on major fund-raising, and suggested the faculty broaden its scope, noting evidence of a "measure of parochialism" in some departments.

The Commission on Higher Education of the Middle States Association is the accrediting body for all colleges and universities in the Middle Atlantic states. There are six such organizations nationwide that collectively represent all colleges and universities in the United States.

Every college and university is evaluated periodically. The evaluation begins with a self-study report submitted by the college that reviews, from the college's perspective, the state of the institution's fiscal health, enrollment and academic quality.

After the self-study is completed and submitted in report form, the Commission on Higher Education appoints a team of veteran college educators and administrators to visit the school for a three-day period. The purpose of the visit is to review the results of the colleges self-study and provide an assessment of the college to the commission, which then votes on whether to accredit the college.

The evaluation team visited Wagner April 7 through 10, and submitted its report last week.

The Commission on Higher Education will review the report and is expected to vote on renewal of accreditation in June.

Staten Island Advance April 29, 1991

The Middle States full accreditation report was a powerhouse affirmation that reached far beyond our wildest dreams. The full Commission would affirm the conclusions and grant Wagner's first unconditional reaccreditation in decades.

The importance of this milestone was as important to the future of the college as had been the refinancing of debt that provided Wagner with a few years of financial stability while pursuing larger enrollments of students who paid a larger portion of tuition.

That Wagner was a bottom tier *US News*-ranked college, and also on the edge of losing accreditation, couldn't have been a worse circumstance for recruiting academically promising students with financial wherewithal who could select from among a wide array of colleges in better condition

Archival

Richard Diamond accepts his Wagner honorary doctorate.

At the spring 1991 commencement, Wagner awarded an honorary doctorate to Richard Diamond, publisher of the *Staten Island Advance,* which he very graciously and happily accepted.

His acceptance speech emphasized advice that all the graduates continue to make reading a habit for life. A Cornell graduate, a member of the Newhouse dynasty family and lifelong Staten Islander, Dick had an informed understanding of what we were trying to do at Wagner and he, too, expressed support as he saw Wagner's success elevating the stature of the community.

Along with Les Trautmann, Dick's advocacy for a better Wagner College was invaluable. The *Staten Island Advance* was key in heralding the college's turnaround that awakened a much broader audience.

Chapter 17
DIY Photography

As the college was now starting to look downright beautiful, I wanted it photographed at its best moments, which turned out to be more difficult that it might sound. On several occasions, Susan Robinson hired professional photographers recommended by Stamats, the gold-standard college marketers that had been hired to design and print the college's admissions materials.

Professional photographers, though, require appointments that typically require scheduling months in advance. And, like clockwork, every time we scheduled a photo shoot, the weather was a spoiler. "If only you had been here last week" was our typical lament.

At Harvard, and at Philadelphia University, I took many of the photographs for publications partly because I knew exactly what I wanted, and I also needed to save money. At Harvard, I was first employed by the Graduate School of Education, which wasn't one of the richest graduate schools. Budgets were always tight, and professional photographers weren't very affordable.

I had been an amateur photographer as far back as I can remember. During my years in Philadelphia when I was vice president of Philadelphia University and later executive vice president of Moore College of Art and Design, I was a frequent photographer and illustrator by avocation. During the 1976 bicentennial celebration in Philadelphia, a collection of my pen and ink drawings of Philadelphia landmarks like Independence Hall and the Betsy Ross House were sold in tourist shops. College administrator wasn't the best paying career then or since.

After repeated failures to capture picture-perfect days via a professional photographer, I decided to always keep a reasonably good camera in my desk drawer. When a perfect day or afternoon or sunset occurred, I would run out onto campus and try to capture the moment. I learned exactly what time of the day each building looked best. Some needed the later afternoon sun to be properly illuminated, while others were at their best in the morning sun.

As the sun set in the west, the Manhattan skyline looked its best, as did the front of the Student Union, Main Hall, and the Library later in the day. You could never photograph Main Hall until the early afternoon. Before then, the front of the building was in a shadow.

To me, photography was not so much an art as it was being in the right place at the right time. Someone once suggested that an infinite number of monkeys typing on an infinite number of typewriters would result in one of the monkeys banging out a Shakespeare play. In that spirit, I would take hundreds of pictures, being satisfied with one or two that could sizzle.

What I most wanted, though, were aerial shots of the campus, especially a photograph of the entire main campus hilltop in the forefront of the New York harbor and the Manhattan skyline. Undertaking such a photograph project, given the cost of an air charter, was a somewhat frivolous expense in 1990 given all the other ways in which limited money could be spent. Renting a helicopter for these photographs would cost a proverbial fortune and would be hard to schedule at the exact right moment on the exact right day.

On occasion, though, I would see the Met Life blimp flying in and out of the New York harbor and right past my office windows. Presumably, this craft was on an advertising mission, but their travel path was directly past our campus and seemed to be appearing only on days when the weather was right. Could we maybe get a free ride in exchange for some sort of commercial consideration?

The next time David Long wandered into my office, I mentioned the prospect to him at exactly the moment that the Met Life blimp was flying by. David said he would get to work on it and, sure enough, he found a way to persuade them to take me on a no-cost flight to the college. However, I would have to drive out to their airfield on Long Island, about an hour and a half away.

The date was set. I wasn't sure my equipment was good enough for aerial photography, so I asked a professional photographer who was a Wagner alumnus whether he wanted to accompany me. Robert Zentmaier, '66, said he would come along at no charge because he would be able to shoot other photographs for his own collection.

We arrived at the airfield on a crystal clear morning and faced the MetLife blimp bobbing about its mooring being held in place by about a dozen young kids whose job it was to hold an array of ropes to keep it steady. That was as high tech as docking was. I developed a little case of cold feet when it came time to climb aboard. Even that exercise had to be finessed according to the bobbing of the balloon. It was something like stepping onto a small boat when the wind is blowing, and the water is choppy.

We all managed to get on and spent the afternoon in the air. Once airborne, the blimp felt surprisingly steady, much like being in a high-rise building.

To get clear photographs, we were able to remove the windows, sticking out our heads and cameras.

I can't believe we were actually bold, or crazy, enough to do that, but we were with an emphasis on the latter.

Archival

Bob Zentmaier (left) and his assistant, center, join me for a pre-flight photo as the crew holds down the balloon and "patiently" await our readiness to board.

We flew? floated? along the southern shore of Long Island to the Verrazano-Narrows, and then directly over the bridge while I was in the co-pilot's seat, which featured a fully transparent floor, giving one an eerie feeling of being a Superman. We then arrived above the Wagner campus and spent considerable time photographing it from different angles.

I still get sweaty palms when I recall removing the side windows of the blimp's cabin so that we could lean out to get panoramic vistas. Once in the blimp for a while, we had become perhaps carelessly secure. With three photographers rapidly moving around for the ideal shot, it is a miracle that one of us wasn't bumped out the window and sent into a freefall.

My Nikon SLR was always in my desk drawer waiting to be called on picture perfect days. On the following pages are some of my favorites captured on rare occasions when conditions were exactly right.

Norman Smith

I took this aerial shot of the campus highlighting the buildings surrounding Sutter Oval, including the college's signature Main Hall. I shudder to remember that I was actually hanging out of the open window of the Met Life blimp in order to get a perfect photograph.

In the center of the Sutter ellipse is Main Hall just to the lower left of the baseball diamond. The library is to the left and the Communications Center (six-sided) to the right of Main Hall. On the far-right side is the tiny Sutter gymnasium that had to be expanded and upgraded if we were going to be able to compete for top residential students.

The dense tree cluster to the far right is the Augustinian estate, which will be the topic of chapters upcoming.

Norman Smith

Bucolic photos like the above require a perfect day.

The sun illuminating Main Hall was possible for only about two hours a day.... The trees were this lush for only about three months a year. And very few of those infrequent days had a clear sky with perfect clouds.

Perfect spring blossom moments are also rare.

I took this photo from the Brooklyn side of the Verrazano-Narrows. Wagner is directly above the sailboat just under the airplane.

Year FOUR 1991–1992

Chapter 18

My "Senior Year" Arrives ...

along with Our Baby Girl!

As I faced the beginning of my fourth year, my "senior" year at Wagner, Middle States had already affirmed our first unconditional reaccreditation and we used the accolades throughout the summer to try for a higher yield among the students we had accepted for the fall 1991 semester. While it was too late to find additional applicants, it wasn't too late to experience a higher yield among those students admitted.

Anyone in independent college admissions knows inquiries and applications are only the beginning of a lengthy enrollment recruitment program. Even admitted students provide no guarantees of who will actually enroll. Admissions offices too often mislead their institutions, trustees, and rating agencies like *US News* by declaring that their inquiries and applications are skyrocketing. Inquiries can readily be increased by attending mass college recruiting nights where as many as several hundred colleges and universities will be in a convention center or shopping mall while high school juniors and seniors wander about filling their shopping bags with expensive college publications they will likely never even read.

Some colleges have been known to hand out T-shirts, monogrammed pencils, and other logo items to any student who fills out a postcard with their name and address. This postcard then officially becomes an inquiry. A night of this sort of "inquiry buying" can generate thousands of alleged prospects, most of whom don't even remember the names of the colleges for which they completed postcards without double checking their souvenir pencils.

The admissions office will then be faced with the costs of following up all these phantom inquiries, most of which don't make it to the applicant phase. Similarly, minimizing application fees and inviting applications from students unlikely to be academically qualified can generate applicants. Responsible colleges will focus on the quality of inquiry and application pools so that they have a group of prospects more likely to enroll.

The most important part of the admissions process is what professionals call the "yield." That is, from among those students who have applied and been admitted, how many of those admits select your school over the many others to which they have also been admitted? Generally, academically promising students aspiring to a private college experience apply to at least five or six institutions, and often many more than that. If they are indeed academically promising, chances are that every college like Wagner College will have admitted them. They then are faced with choosing one from among them all.

For colleges like Wagner, yielding 30% of those admitted is a great outcome even though it means that seven of every ten admitted students decline the offer. Wagner was yielding far less than 30% and needed to improve outcomes. More of Wagner's applicants needed to view the college as their first choice.

The ***A+ for Wagner College*** article was a breakthrough in helping the College to experience its first major surge in new students in the fall of 1991. It also helped that the NYS Department of Education had reversed their view of Wagner and was applauding the college's return to fiscal balance. Of course, the improvements to the campus were also a major plus. And in the forefront was the completely new admissions team, headed by Susan Robinson, which had now been working on the problem for the past two years. Their efforts were beginning to pay off in what most would consider a very short span of time.

As it turned out, freshman enrollments were up 15% in the fall of 1991 and, even better, total new student enrollments were up 19%. A growing number of state college students, mostly from SUNY and CUNY, were disenchanted with the overcrowding where some of their freshman courses were taught in auditoriums, by graduate students, with as many as 300 students or more in a class. I recall two SUNY-Stony Brook students who transferred to Wagner after their first year. Both had been in the same class but had never met each other.

Even *US News* had started to pay attention and had elevated Wagner from their bottom tier to the third tier. Third tier was still in the bottom half, but at least it wasn't the very bottom, where CUNY-Staten Island remained. For the first time in decades, Wagner wasn't the lowest *US News*-ranked institution among CUNY-Staten Island, St. John's Staten Island, and Wagner.

Unfortunately, the rest of the world was not faring as well as Wagner College. The year 1991 marked a period of major economic recession that was adversely affecting colleges and universities throughout the country, all of whom were reporting budget cutbacks. Savings and loan banks were in trouble, many of them being taken over by the FDIC, the result of having made too many bad loans to debtors who would then declare bankruptcy. Then there was the collapse of the Soviet Union, resulting in a 70% drop in U.S. trade, along with spiking oil prices and the first Gulf War, Operation Desert Storm.

Although Wagner was swimming against the current and experiencing its first enrollment increases, the growth was modest and not enough to represent a financial breakthrough. Additionally, the debt that had been incurred by the bond refinancing would result in a major debt service being added to the operating budget in 1992, just a year away. We were going to need a significantly greater enrollment surge in the fall of 1992 to remain in fiscal balance and also pay the annual bond debt service.

If that were not enough, we also needed to continue to address those aspects of the College's campus that remained in disrepair. One building that had become a more notable eyesore was called the Communications Building. This hexagonal, two-story structure was built in the 1960s largely as a classroom building. It was in the heart of the campus, on the main Sutter Oval immediately adjacent to Wagner's one classic, iconic structure, Main Hall.

The building was in terrible disrepair and had not been upgraded since its construction. The walls were exposed brick, littered with graffiti that could not be removed. The carpet was ragged. The lower level of the building comprised heavily "raked" amphitheaters. The seats, however, had long been worn out, torn, or vandalized. The disrepair became that much more apparent after we had installed a student computer center on the second floor, thanks to Don and Evelyn Spiro. That center looked great, but also served as a contrast to everything else in the building that looked terrible.

Don Spiro, being chairman of the Board of Trustees, visited the college frequently and would routinely check out the student computer center, which had been dedicated in his honor. "We've really got to do something about the rest of that building," he would remind me. I told him I completely agreed and that, like so many other job jar-projects throughout the campus, all it took was money that we didn't have to spend. I then reminded Don that the building, like most structures at the college, had not yet been named for anyone. If we could get someone to donate one million, we could completely upgrade the building and name it for the donor. That the building was so centrally located made it a natural for such a fundraising project.

David Long agreed and started promoting the prospect among the trustees and other major donor prospects we were cultivating. David had already built an extensive list of donor-naming opportunities. The

Communications Center, while central, was not what we considered to be the costliest naming opportunity. Main Hall should be the most expensive naming opportunity, because of its iconic status.

The college needed both a sports/recreation center and a performing arts center. They would be expensive to build and would require at least five million each to be named after a donor. In 1991, one million dollars was a lot, considering the fact that Wagner College had never in its one-hundred-year history received anything close to that amount of money from anyone for anything.

As the year proceeded, though, David and I were driven to locate the college's first one-million-dollar gift. It seemed like the logical next milestone to achieve. We were now unconditionally reaccredited for the first time in decades. Enrollments were starting to move in the right direction. Our rankings in *US News* and *Barron's* were rising. The campus was looking as good as it had looked in decades. There was a prevailing air of optimism, even though we were still living hand to mouth. It's all relative.

Don was taking an enthusiastic lead in forwarding Wagner, and continued to be particularly focused on finding new trustees who could advance the college. One big find was Donna Hanover, wife of Rudy Giuliani, who in 1991 was forwarding his candidacy to become the next mayor of New York City. A Republican, Rudy needed Staten Island to win. Staten Island was New York City's Republican stronghold, overseen, politically, by Guy Molinari, borough president, former U.S. congressman, and Wagner College class of 1949 alumnus, the same year Don Spiro graduated. When Molinari became borough president, his powerful oversight of the Republican party made it easy for him to pass his congressional seat to his daughter, Susan, who for a moment became a national political figure, including a keynote speaker at the Republican National Convention.

Giuliani spent a great deal of time on Staten Island, including a visit to Wagner College with Donna. Donna was a media figure in her own right, having been a television news anchor before marrying Rudy, and continuing to pursue a media career. In a conversation that preceded his address at Wagner, Rudy informed me that he had proposed to

Donna on the Wagner College campus. Donna, he told me, had reservations about moving from her Florida news anchor job to New York City. To settle her nerves about the intensity of New York, Rudy claimed that he drove over to the Wagner campus with its panoramic view of the New York harbor and Manhattan skyline.

Donna joined the Board of Trustees and, for years thereafter, she would be an influential cheerleader for Wagner. Shortly after Rudy was elected mayor, she arranged for Rudy to wear a Wagner sweatshirt during a photo opportunity when he was playing football with his son Andrew on the Gracie Mansion grounds. That photo was a full front-page display in the New York *Daily News*.

Donna also was a frequent radio talk show host, including on the widely listened-to WOR station in Manhattan. She invited Susan and me to come by and plug Wagner College. She would also invite us to Gracie Mansion dinners, the most memorable one being a small dinner party in honor of superstar Julie Andrews and her husband, producer-director legend Blake Edwards, director of all the Peter Sellers' **Pink Panther** movies and the blockbuster movie of the 1980s, ***10***.

Archival

New York Governor Mario Cuomo with Les Trautmann '40 and me in my Wagner College office on the occasion of the governor's visit to Staten Island

To remain bipartisan, leaders from both parties were always invited to the College. Another major media event for the college was Governor Mario Cuomo's visit. Les Trautmann had arranged for that event, which included more opportunities for Wagner to get its name in the limelight.

As we entered the winter semester of my 'senior year' at Wagner, a major heartbreak occurred. Les Trautmann died in his sleep on a February night in 1992. Richard Diamond, the *Staten Island Advance* publisher to whom we had given an honorary degree a year earlier, invited me to be a speaker at Les's memorial service.

Fortunately, we had managed to give Les an honorary degree before he died. Les went the way I guess everyone would prefer. He didn't appear to have any illnesses, although he had been a heavy smoker. He just went to sleep one night and never woke up.

Wagner would miss Les's advocacy. While there were many *Staten Island Advance* articles to come that were positive about Wagner's progress, they were less frequent than they had been during my first four years. But those early years were when we needed Les the most.

Les's legacy needed to be acknowledged at Wagner. What had been accomplished during my first four years had been accelerated because of the way in which the *Advance*'s reports had affirmed the progress that was being made. On the one hand, the newspaper was just doing its job reporting factual events.

The *Staten Island Advance* never misrepresented Wagner's turnaround. But there is no denying that the articles were encouraging and enthusiastic because of Les's love for his alma mater and his joy that Wagner was had pulled itself out of near bankruptcy and was back on the map at a level of stature it had never before experienced.

Trautmann Square, Wagner College

An ideal memorial for Les was outside the front door of my office: a small central square facing the Student Union and adjacent to the library and Main Hall. This small plot of grass and trees was unremarkable and needed an upgrade, including some attractive benches and, ideally, a clock. I had for some time envisioned a cast iron, multisided Victorian clock. Installing such a clock would cost about $40,000 and was the kind of frill that ranked low on the must-have list at that time in the college's evolution.

I took the idea to *Advance* publisher Richard Diamond. He organized a fundraising campaign that produced all the money necessary for renovating the square, as well as installing the clock and a memorial plaque honoring Les. The improvements greatly lifted the character of the entire area and left a well-deserved legacy for Les. Former New York City mayor Ed Koch was among the dignitaries assembled when we formally dedicated Trautmann Square.

Archival

Former NYC mayor Ed Koch under the Trautmann Square Clock at the formal dedication ceremony

In March 1992, after David and I had been working since the previous fall in search of a breakthrough gift that would set a new standard for giving at Wagner, Don and Evelyn Spiro informed me that they were making the milestone gift we had been seeking. In truth, David and I had hoped the Spiros would be the ones, as among the alumni and trustees, Don and Evelyn were in the best position to make such a gesture.

$1 million for Wagner

Spiros' donation is college's largest

ADVANCE FILE PHOTO

Wagner benefactors Evelyn and Donald Spiro pictured at a past visit to the campus.

BY ADVANCE STAFF WRITER

Wagner College has received a $1 million donation, the largest single gift in the college's history, Wagner President Dr. Norman Smith announced today.

The donation comes from Donald and Evelyn Spiro, both graduates of the college.

Spiro, a native of Staten Island who presently lives in New Jersey, is chairman of Wagner's board of trustees and has had a longtime involvement with the college. He also is chairman emeritus of the Oppenheimer Management Corp., Manhattan.

A 1949 graduate of Wagner, Spiro spent most of his career at Oppenheimer, where he began as a field representative. Spiro served in the Army Air Corps during World War II and attended Wagner under the G.I. Bill.

"Needless to say, I'm deeply gratified by the Spiro gift," Smith said. "Private colleges cannot flourish if they must rely on tuition alone. The colleges with which Wagner is now being compared have strong endowments.

"The Spiro gift takes us over the $1 million hurdle we've been waiting for four years to overcome."

Smith noted that the college in recent years has been raising about $2 million annually in gifts, but has never before received $1 million from a single donor.

Commenting on the gift, Spiro

It's good news!

said: "The progress Wagner Co lege has been making in recen years shows that it can be amon the top private colleges in th East if it has the same resource as its competitors. Evelyn and hope that our gift is the beginnin of many such donations that wil together, give Wagner College th strong endowment it should right fully have."

This is not the first time th Spiros have come to the aid of th college.

"They've been instrumental i getting us to important plateaus, noted Smith.

Smith said that since he arrive at the college in 1988, the Spiro have come forward a number o times with support for importan needs. In September 1989, the presented Wagner with a state-of the-art computer technology cen ter.

This was followed by a fitnes center that was dedicated i memory of their friend and fellov Wagner graduate, Navy Capt. Jo seph Parise. Most recently, th couple erected a flag at the en trance to the college in honor o the men and women who served i the Gulf War.

STATEN ISLAND ADVANCE
WEDNESDAY, MARCH 4, 1992

The Spiro's one-million-dollar donation was Wagner's first seven-figure gift

Don had been repeatedly telling me how concerned he was about the condition of the Communications Center, and I couldn't have been more pleased to comply with its repair needs. The building was largely an eyesore and far too centrally located to be ignored, including during admissions tours. As important, though, was the stature that the gift represented. We needed to take the onus of never having received a seven figure gift off the shoulders of the college. Even when soliciting foundations, as David Long would tell all trustees and alumni, one of the first questions asked is how much the alumni and trustees are giving to the College and what was the largest gift ever received.

The *Staten Island Advance* covered the Spiro gift as the major story that it was. Don, though, would have preferred not getting on the front page for this kind of news. I recall him telling me that shortly thereafter he started getting letters from charities and schools all over Staten Island hoping that they, too, could get a million dollars from the Spiros.

He was especially taken aback by a solicitation he received from a College of Staten Island professor who sought Don's support for his research of garlic.

My senior year at Wagner was also consumed with another major milestone in my life. At 45, I was about to become a father for the first time. Susan was expecting our first—and what would be our only — child, whom I learned in February of 1992 was a girl due in late April.

Both Susan and I were thrilled that we were going to become parents, a gift we almost let slip through our fingers by waiting as long as we did. Susan was only forty, relatively late in life for her first child, but thankfully not too late to deliver perfection.

We spent Easter Sunday awaiting Caroline's birth, which came shortly after midnight on the following day. The *Advance* announced Caroline's arrival in that day's gossip column, where she was the lead story, beating out Cindy Crawford and Elizabeth Taylor.

From that point forward, Caroline became our pride and joy, just like all parents. She was healthy and happy.

I too frequently shudder to think that we nearly missed out on the most important priority in our lives by waiting as late as we did.

For the next ten years of my presidency at Wagner, Caroline was a fixture known to everyone on campus. We introduced her in person at the 1992 commencement ceremonies when she was little more than a month old, wearing her first Wagner T-shirt.

Year FIVE 1992–1993

Chapter 19
Let's Invest in the Product
...But You Say Save?

My 'senior year' at Wagner also marked the beginning of a debate among trustee factions that would persist, to my disappointment, throughout the rest of my tenure. Whereas essentially all trustees agreed that the college should continue to aspire to higher plateaus, thereby becoming a more financially secure institution, the fundamentals as to how that goal could best be achieved were not as universally agreed upon.

I contended that to be a first-rate college, all aspects of the college had to be first rate. The facilities had to be in good condition. The grounds had to look great. Technologically, the college had to be up to standard. The recreational and living facilities had to be comparable to what top-tier colleges were offering their students.

The reality was that colleges like Wagner were in an extremely competitive marketplace that was destined to intensify. In the quarter-century between 1965 and 1990, the number of students attending private colleges had flipped from about 65% private in the 1960s to 65% public in the 1990s. New York was a case in point. The SUNY (State University of New York) and CUNY (City University of New York) expansion during these twenty-five years was typical of most states. SUNY and CUNY campuses surged during this time, offering low-cost public university degrees that were in part accommodating a concurrent expansion of students attending college. But they were also pulling students out of the much more expensive private college community.

Even affluent parents would often be drawn to sending their children to state colleges. Politicians would portray public education as giving access and opportunity to the economically less advantaged. However, the fact was that in New York State at least, over 70% of the public university students attending SUNY and CUNY came from families that could afford private college tuition but opted instead for the lower costs of CUNY and SUNY.

The media would frequently cite parents who gave their child the option of a private college, but if they instead chose a CUNY or SUNY, could have a car because of tuition savings. Giving an eighteen-year-old that kind of offer almost guaranteed what the choice would be. Driving through the SUNY student parking lots and seeing the array of new cars affirmed that private colleges had their work cut out for them if they were going to successfully enroll paying customers who also had the wherewithal to attend and graduate from a college.

We had cleaned up Wagner, but the college was far from having all the bells and whistles that most successful competing colleges had. Wagner had virtually no recreational facilities other than an indoor basketball court, some remote tennis courts, and a few playing fields. There was no comprehensive recreational facility. The world-class theatre department continued to perform in a virtual high school auditorium if that. The bands and choir had nowhere to perform on campus and usually went to churches in the community both to practice and to perform. The residence halls, although at least refurnished, needed to be upgraded, especially regarding bathrooms. The business and nursing programs were housed in a former dormitory that lacked just about everything that a quality academic program needed. That the business program was the most enrolled in the college, but in the worst facilities, again, represented a shortcoming that needed to eventually be corrected.

All this was going to cost much more money than the bond issue had made possible. Fundraising was the only solution. Let's list all these needs in a catalog, I concluded, and start selling them to major donor prospects, including the Board of Trustees. And this is where a difference of opinion emerged. A disappointing number of trustees were troubled that the college had essentially no endowment. They believed that, first and foremost, Wagner should build an endowment that would someday relieve the college forever of being overly dependent on tuition revenues.

I agreed that a large endowment is desirable. As a measurement of institutional quality, one of the first questions typically asked about a college is the size of the endowment. The larger the endowment, presumably, the better the college. When presidents step down, the growth in endowment during their tenure is one of the most frequently cited measurements of success.

Almost anyone who is asked to cite the most prestigious colleges in America would likely pick Harvard, Yale, Stanford, and Princeton as among their top ten. Their endowments are the top four. With the University of Texas and MIT, these six institutions, in the early 1990s, were the only ones with double-digit billion-dollar endowments. Of the over 2,500 colleges and universities in America, however, only 250, in 1992, had more than $250 million. The other 90% had less to no endowment. But all these heavily endowed colleges and universities also have state-of-the-art facilities, faculty, and campuses.

So, what comes first, the chicken or the egg?

My "first" was the quality of product instead of the endowment. If Wagner was going to grow to enrollment capacity and become a top-tier college, it had to ***be*** one. All the facilities had to be in place. The condition of the grounds and the buildings had to reflect a well-managed, first-class institution.

Not everyone wants to think of a college this way, but I saw Wagner as a very expensive, consumer product. The college choice decision, if it is a private college, is one of the costliest acquisitions in life, up there with buying a house, and bigger than buying an automobile. Any automobile company trying to sell a car that doesn't have a radio, air conditioning, automatic transmission, or any other features considered standard nowadays is going to have a problem competing with all the other companies that provide fully equipped automobiles.

Colleges face the same challenge. Few prospective students and their families, if any, make a college decision without a campus visit. That visit has long been established as the single most important factor in the final decision. If the prospective student family doesn't see a campus that is well cared for and with all the features that other colleges have, the sale is lost. By those standards, Wagner had a long and expensive road to travel to become truly competitive. For decades, nothing had been kept current, and everything had deteriorated to unacceptable levels.

I didn't exactly come up with a price list, but tens of millions of dollars in upgrades were needed, heavily directed toward facilities including a theatre and concert facility, a sports and recreation center and a business school. Wagner also needed an admissions center, an alumni center, and a development complex. Additionally, many of the buildings required major renovation, including the historic Cunard Hall, a former dormitory now called Campus Hall, and the Student Union, which needed to be expanded, perhaps by covering the outdoor terrace thereby creating a large, multipurpose gathering center that would be the campus social hub.

Many of the trustees concurred with my rationale. The most supportive were business executives who ran companies that had to compete in the open market, like John Lehmann, Bill Reynolds, and Bob Evans. Those trustees favoring endowment contended that the campus had been adequately upgraded and that enough money had been spent on that part of the turnaround. "Let's stop spending and start saving," they declared.

There was no question that Wagner looked at least 300% better than it did just three years ago. But compared to the top-tier small private colleges, where I saw Wagner belonging, the work had just begun.

From the day David Long had come to Wagner, I had hoped that he could help me get everyone rowing in the same direction, and he tried. In almost every way, what Wagner needed to do was what Skidmore had done during David's years there with President Joe Palamountain. In the late sixties, Skidmore didn't have all that much going for it.

Not wanting to put the cart before the horse, Palamountain called for the top priority NOT to be endowment, but a complete college infrastructure that would attract sufficient students. Only then should there be a pursuit of an endowment. Skidmore proceeded to abandon its campus of houses up and down the streets of Saratoga Springs and instead built a completely new campus about one mile away from the town center.

The new campus has everything a college needs to offer a complete educational experience. As a result of that strategy, Skidmore became and remains one of the most desirable colleges in the northeastern United States. Additionally, putting infrastructure first drew donations that resulted in a meaningful endowment. Especially when it comes to endowment, benefactors are most inclined to give to winners. Winners are those schools with highly competitive rankings that top students want to attend. That kind of student demand is more enabled when the college offers comprehensive resources rather than a large endowment. Having both is even better, of course. But — first things first.

I further argued that endowments are not overnight undertakings. Additionally, they don't do much to improve a college's financial security until they reach at least several hundred million. Most colleges annually spend no more than 5% of the endowment principal, an amount that the endowment should at least be earning each year. Thus, only five million annually is likely from $100 million which, for virtually any institution with such an endowment, represents less than 10% of annual operating revenues. A mere 100 additional students realizes the same revenue and is much easier to come by than $100 million in endowment.

A big problem for colleges is the dependence that can arise from a large endowment. Because costs go up each year, the endowment, or the interest rates, or both, must grow each year as the institution becomes dependent on this source of revenue for annual expenditures. At the end of the first decade of the twenty-first century, those colleges and universities with the largest endowment dependence are perhaps suffering the most as they have seen their endowment principal drop by as much as half while interest rates have also plummeted to levels of just one or two percent annually. As a result, these institutions are faced with massive cost-cutting programs that include major staff and faculty cuts. Even wealthy Harvard eliminated hot breakfasts for the undergraduates because of their endowment dependence, although the protests from students had them restore that "benefit."

All that said, having an endowment is better than not. But not at the expense of lacking all the key features that "close the deal" with the 30% of college-bound students and their families who aspire to a non-public college experience and, for the most part, have the pick of the litter. Any college lacking in state-of-the-art facilities and resources will find themselves among the first to be dropped from the list of choices that most good students, with financial wherewithal, have available to them.

I liken the argument to Maslow's hierarchy of needs. Simply put, Maslow observed that some choices precede others according to relative urgency. The most basic needs relate to survival. Anyone who is drowning, starving, choking for air, being shot at, and so on, is thinking about nothing else except survival. Once such basic threats are removed, the next hierarchy is security and comfort—namely, knowing that there is little likelihood of being without food, air, and safety. Following these first two basic levels, when fulfilled, emotional wellbeing becomes important — concerns like being loved and belonging. Next, there is the state of actualization, meaning a felt sense of confidence and status. Finally, there is the level of total fulfillment.

My view of Maslow's hierarchy as it related to Wagner College's endowment was that endowment represents the peak level of total fulfillment; meaning, by my interpretation, only when all else is in order and there are no fundamental needs related to survival, security, and status, should money be channeled to the endowment. Until then, invest in all the facets that help secure survival, status, belonging, and confidence.

If one hundred million in donations could ever be realized, spending that money to build a sports center, a business school, an upgraded library, a performing arts center — while renovating all other facilities including Cunard Hall, Main Hall, and the Student Union, not to mention the residence halls — would be a better investment in Wagner's long-term security.

Endowment gifts usually come from bequests that can take decades to be realized, since such donors first must die. Wagner didn't have decades. The probability of such an endowment windfall is also daunting. In the past forty years, in 1992, there had only been 175 gifts of fifty million or more, according to the *Chronicle of Higher Education*. That's about four such gifts, nationwide, among thousands of colleges and universities per year. Out of those 175 gifts, fewer than ten — *in forty years* — have been realized by small colleges like Wagner. Most have gone to major national universities like Harvard, Yale, NYU, and USC.

I contended that pursuing a hundred-million-dollar endowment, which would be a modest endowment, just didn't make sense.

Wagner enrolled only 1,188 students at the time of my arrival but twenty years earlier had accommodated twice that many students. There were empty dorms that, in my judgment, could support an enrollment of well over 2,000 students. Wagner was only realizing a net enrollment of 550 that 1,188 students being discounted at 50+% represented. A 2,000-student enrollment at a 35% discount rate could increase the net enrollment from 550 to 1,300. An additional 750 net students could bring in an additional seventeen million dollars annually. Realizing seventeen million dollars annually from endowment would require a $350 million endowment.

So, let's first go after the full-to-capacity enrollment. Then, once we achieve that plateau, we can start channeling surplus revenues, including giving, into an endowment. This may take decades, but again — *first things first.*

Chapter 20
Fifth Year Report Card

Nationwide, September 1992 demographically marked the fewest number of first-year college students before a trend that would slowly grow from that year forward. In that respect, it wasn't the best of times for Wagner to be aspiring to a larger enrollment. The fall also marked the beginning of what would be my fifth year as president.

There is nothing sacrosanct about the fifth year. It does represent, however, a form of benchmark where I would undoubtedly be measured by someone for what kind of progress the college had made over that period.

Although everything we had aspired for Wagner had not yet been realized, the college was being largely viewed as having come a long way in a short period of time, particularly when the near fatal starting point is taken into consideration. Five years ago, most observers considered Wagner's remaining days to be few.

The fall 1992 enrollment, as a five-year benchmark, had quite a few positives to report. The character of the student body was moving in the right direction on several key measurements. To begin with, the enrollment had grown, from 1,188 when I arrived in 1988 to nearly 1,300. Of note was the academic quality of new students, which, when measured by SAT scores, had increased from a combined average of 788 in 1988 to over 1,000 five years later.

Although 1,000 is no better than the national average score, 788 was so far below that average that most of Wagner's students in 1988 were not really qualified to pursue college studies. The high dropout rate that Wagner had been experiencing confirmed that fact.

Another big breakthrough was the increase in resident students. In 1988, 60% of Wagner's 1,100 students were commuters; only 475 were residents. Of the 1,300 students enrolled in the fall of 1992, 66% (860) were residents.

The residential population had nearly doubled since 1988. This justified, in just a five-year span, the retention of the Harborview Hall dormitory that had nearly been turned over to the Eger Nursing Home.

These measurements alone made a strong case for a successful first five years.

Additionally, Wagner had earned its first unconditional reaccreditation and had posted four consecutive years of fiscal balance.

Another great breakthrough was the *US News* decision, in the fall 1992 edition, to promote Wagner from third tier to second tier.

The college was finally out of the bottom half and into the top half, in less than five years, which seemed unprecedented in *US News* history. Mel Elfin, the *US News* editor, who had become a Wagner fan, personally called me up with the good news — and good news it was.

Financially, prospects were also looking much better than 5 years earlier. Through a combination of enrollment growth, major residential growth, and cutbacks on discounts, the net enrollment revenue had increased from $9 million in 1988 to $15 million in 1992–1993.

Having an additional $6 million every year was comparable, in 1992, to having a one hundred-million-dollar endowment earning 6%.

Thus, having invested in infrastructure and improvements to recruit and enroll paying customers was proving a much better strategy than putting all gifts in endowment.

Speaking of endowment and giving, the first five years of fundraising totaled nearly twelve million dollars, more than two million each year.

Although this level of giving was far below what many comparable colleges might have been realizing, it was far and away the most successful five years of giving in Wagner's history.

As each year going forward continued to bring about additional advances, the spirit of giving would hopefully improve accordingly. A large part of that twelve million came from Don and Evelyn Spiro, whose many gifts included last year's one million dollars, Wagner's first seven -digit gift ever.

Over the summer, we completely renovated the Communications Center according to their wishes, and one of the highlights of the fall semester was rededicating the facility and naming it *Spiro Hall.*

The building looked so much better, as it should have. All the interior exposed brick was painted off-white, removing decades of graffiti and brightening all the classrooms. New chalkboard and speaker systems were installed in all classrooms. All the amphitheaters on the first floor were recarpeted with new plush theatre seating.

Wagner building gets new name in honor of alumni

Communications facility now Spiro Hall

By AMANITA DUGA-CARROLL
ADVANCE STAFF WRITER

Old friends and colleagues joined students and faculty yesterday as the newly renovated communications building at Wagner College was renamed in honor of an alumni couple who donated money for the refurbishment.

Drs. Donald and Evelyn Spiro, both members of the class of 1949, met while attending Wagner. The pair have been generous with their time and money since graduating, donating more than $500,000 for this latest project.

The building, officially dubbed Spiro Hall during yesterday's ceremony, has undergone a refurnishing of all its amphitheaters, the installation of reverse-projection audiovisual equipment and the addition of a 100-station personal computing center for student use.

"We wouldn't be here today if it weren't for the Spiros," said Dr. Norman Smith, president of the college.

Spiro said he and his wife believe it is important to help students, because each successful one will then make a difference in the world.

"I think this is what people should think about," Spiro said.

Both Spiros are native Islanders. Spiro made his fortune by building the Oppenheimer Company for mutual investment funds into one of the nation's largest, while Mrs. Spiro once held the distinction of being the youngest supervision nurse in the Staten Island University Hospital operating rooms.

Among the Spiros' classmates was Borough President Guy V. Molinari.

"He felt that he owed something to Wagner College, where he got his foundation — he never forgot," said Molinari of his old school chum, Spiro. "We're very proud of you."

Leon Levy, business partner to Spiro for more than three decades, also was on hand to honor his old friend.

"Don exemplifies what we would hope that many Wagner College students would choose to become," Levy said, adding that Spiro's strength of character and values distinguish him from the legions of less-than-honorable businessmen of recent years.

As for the fruits of the Spiros' generosity, the computer center is "full day and night," said Dr. Mordechai Rozanski, school provost.

"I want you to know what you have done for Wagner does not go unnoticed . . . I want you to know it is appreciated," said James Hickey, student body president.

College president Smith added that higher education is clearly a bipartisan issue, drawing support from both Molinari, a Republican, and Democratic Party chairman Bob Gigante, who also attended the ceremony.

Staten Island Advance Fall 1992

Don Spiro and I witness the unveiling of **Spiro Hall**

Another remarkable five-year benchmark was the way in which the Board of Trustees evolved. Of the twenty-seven trustees in 1992–1993, fifteen were new since my arrival as president. Don Spiro and Kevin Sheehy had been especially energized in recruiting new trustees from among successful Wagner alumni, and an impressive cohort of quite successful graduates were found, most of whom were enrolled during Wagner's flourishing baby boom 1960s and then went into Manhattan to build their careers.

Ten trustees were CEOs of major corporations. Wagner had the kind of board leadership needed to aim for high plateaus, and it all happened within the first five years. If the next five could be as successful, Wagner would be one of the most remarkable turnarounds in higher education.

On the downside of year five was the too-soon departure of two star executives, David Long and Mort Rozanski. David's departure was inevitable from the day that he came on board. He was nearing retirement when he joined Wagner and informed me that he could give me three to four years maximum before he would retire. It's less than ideal, but a bonfire for a few years is better than wet wood for decades.

What David had accomplished raised the bar for Wagner.

Mort's departure came as more of a surprise to me. Mort had done a great job getting Wagner through its first unconditional reaccreditation. He and I had a great working relationship that was a partnership in every way. Over thirty years later, we remain good friends.

But Mort was very able and very ambitious, as he had the right to be. Coming to Wagner was seen by many as a step backward for him. His vice presidency of Fairleigh Dickinson University was a much bigger job. He had come to Wagner to get away from a problem, and to that end we were something of a port in a storm.

Mort was on to greater horizons. He had accepted the presidency of the University of Guelph in Ontario, Canada. Mort, like me, was a native Canadian, having earned his undergraduate degree at McGill University in Montreal before earning his doctorate at the University of

Pennsylvania. The University of Guelph was one of the largest universities in Canada, about forty miles west of Toronto. Famed economist John Kenneth Galbraith was an alumnus. Mort was taking on a major assignment, and I was very happy for him.

Susan and I were part of the Wagner contingent at Mort's University of Guelph presidential installation

Everyone at Wagner was disappointed to see Mort go, but his new presidential appointment was a feather, of sorts, in Wagner's cap.

Wagner was now the kind of college that was populated by top-shelf faculty and staff. Although Guelph, Ontario was quite a distance from New York, a surprising number of faculty and staff went up to his formal presidential installation. I was a keynote speaker.

Some big shoes had to be filled. It wasn't going to be easy to replace either Mort or David with anyone comparable.

Lyle (center) and Deidre Shaffer (left) head up a student affairs team that includes Taku Poto, Susan Hudec, and George Sherman.

By now, Lyle Guttu had become Vice President for Student Affairs and had assembled a very solid team. Lyle had once been Wagner's Dean of Students but more recently had limited to his duties to chaplain. That he was living on campus, and, more importantly, was so skilled, made me want to put him to better use.

In addition to being a faculty ombudsman, I also looked to him to serve as my liaison to parents. He had a calming way of dealing with parent concerns, which had me conclude that student affairs were well suited to him. He, in turn, hired a dean of students, Deidre Shaffer, from Philadelphia University (now Thomas Jefferson University), where I had once been Vice President for Student Affairs. The team was in place and felt like the best student affairs staff that Wagner ever had.

Early in the search for David Long's successor, someone emerged who looked too good to be true. Lightning never strikes twice in the same place, although Victor Chira's credentials appeared to come close. Chira was vice president for development at Philadelphia's venerable Pennsylvania Academy of the Fine Arts, America's oldest conservatory, which had a faculty history that included two American artists of renown, Mary Cassatt, and Thomas Eakins. Before the Academy, Victor headed the fundraising arm of The Joffrey Ballet and had begun his fundraising career at Haverford College, one of the finest, small residential colleges in America. These were prestigious credentials for Wagner and seemed to live up to the standards that had been set by David. We hired Victor.

The development team also included Mona Motte, who had headed fundraising at Staten Island's Snug Harbor Cultural Center and was rounded out by a veteran corporate/foundation fundraiser, Charles Rose, and a young annual fund director, Kerrin Kelleher. My hopes were high that we had a results-oriented team in place that, with fifteen new trustees, could continue the momentum that David had launched over four years ago.

Replacing Mort would be somewhat more complicated. To begin with, the faculty rightfully expected to play a role in the selection process, which adds to the delay in appointing a replacement. Another positive five-year benchmark was that thirty-one new faculty members had been hired during that period, greatly strengthening the quality of the college's academic program. They all had a vested interest in who the chief academic officer would be and, like David, Mort had set a new standard that his successor would have to match.

Among the faculty appointed to the search committee were veteran humanities professor Anne Schotter, and a new history professor, Alison Smith. Alison came to Wagner from Vassar College, having earned her PhD at Johns Hopkins University. She was an impressive addition for

Wagner, as were virtually all of the thirty-one new professors.

After a relatively exhaustive search, one candidate emerged as a runaway favorite among the members of the search committee, especially Anne and Allison. Linda Basch was dean of the faculty of arts and sciences at Manhattan College and had previously been head of the faculty resource network at New York University. Before that, she had been director of the United Nations Institute for Training and Research. Basch was an anthropologist with an NYU PhD and a master's from Columbia University. She was also well published.

Like the search committee faculty, I too was drawn to her credentials along with the prospect of a female chief academic officer. All the other senior members of the college staff were male, which had been the case since Ellie Rogg returned to the faculty. Even in the early 1990s, an all-white, all-male leadership team wasn't ideal.

Linda became a unanimous faculty committee recommendation and was hired. Mildred Nelson had been serving as interim. Mildred hadn't wanted to be the permanent vice president and was happy to return to her job as registrar, which had been upgraded to Associate Provost.

On the financial front, Wagner's fifth year was finally starting to provide some breathing room. Enrollment revenues were up six million dollars, and the net operating budget had, over five years, more than doubled from under ten million to twenty-four million. On the negative side, though, the college now faced a hefty annual debt created by the bond issue. The bonds had been issued at a time when interest rates were particularly high, and the college consequently faced an annual payment of nearly three million dollars. Interest rates, though, had since dropped several percentage points.

First Boston's Dave Czyganowski called with a proposal that we obtain bond insurance from Asset Guarantee that would permit us to refinance the bonds. Given all the quantitatively measurable outcomes of the first five years, Czyganowski believed that the debt service could drop by as much as six hundred thousand a year. We proceeded with this and indeed won the bond insurance that permitted the refinancing.

As a result, the annual debt service dropped to $2.4 million, still a large portion of the operating budget, but more manageable.

On the plus side, another annual debt service was paid up, namely a longstanding New York dormitory authority bond that was taking several hundred thousand dollars out of each year's budget.

But what the Lord giveth, the Lord taketh away. Over the first five years, health insurance for employees skyrocketed from $250 thousand in premiums annually to $800 thousand. This was largely the result of a benefit that had been given to all Wagner retirees who were permitted to remain on the college's health insurance plan for life at no cost ... an unprecedented retirement benefit and a financially unsustainable one for a small college like Wagner.

As each year progressed and this retiree cohort age got higher, health care claims soared, which, in turn, notched up the college's premium. That situation was doomed to worsen as each year went by.

At some point, the college was going to have to rethink the benefit and perhaps cut back on benefits, which would not be well received by retirees.

Workman's compensation was also skyrocketing. Over the first five years, the annual payment had increased from $58 thousand to $390 thousand. Tuition increases just couldn't keep up with these sorts of involuntary inflationary sums.

Luckily, the first five years of enrollment growth and reductions in discounts had built a much larger budget base to support this inflation. Without those improvements, Wagner would have been put out of business, unable to keep up with costs over which it had no control.

Chapter 21
WAGNER–*The Movie*

Sometimes the best intentions blow up in your face. The college's need for a recruitment video was where it all began. 1992 predated DVD technology, and websites for colleges and universities hadn't yet been born. View books with beautiful photography and VHS videos were the standard and only ways to widely market colleges.

During the first five years, Susan Robinson had overseen a total revamping of the college's publications, and they looked great thanks in large part to the Iowa admissions marketing company Stamats and their remarkable Sr. Vice President Marilyn Osweiler who worked closely with Susan. Together, they created one of the best marketing packages that any college could hope to have.

But the only video we had was essentially a slide show with voiceover. We knew it was nowhere close to being as effective as some of the very professional videos that competing colleges had already introduced to our disadvantage.

We needed a promotional video, and it had to be first rate. Some of

Wagner's most distinctive characteristics had to be seen to be believed; namely, its location on a hill overlooking Manhattan, and its bucolic campus emulating the best of New England rural settings. A video could capture this and lure viewers to come and see for themselves. Several production companies specialized in college recruiting videos and, as we canvassed them, we learned that a top-shelf video was probably going to cost at least one hundred thousand dollars.

Our trustee Phil Dusenberry had been very helpful in designing some print media ads for us that we were running in the educational supplements of the *New York Times* and other major daily newspapers. Phil's agency, BBDO, was much more than a print media organization.

BBDO was famed then for a series of Pepsi commercials they had produced that featured Michael Jackson at the peak of his popularity. A lot of publicity surrounded the commercials because Jackson had been seriously burned by pyrotechnics, an injury he would reportedly suffer from throughout the rest of his life and which was, perhaps, the cause of his addiction to painkillers that many believe finally caused his death.

I approached Don Spiro about the advisability of asking Phil to produce a video for us. We had just given Phil an honorary degree the previous spring. He and Evelyn Spiro were joint recipients.

Don was all for approaching Phil, and upon being asked, Phil agreed but would only donate professional expertise. The camera crew and related production costs would have to be paid by the college. Phil estimated those costs, if we wanted to go first rate, would be about $100,000.

Don considered that a bargain from Phil and proceeded to call the trustees to pitch in and come up with the $100,000.

Don and Bob O'Brien took the lead in donating to the cause, followed by several other trustees including Bob Evans, John Lehmann, and John Myers.

The $100,000 was quickly realized, and Phil got to work.

Evelyn Spiro and Phil Dusenberry receive honorary doctorates conferred by Don and me

I sent Phil a number of college recruiting videos comparable to what we would need for Wagner, noting that the beauty of the campus was an important characteristic that had to be captured, along with Wagner's location overlooking the Manhattan skyline. An ideal closing shot would start at Main Hall, then rise into the air until the Manhattan skyline became visible. We could voice over this shot with a comment like, "At Wagner College, your most ambitious goals are within reach"—namely the career opportunities in the most powerful city in the world.

Phil was a very soft-spoken and understated man. He listened to me but didn't really nod his head in an understanding way. No doubt he was used to clients laying out their view of what the commercial should be, which was probably contrary to what his creative mind saw. The big Pepsi slogan he created was *Uh-huh*. The Pepsi CEO probably gulped disapproval when Phil came up with *Uh-huh*, but I guess it sold Pepsi.

Phil sent over what he said was his best production team, a group of about five people. Phil himself was not on campus during the production planning or shoot. Susan walked the team through the campus, pointing out what we considered to be the locales that seemed most photogenic. Susan also assembled dozens of students, faculty, and staff, all of whom we thought put Wagner's best foot forward. The production team then went about assessing and casting everyone.

The shoot lasted several days during a period when, thankfully, the weather was on our side. Each day was sunny and clear. The campus looked great. We were going to end up with a great video. Phil had decided to use 35mm film instead of video, and then transfer to video. This would make everything look more lush: richer colors, better contrasts, and so on. It wasn't easy, but I distanced myself from the shoot while wanting to be in on every facet.

On the final day of the shoot, a helicopter landed on the Main Hall Sutter Oval. (1992 was long before the advent of video drones)

Phil had remembered my closing shot suggestion and had arranged for a camera crew to be lifted by helicopter until they could pan from the campus to the Manhattan skyline. Too good to be true! This was going to be great! Phil also arranged to use Gershwin's *Rhapsody in Blue* for the soundtrack since Woody Allen's movies had made that music synonymous with New York City. That sounded good to me, too.

Now, however, after several days of clear sun, clouds were coming in, and it looked like a storm might be imminent. The camera and helicopter crews rushed their plans and proceeded with the shoot, pulling up from the Oval and over the tree line in what looked like the nick of time to get the shot. The clouds and rain came shortly thereafter. There weren't going to be multiple takes. I hoped they succeeded the first time around. It was unlikely that we could afford to do this a second time on another day.

With the shooting done, we were told it would take a couple of weeks to edit everything into a final cut, so we waited patiently for the call. Eventually, Phil called us and invited Don Spiro, Bob O'Brien, and me to come to his Manhattan offices to see the video. He said they had about twelve minutes assembled, which sounded about right.

We all gathered in Phil's office where the production crew had also assembled. Phil had a television and video player in his bookcase, and we all gathered around. The high point of the video was definitely the ending. The helicopter shot worked extremely well and, with the Gershwin music, was a powerful ending that in every way captured the magic of Wagner's unique location.

Most of the video, though, featured close-up headshots of students and faculty talking about Wagner. The production opened with a group of students tap dancing and, from that point forward, virtually every student was a theatre major talking about the theatre program. There was very little reference to any other part of the college.

For all intents and purposes, anyone watching the video and knowing nothing else about Wagner would assume that we were the Wagner School of Performing Arts. Ironically, theatre was the only program at Wagner not in need of a recruiting video. The program had a great national reputation, and applications always exceeded the limited capacity.

I was also disappointed that very little of the campus' beauty had made it into the video. Except for the final helicopter shot, the video barely featured the rural park-like beauty that we had spent the past five years trying to optimize.

This video wasn't going to work for us.

When Phil asked for my reaction, I praised the ending but noted the overall emphasis on theatre as a problem. Neither he nor his production crew were happy. The head of the production crew walked out of the office in a huff, grumbling that he had had it and wanted nothing more to do with the project. Don and Bob seemed disappointed that I had been critical of the video. I had attempted to be diplomatic but felt strongly that the video had to be re-edited to more accurately portray the breadth of the college.

Others shared my concern. Susan and her admissions recruiting crew loved the quality of the production, which was exceptional, but they agreed that the message wasn't going to work very well except in theatre — where it wasn't needed.

Phil did go back to the drawing board. They had shot tens of hours of film and selected only twelve minutes for the final version. As I had suspected, Susan had provided them with students from throughout the college, not just the theatre department. Although the theatre students were particularly attractive, articulate, and compelling, many of the students from the other disciplines also had made effective presentations.

A few weeks later, Phil sent a revised version that was wonderful. There were now a lot of campus panorama shots they added that had not been in the original version. The changes turned the production into a winner. As we tested the revised version, everyone who saw it loved it. Among those who had seen many college videos, most volunteered that Wagner's was the very best one in the marketplace.

We passed all these accolades on to Phil, with my profound gratitude for the way in which he had changed the video to accommodate my concerns. Phil, however, made it clear to me, without really saying so, that he never wanted to have anything to do with me again. I had challenged his expertise, and he didn't like that, especially since he had been volunteering his expertise.

Who on earth was I to question the reigning dean of advertising?

Phil would back away from all involvement with Wagner and, when his four-year term came up for renewal, he asked not to be renewed. The outcome was the most bittersweet of my five years.

We had ended up with one of the finest recruiting videos of any college in the country, but at a price I wished we hadn't had to pay.

But if I had to do it all over again, I can't think of how I could have avoided a most unfortunate outcome.

The video was mailed far and wide to prospective students out of state having a very positive effect on prospective students. There was an almost immediate surge in campus visit by families who wanted to see the campus to believe it.

While over 30 years old at the time of this second edition, I believe it would work to this day and wouldn't have to be mailed as most colleges now have such videos on their websites ... websites that didn't yet exist in the early 1990s.

While a little grainy as the video has been transferred from VHS cassette to on line and can be seen on the Wagner College website, **www.wagner.edu**.

Or you can simply Google "Wagner College The Movie 1992" and watch through other sources including YouTube.

Year SIX 1993–1994

Chapter 22
Admissions Hits a Home Run

I've often been characterized, probably correctly, as being too impatient, wanting everything to happen yesterday. To remind myself to settle down a little, there have always been three quotes framed and placed prominently in my office.

One, by Jack Kerouac, declares, "Walking on water wasn't built in a day." The second is an anonymous declaration that it takes time for an acorn to grow into an oak tree. The third is from Walter Lipmann: "We must plant trees we may never get to sit under."

Throughout my first five years at Wagner, the need for a stronger enrollment, both qualitatively and quantitatively, loomed above all else. Maintaining the costly size of the campus combined with the vacant dormitories was not financially viable without more paying customers.

Conventional wisdom within higher education was that no private, enrollment revenue-dependent college like Wagner could be even minimally financially viable without at least 1,000 paying customers. One thousand full-paying students meant 2,000 at 50% discount

The good news was that we had made meaningful progress over the first five years. The enrollment had slowly risen from 1,100 to 1,400 students. That was 300 more students over a five-year period.

In 1992, 1,400 students, receiving an average discount of 20%, calculated to nearly 1,100 full-paying customers, which was above conventional wisdom's magic number of 1,000. But the cost of living in New York City was much higher than the national average, so the average minimum for Wagner had to be higher too.

Try as we did throughout the first five years, though, pushing the enrollment faster just didn't happen. We were faced with our need to increase academic standards, thereby having to deny admission to many students whose tuition we would have loved to collect. And we couldn't afford to sell the product for less than it cost to make. It was tempting to increase the discount rate, but an enrollment increase achieved at too high a discount rate would increase our operating costs.

That is, our 1,400 students generated 1,100 full paying customers at 20% average discount. Had we stayed at 50% discount, we would have needed to enroll 2,200 students for that same income level, but would incur the costs of educating, housing, and feeding 800 additional heads that were, for all intents and purposes, paying nothing. Because we weren't doing the latter, we had managed to stay within budget for five consecutive years. I kept hoping, though, to realize larger enrollment growth faster.

Finally, the sixth year delivered an oak tree—maybe not a massive oak tree, but four consecutive years like 1993-1994 would produce a very grand oak tree. Fall 1993 saw an enrollment of 1,600, 200 more students than the previous year.

We had just experienced a whopping 600% increase in new students in one year.

Susan Robinson had predicted the enrollment outcome since last spring but I had to see it to believe it. Susan had been reporting breakthrough statistics throughout the recruiting season. We had also all been sensing a new attitude about Wagner among prospective students and their families.

This spirit was especially discernible during the on-campus open houses. These all-day programs, both in the fall and the spring, had been full to capacity with families that were geographically farther from New York City than ever before. Visitors were driving from as far away as New England to the north and Virginia to the south.

Susan and her staff were witnessing parents calling on their cell phone declaring, "You should see what we've just found! Wagner is a well-guarded secret you must come and see for yourself. This place is gorgeous."

One Connecticut parent confided in me that she nearly turned around two or three times while driving through Brooklyn and onto Staten Island because of the high-density blight of these boroughs. But when she turned onto Howard Avenue and started driving to the top of Grymes Hill where Wagner was perched, "The whole aura changed from urban blight to rural beauty. I couldn't believe the metamorphosis and fell in love with the setting."

The campus did look great, no question about it. Walter Earl, head of grounds for five years, had systematically transformed the college into a botanical garden. The grass, trees, and shrubs were the most carefully attended of any college I had ever visited. But other breakthroughs had been occurring that added to Wagner's new appeal. Moving into the top half of *US News*-rated colleges made a big difference.

Our marketing materials unquestionably put Wagner's best foot forward and were drawing the curiosity of a new audience who had never heard of Wagner.

I was beginning to realize how lucky we were that Wagner had such a local enrollment during its worst years. With an enrollment that was 90% Staten Island and Brooklyn, most prospective students for Wagner never knew of the college in its worst condition. Had Wagner been more widely known during those bleak years, it could have been that much more difficult to change people's views.

Phil Dusenberry's video awakened families that had never before considered Wagner. We widely distributed the lush production, and many visitors commented that the video piqued their curiosity to come and see for themselves — exactly what we had hoped would happen.

Susan Robinson and her staff deserved a lot of credit for the breakthrough. Susan had recruited an entire new team of personable, attractive, intelligent young people, all of whom made exactly the right impression. Susan's ability to manage complex databases and monitor the thousands of inquiries through the process of becoming applicants, admits, yields, and enrollees also was starting to contribute to the payoff.

Another important piece in solving the admissions puzzle was the revised grant aid strategy we implemented that diverted our limited discounts away from high-need students (who couldn't afford their share of tuition anyway) and A students, who were getting more generous grants from competing colleges with a stronger financial history.

Instead, we were making grant offers to B students without consideration to need. As expected, the yield among these students skyrocketed and contributed to the fall 1993 tidal wave of new students.

Even parents were remarking how proud they were that their son or daughter was a scholarship student. This "bragging right" was more important than the money itself, which, after all, averaged only 20% per student. But these families could afford the other 80%, and the scholarship, added to everything else that Wagner had now become, was making it all come together to turn Wagner into a more frequent first-choice institution.

If this trend could only hold from this point forward, Wagner was within five or six years of being at optimum enrollment. As oak trees go, that is a pretty fast evolution from acorn status.

STATEN ISLAND SUNDAY ADVANCE • SUNDAY, SEPTEMBER 19, 1993

Wagner College president Dr. Norman Smith points out the school's growth.

WAGNER COLLEGE

Things are looking up on Grymes Hill campus

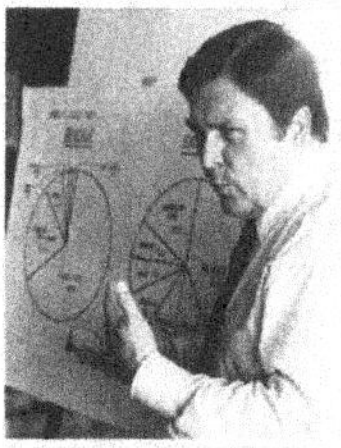

Dr. Smith uses a chart to detail Wagner College's turnaround during the last five years.

ADVANCE STAFF REPORT

After five years at Wagner College, president Norman Smith is up.

Admissions are up, the average Scholastic Aptitude Test (SAT) score of new students is up, and Smith says Wagner College is up to the challenge of getting "to the top of the lists" of small colleges nationwide.

The president of Wagner met with members of the Advance Editorial Board recently, to show off his campus and to discuss the past five years at Wagner under his leadership.

In his paneled office, which allows a remarkable view of Staten Island from atop Grymes Hill, Smith stressed a forward look. He plans to increase the school's endowment and wants to build a new athletic complex.

The president boasted that this year's entering class has an average SAT of 1,000 points, higher than in any other year. However, SAT scores reportedly have risen in the past year nationally.

Freshmen who began the fall term three weeks ago were positive about entering Wagner. Many echoed selling points that Smith has been using to build the college's image.

Jacqui Rodda came to Wagner "for the theatre program."

"I'm a singer and when I visited I got a really good feeling about it," she said. Ms Rodda also said she was influenced by a friend she made who "really wanted to go here."

Many students who spoke with an Advance reporter said that Wagner was their first choice.

One 18-year-old prospective business major from Stamford, Conn., put it this way: "This is the only college I applied to. It's a small school and it's close to New York."

The student computer center in Spiro Hall

Smith: A man on several missions

Wagner president a fund-raiser, administrator, cheerleader

Dr. Norman Smith moves through Wagner College's Grymes Hill campus on a mission. Which mission, depends on which Smith one encounters.

Smith segues from being a fund-raiser, an administrator concerned about day-to-day duties, a cheerleader for for his school, and for private colleges in general. Throughout it all, the former assistant dean at Harvard University's Kennedy School of Government is animated and relentless.

Wagner College President Dr. Norman Smith takes members of the Advance Editorial Board on a tour of the Grymes Hill campus.

The main dining hall in the College Union.

Excerpted: After 5 years at Wagner College, President Norman Smith is up. Applications are up. The average SAT of new students is up. Dr. Smith moves through Wagner College's Grymes Hill campus on a mission. Which mission depends on which one he encounters. Throughout it all, the former Harvard Kennedy School of Government Asst. Dean is animated and relentless.

Chapter 23
The Door Keeps Revolving

The enrollment tidal wave experienced in Year Six was an enormously successful one, yet there were a couple of disappointments that sent me back to the drawing board. I had known from the get-go that successfully replacing David Long and Mort Rozanski would be tall orders. Both had left very big shoes to fill that put their successors in unenviable positions. To my disappointment, it became too quickly apparent that both of their successors were finding Wagner to be a wrong fit for them.

Victor Chira was not in his cultural milieu at Wagner, and he knew it. I had relied too much on his early career experience at Haverford College to have embedded itself in his essence. Haverford was very much the model for what I envisioned Wagner would someday be. With Swarthmore, it ranked as one of Philadelphia's two most highly regarded, small, private, residential liberal arts colleges. Victor's more recent, and more senior, positions at the Pennsylvania Academy of the Fine Arts and at the Joffrey Ballet more completely defined who he was and where he was most comfortable. He was an urban cosmopolitan who really didn't fit in with the small-town atmosphere of Wagner College. He appeared to have little interest in sports, although Wagner was a Division I program, and many of the most successful alumni and donors were former athletes. Most alumni trustees had been athletes.

Victor just couldn't find his audience because it largely didn't exist at Wagner. He was more suited for the Metropolitan Museum of Art or Lincoln Center. Without question, part of the problem was how much the trustees already missed David Long. David knew exactly how to integrate himself into the family of college life. David had been omnipresent at Wagner, night and day, seven days a week.

Linda Basch was also finding Wagner to be less than a perfect fit for her. Perhaps Linda's biggest handicap was her decision not to move close to the college. Her home was in Bronxville, an upper-crust neighborhood north of Manhattan where her former institution, Manhattan College, was located. Bronxville and Staten Island are both in New York City, but they may as well be in different states. With Manhattan in between, there is no easy and quick way to get from one to the other. Staten Island is the southernmost corner of New York State, and on any map looks like it should be part of New Jersey. Legend has it that even New Jersey thought it should be part of New Jersey. New York won a boat race around Staten Island and that, according to the legend, is how the Island became part of the Empire State.

Even a drive from Staten Island to Manhattan, which is only twelve miles via — for the most part — the Brooklyn Queens Expressway (BQE) can take over an hour because of traffic congestion. Add another hour from Manhattan to Bronxville and you have a minimum four-hour daily commute. On wintery days, and there are many throughout the academic year, getting from commuting to Wagner was fundamentally impossible on a same-day basis.

Almost immediately, Linda was having trouble getting to the college. Her morning appointments frequently had to be cancelled and rescheduled, as she would be delayed in traffic. Because she had a long ride home, she left early to have some of the night with her family. Her motive was understandable, but the college never closed. Almost every evening of the regular academic year there was an event on campus, from choir recitals to theatrical performances. I rarely missed any of them and neither had Mort, David, or Lyle. Linda couldn't stay for evening events and then undertake her commute without consuming the entire night and arriving home at midnight. She was too infrequently seen at college events, which adversely affected her support from faculty who expected her to attend their events.

Again, I should have more carefully considered her prior affiliations. Linda lived down the street from Manhattan College in a community she favored and didn't want to leave. Her closeness made it easy for her to attend evening and weekend events without facing a four-hour commute. NYU is massive and very urban. Linda's NYU position was much less demanding on her time. She could focus on her specific responsibilities and enjoy more evenings and weekends at her home, which was only half as far from NYU as Wagner would prove to be.

Then Linda was offered the presidency of the National Council for Research on Women in New York City. Here was a nationally prestigious academic position that she probably would have taken even if her commute hadn't made Wagner such a difficulty. She was back to the commute she had undertaken while at New York University.

But for Wagner, the provost's job was once again vacant, and that wasn't good.

I learned from my experience with Linda and determined that the provost, like the president, had to live near the college. Such had been the requirement for the chief student affairs officer, but at small, residential colleges like Wagner, the provost was just as important part of the 24/7 community. David Long's on-campus residency had also proven to be a plus. Since his wife remained in Saratoga Springs so she could maintain her career as deputy superintendent of Saratoga schools, his campus presence made him a routine fixture at events where he also mingled with alumni and parents who would become benefactors.

I was not drawn to the prospect of undertaking two national searches for yet more new faces. A more familiar and comfortable solution seemed a better answer. Were there two Wagner people who could fill these positions for the next couple of years before we launched searches for outside people? My first thought for provost was to go back to Mildred Nelson who had filled this gap previously, and whom everyone loved and respected, including me. Mildred asked not to be asked. She had personal health concerns that she believed would slow her down. Without pursuing it, I accepted her decision and looked elsewhere.

Within the Wagner community, who had stood out as a leader? Walt Hameline continued to run an impressive Division I athletic program on fumes while also serving as head football coach. However, Walt wasn't an academic, and removing him from athletics would be robbing Peter to pay Paul.

What part of the college's academic program is well run? Of course! Theatre! Wagner's theatre program had won national accolades and, like Walt's program, was producing diamonds from coal. Professor Gary Sullivan had been overseeing the program for years since its founding father, Lowell Matson, had retired.

The theatre faculty was first rate. The shows were Broadway class. And Gary was also the producer extraordinaire who had managed to build an audience of paying customers for every show's two-week run. Four fully staged shows were presented each academic year. Each show was presented six times a week for at least two weeks. Most were typically filled to capacity and won rave reviews, deservedly so.

No one disliked Gary. He was soft-spoken, low-keyed, and steady under pressure, a commonplace circumstance in theatre. He just got the job done. As I canvassed the faculty, the majority thought it might be the right interim move, but (noting Gary was without a PhD, as was typical among performing arts faculty) insisted that another Mort Rozanski eventually be found.

The academic culture was conducive to Gary's assumption of the provostship. Dozens of new professors had been appointed in recent years. The quality of the student body was making teaching more exciting for everyone. In many ways, nothing was really broken within the faculty, so there wasn't really a need for anyone to come in and fix anything. A steady overseer that everyone knew, trusted, and respected seemed to make a lot of sense to just about everyone.

Gary agreed to take on the position and we happily announced that we would be enjoying continuity immediately rather than spending most of the coming year searching for a provost.

Norman Smith

Theatre's Professor Gary Sullivan assumes the provostship.

There was no point searching for anyone currently at Wagner who could head up fundraising. Spending the next six to nine months searching for someone didn't appeal to me or to the trustees. We both knew the urgency of continued fundraising outcomes. We needed another David Long and everyone knew it.

So, I called David Long to see how he was making out in retirement and to pick his brain on the prospect he might know of someone who would be close to being him. I told him what had happened with his successor and how much everyone missed him. To my surprise and gratification, he admitted that he missed Wagner too.

"David, would you please return for a couple additional years," I asked him. Maybe I was begging. Whatever the case, David agreed to return. He reminded me that he could only stay for a couple of years — I would have agreed to a couple of months. With David returning, not only did we dodge the bullet of being without a chief development officer for the large part of the coming year, but we had the guy who all the most important donors and donor prospects missed.

The board was elated. For that matter, everyone was elated. David was coming home.

On the occasion of his return, David Long with Alumni Director, Lisa DeRespino '85 and Annual Fund Director Kerrin Kelleher. Lisa would leave higher education work to join an investment bank where she has had a successful career and serves today as a Wagner Trustee.

Chapter 24
Immortalizing Our Heroes

Year Six was undoubtedly the breakthrough year affirming that my alleged delusions of grandeur were being realized. There were some who remained on the sidelines, wanting assurances that the enrollment surge wasn't a one-year fluke. Susan and I understood why the surge had occurred and knew it could, and would, continue.

The admissions staff couldn't have generated their results had it not been for the benefactors and trustees who had believed and put their money on the line. They deserved to be lionized and most certainly never forgotten. Many of them had already received honorary doctorates during the past five commencements since my arrival.

Except for the Spiro student computer center, Megerle Hall, and Trautmann Square, no other campus facility had been named for anyone. We were reserving building names for what we hoped would be future multimillion-dollar gifts.

During visits to other colleges like Wagner, I noticed that most had impressive historic portrait galleries chronicling past institutional leaders, including trustees and benefactors. The Harvard Club in Manhattan had portraits of club leaders throughout the facility. Wagner should begin its tradition.

Richard Gaffney, chair of the arts faculty, suggested that Professor Bill Murphy was a very talented artist who might be interested in some commissions. Bill had been a protégé of famed Staten Island artist, John Noble. Bill said that he hadn't done many portraits, but he would be willing to give it a go.

Cost was my greatest concern since I had been told that a professional oil painting would probably cost $20,000. Wagner was in much better financial condition than anyone could have hoped, yet the outstanding needs still exceeded available resources. Spending $20,000 per portrait would not be received well by those awaiting everything from better bathrooms to salary increases. Bill cited a fee that was a fraction of conventional costs, making the undertaking affordable.

We decided that the first portrait should be of Al Corbin, the veteran trustee who had rung the alarm bells on the financial condition of the college. Al had played a key role in mobilizing, with Don Spiro and others, the Staten Island bankers to provide the short-term loan that enabled Wagner's survival during my first two years.

Al was treasurer of the board for my first few years and was an instrumental advocate in a host of issues including the reversal of plans to sell buildings and campus property to the Eger Nursing Home and the Coast Guard. He was also the oldest turnaround trustee, and I wanted to ensure he would be around to see the unveiling of this tribute.

We decided we would aim for an unveiling of this first portrait at the December black-tie gathering in the president's house, which was attended by trustees, major donors, and senior faculty and staff.

This event had already become a well-received annual tradition that would endure through my tenure.

Al Corbin's portrait is unveiled, and he is presented with a framed photograph of the painting.

Bill completed the portrait in time. To complement the painting, we presented Al with a framed photograph of the finished portrait. We then hung the painting in the president's office although my long-term hope was to find a suitable area somewhere else on campus where more people would more frequently see the collection. Since Al's would be the first and only for the moment, there would be plenty of time to find a space that, I hoped, would someday have dozens of such honorees.

Al was thrilled with the honor and for his remaining years would tell me that having received an honorary doctorate and then having a portrait hung at the College, along with having married his wife, Buttons, were the most important events in his life. Al wasn't a young man, and I was happy to have been in the position to enable his rightful acknowledgment within his lifetime. He certainly deserved it.

From the day of the unveiling, every time Al walked into my office, I saw him glance over at the painting, and I would see emotion well up in him. Al loved Wagner, but something more intense had happened to him. He would talk frequently of his intentions to leave his estate to Wagner, a decision I felt was inspired by these honors. As I had thought would be the case, an oil painting does have a powerful effect on many, if not most, people.

Dr. Donald Spiro, '49

During this same year, Bill completed two other portraits. Had it not been for Al's age, Don Spiro would have appropriately been the first so honored. Don had no problem with the decision to paint Al's portrait, but understandably resisted the prospect of his painting, thinking it should wait until after he was no longer chairman of the board. I persuaded him, though, that these paintings are more than a tribute and could maybe serve as an incentive for major giving from others who had not yet come to the plate. With that condition, Don agreed.

Another benefactor had also been extremely generous during the past few years, and she was also at an age when time was a factor. Martha Megerle had become very re-engaged with Wagner.

As Martha saw each year getting better than the former year, she became very bullish and enthusiastic. She loved the college choir, and we would almost always attend their recitals together. She even took the choir to her hometown in Germany, which she hadn't visited for decades. The choir performed on the city hall steps and Martha received a key to the city from the mayor.

Martha had been very touched when we awarded her an honorary doctorate and, like Al Corbin, I could see that she was even more affected upon seeing her portrait unveiled. The event came as close to bringing her to tears as any moment I had spent with her. A warm and caring woman, Martha nevertheless was a strong-willed German who rarely let her emotions overwhelm her.

The next time I met with Martha alone, she informed me that she had decided to bequest a multimillion-dollar endowment for Wagner upon her death. She told me that she was making the bequest because of what had been accomplished since my arrival, and that she too believed Wagner had a promising future that she wanted to help underwrite. Like all such bequests, the proceeds are not realized by the college until after death. I was certainly in no hurry to lose Martha and she was in excellent health for her age. In fact, she would live for another eight years, although sadly she deteriorated to an Alzheimer's type of memory and recognition loss. For her final four years, she was kept away from all but her closest family.

Martha died in 2002 shortly before I left Wagner for London. She was true to her word and had indeed left a substantial bequest of over ten million dollars, which her son and daughter requested be announced as having come from an anonymous source. Executor proceedings delayed Wagner's receipt of the bequest until after I had left Wagner.

Don Spiro unveils Martha Megerle's portrait.

The college respected the wishes of Martha's family and announced the anonymous gift as the largest endowment gift ever received (which it was). The largest single gift in the college's history, the local media cited it as an endorsement of new leadership.

Hmmm. I wonder where they got that idea?

I may be wrong, but I am almost certain that in Martha's failing years before her death, she had no idea that I departed and that there was a new president, so I can't fathom how she could have been applauding new leadership she couldn't have known about.

I remember that Jay Oliva, the former president of New York University, once shared with me that his first year as president had been the most successful fundraising year in the University's history. I congratulated him and asked him how he did it. "I did nothing," he admitted. "My predecessor, John Brademus, deserves all the credit as he built the relationships with the benefactors who died during my first year as president. John made me look good."

As I think back to my first year as president of Wagner College, I was without even one prospective gift that had been cultivated by any of my predecessors.

Beginning in 1987, I began with not one major donor or bequest in the pipeline and, with David Long, launched the most successful fundraising outcomes in the college's history that ultimately became a major source of the College's endowment years after David's and my departure.

Chapter 25
Our Early Childhood Gem

Like theatre, athletics, and nursing, another diamond in the rough that preceded my arrival at Wagner was the college's early childhood center, a modest but very popular school that operated quietly in a far corner of the campus. Quiet, that is, except during drop-off in the morning and pick-up in the afternoon. Long lines of cars would form each day, as the program flourished and was always full to capacity.

I was aware of the program, having visited the center on several occasions, but my esteem grew when our daughter enrolled when she was little more than two years old. Susan was still working full time in admissions, and we jumped at the opportunity to enroll Caroline. We were thrilled with how well it served her and how happy she was attending each day. I became so enthused that I didn't want to face the prospect of Caroline attending school anywhere else. In fact, there weren't many choices after early childhood, and Caroline would outgrow Wagner in just a year or two from now. Once ready for kindergarten, that would be the end of the Wagner program.

I started to explore whether Wagner could organize a continuing program that would run into elementary school. As I surveyed the parents of students enrolled in the early childhood center, most indicated that they, too, would keep their child at Wagner were the upper grades to become available.

Among the deterrents was space. The program was already overcrowded and there really wasn't any other department or program at the College that could be readily relocated. If anything, the enrollment growth was calling for more classroom space. We were bursting at the seams just about everywhere and were facing the likelihood of four more years of significant enrollment growth.

Year six was but the first bumper crop of new students. As those students become sophomores, juniors, and seniors, along with continued large freshman classes, Wagner would have a space problem that prevented any serious consideration of opening an elementary school, especially since the trustees continued to resist further infrastructure development.

I found myself eyeing the Augustinian property, a former private school and seminary to the immediate southwest of the Wagner main campus. The lower level of the property was well suited for athletic fields, but the upper level included a massive building that had been used as a monastery, prep school, and residence hall. The building must have been grand at one time but had been abandoned for over a decade and was scheduled to be demolished by a developer who was planning to build high-density town houses.

During the years it was abandoned, vandals stripped the building of anything of value including copper pipes and brass hinges. Nothing was left except a gutted hulk that had also been a victim of several fires. Sadly, the building had been fully useable when the Augustinians offered it to Wagner years before I arrived. But those were years when the trustees were concluding the college already had more of a campus than it needed. Had Wagner acquired the property then, the building would have made a marvelous business school, and the space occupied by the business department could have become an elementary school since it already also housed the early childhood center.

Joan O'Connor (left) and Claire Maher (right) led the Center with Pamella Dicke and Marguerite Woodward.

Caroline in her first year at Wagner's Early Childhood Center.

Year SEVEN 1994–1995

Chapter 26

Infrastructure or Endowment?

The Debate Intensifies

A particularly unenviable aspect of college admissions is that there is never a moment to rest on one's laurels. Recruiting is a year-round undertaking. The fall is spent in search of applications. The early winter is selection time. Then, all the admitted students become a group requiring individual cultivation for yield. A college like Wagner is doing well if 25% of the students who have been admitted decide to accept the admit offer and enroll.

So as soon as last year's record-breaking crop of new students arrived in September of 1993, the admissions staff was underway to ensure that the new level repeated itself for the fall 1994 freshman class. The good news throughout last year's recruiting season was that all indicators pointed toward a repeat. Nevertheless, we were all on edge throughout the year bracing for something to go wrong.

We needn't have worried. When the fall of 1994 arrived, so did another bumper crop of first-year students. Admissions had repeated and expressed every confidence that 400+ new student enrollments appeared likely to be the routine each year going forward. The opening enrollment hit 1,700 students, up nearly 500 students from seven years ago — higher if counting net students. In 1988, when I arrived, the 1,188 students were being discounted at 50+%, yielding less than 600 net students. The fall 1994 student body had been discounted an average of only 20%, thereby yielding 1,300, more than double the number of net students.

The operating budget had grown from a mere ten million in 1988 to over thirty million in 1994. In just the past two years, revenues were up seven million, an amount that would have required an endowment of $140 million, assuming an annual 5% spendable interest income level, which was the standard expectation in 1994. While admissions had pulled off another record year, its second in a row, the total enrollment had only increased by one hundred students. Unfortunately, the attrition rate continued to be too high. That is, too many first-year students weren't returning for their sophomore year.

Too many freshmen weren't getting themselves rooted. The problem didn't reach throughout the student body, though. Virtually all the students interested in theatre had returned, as had athletes. There was also a high retention rate among nursing students. We tried to survey the students who didn't return, but no clear pattern emerged among their reasons for not returning. Some cited financial reasons that had them having to transfer to a less-expensive public university. Some said they wanted to be closer to home.

On the positive side, many indicated that they were transferring to a top-tier institution, and they credited their year at Wagner as having enabled that outcome. I received a telephone call from one parent who could not have been more complimentary about her daughter's freshman year. The student had earned a 4.0 grade point average, enough for her to be admitted to the University of Pennsylvania for her sophomore year.

Although there is a positive side to Wagner springboarding some of its students into the Ivy League, most students were leaving for other reasons — perhaps reasons they didn't want to share or maybe didn't even realize. Lyle Guttu, now vice provost for Student Affairs, had been reporting student unhappiness for some time. Many of the first-year students were unhappy with the bathroom conditions in the dorms. The bathrooms had not been upgraded since the buildings were originally constructed, nearly a half century earlier. We had painted and refurnished the dorms, but upgrading bathrooms was on the lengthy to-do list of particularly costly ventures.

Another bathroom problem was their lack of privacy. Unlike the students who attended in the 1960s, this new generation of students more frequently came from relatively affluent families. When surveyed, Lyle discovered that virtually every student in the freshman class had a private bedroom and private bathroom in their home.

The women were especially unhappy with the public showers and toilet stalls. We had realized the problem with the dorm bathrooms but renovating them represented a multimillion-dollar undertaking that had not yet found a funding source. Admittedly, the bathrooms were a problem, but were they THE problem? Male and female athletes didn't seem deterred by them, nor did the theatre students.

The overall experience for first year students was inconsistent. Those who were involved in a team sport or theatre productions were kept busy both in and out of the classroom. Those who had not yet selected a major, which is typical of most first-year students, were not kept busy enough. Adjunct faculty were teaching too many freshman courses, and some of the most popular senior faculty members never taught freshman-level courses. As a result, first-year students were not always experiencing the best that Wagner had to offer.

Another big problem was how little there really was to do on evenings and weekends. Wagner's beautiful campus was more remote than initially appeared to be the case. There was no town center within walking distance. There were no movie theatres nearby. There was no shopping center or mall that was readily accessible. Those students without their own car were isolated. We had tried to resolve this by offering a free shuttle bus that would take them to the Staten Island Ferry terminal (so they could go over to Manhattan). The shuttle also stopped at the Staten Island Mall. While many students did use the shuttle, it wasn't enough of a solution.

On-campus extracurricular resources were limited. The Student Union, for example, was largely a dining hall, snack bar, and administrative offices. The snack bar had an agreeable hangout atmosphere, but it wasn't enough for seven-day-a-week residents.

What students most found lacking was recreational space. We had installed a fitness center in the Student Union, but there were no changing rooms or showers. That didn't pose as much of a problem in the early fall and late spring, but working out during the winter months, which represented most of the academic year, was inconvenient.

Students also lamented the lack of a swimming pool and the limited access they had to indoor intramural facilities. The gymnasium was essentially an indoor basketball court that was used heavily by the athletic teams and was rarely available for walk-in student use.

Wagner was about the only college, among those with which it was being compared, that lacked a comprehensive recreation center large enough to accommodate not only the sports teams, but also the non-athlete students. Staff at other colleges would report that the recreation center, more than the student center, had become the most popular hangout for students. Fitness was a bigger concern to more students from this generation, and fitness centers had become a social hub for students. Working out was something a student could do without feeling the need to be part of a group, while concurrently presenting opportunities to engage new friends.

The beauty of the campus that was selling at the front end was not enough to sustain student interest for four years. The car looked great and was respectably ranked, but once the buyer started driving it, the lack of power steering, automatic transmission, and air conditioning took the gilt off the lily.

The trustees were not surprised to hear my assessment. They had endlessly heard my views that Wagner, if it was going to be competitive in the very challenging Middle Atlantic private college marketplace, needed to build an expansive sports and recreation center, among other things, that was large enough to be accessible to all students. From my first few years at Wagner, I had approached architect/builders who visited and provided free conceptualizations on the prospect of obtaining the contract to design and build. One company, Stanmar, was particularly forthcoming. In my tours of competing colleges, Stanmar proved to be a frequent contractor. Stanmar specialized in sports centers, and a familiar style showed in their work. They had an almost cookie-cutter pre-fab approach to their buildings, which, they explained, resulted in significant cost savings.

The template/prefab approach to building did not deter the attractiveness of Stanmar buildings, and their preliminary, no-obligation free designs added to their appeal. They even built a three-dimensional model that I had on display in my office. There was a lot of sentiment for the building.

Because so many of the trustees had been athletes during their undergraduate days at Wagner, a sports center, and a permanent stadium for football, drew more interest than some of my other wish list items, like a performing arts center. Stanmar's estimate for the sports center and stadium project was roughly fourteen million dollars. David Long and I started to lobby for support to undertake a capital campaign to raise the money.

This early Stanmar concept was a 75,000 square foot, all-new construction building that would be erected on what was called the west campus, across Howard Avenue from the main campus and adjacent to the football field.

As always, there were differing views on where donations should go. One contingent of trustees continued to advocate their "endowment first and foremost" policy. The business executives led by John Myers, John Lehmann, Bob Evans, Bill Reynolds, and Don Spiro accepted my view that the institutional product had to be first class if optimum enrollment and enrollment revenues were going to be realized and sustained.

Don Spiro and John Myers agreed to co-chair a campaign coordinated by David Long and me. Nothing, though, would proceed until the money had been at least pledged. David and I went through the designs and put price tags on all aspects of the project. The building itself could be named anything a $3.5 million donor wanted. The swimming pool would cost $800,000. The basketball court would cost $750,000, and the main entrance would cost $600,000. Even the locker rooms could be named for $150,000.

The football stadium project was particularly popular among trustees, especially those who had been football players, which included at least half a dozen men, some of whom were otherwise pro-endowment. When completed, the stadium would include team lockers under the seats and a synthetic track around the field. The existing track was a cinderblock mess fraught with potholes and more of a hazard than a sports facility. The stadium would also have a press box and would feature a fifty-yard-line section of premium seating that could be sold for a higher price.

At one point in the campaign, Don Spiro questioned why the facility was being constructed across the street from the main campus. Wouldn't it be more accessible if it remained where the current gym was, right on Sutter Oval near Main Hall and the library? Wouldn't residential students have an easier and safer walk?

Don rightfully expressed concerns about the dangers of crossing Howard Avenue. He had a point. Our original thinking was to create a centralized sports complex that included the football field and stadium within the mix. On second thought, the building probably would be too far away from the hustle and bustle of campus life. More students, especially non-athletes, would likely use a facility that was closer to the traffic patterns of the college.

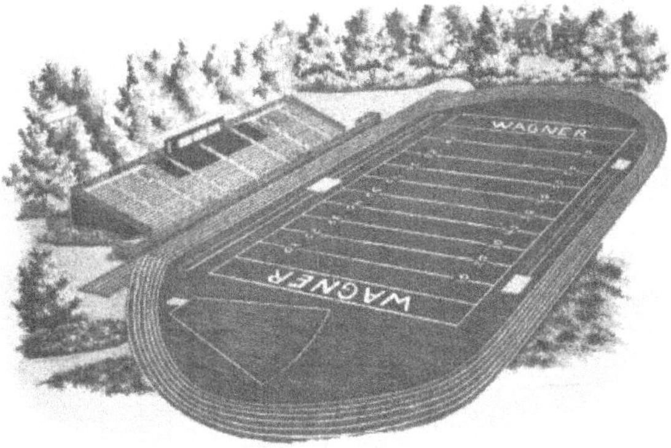

The new football field with permanent stands for the first time in the College's history

Old Sutter Gym comprises the left side of the building. The right side, which includes the swimming pool to the far right and the fitness center to the front right, would be all-new construction.

Stanmar went back to the drawing board and came up with an idea that would retain some of the existing gymnasium structure, which would also bring costs down. The west campus was not as well developed for utilities, so there would also be infrastructure savings by building on the existing site of the gymnasium.

Don's idea provided for more than one bite out of the apple. We would now proceed with a cheaper and more accessible building that might be underway earlier because less funds had to be raised.

Chapter 27
Bad Timing—But a *Must-Do*

From the day of my first visit to Wagner, I was struck with the beauty of the College, perhaps its greatest asset. Once on the campus, you were transported out of the high-density atmosphere typical of Staten Island and all of New York City. You felt like you were in upstate New York.

This bucolic character had been key to Wagner's recovery and would continue to be essential to future success. But it had to be protected. The atmosphere so important to Wagner was fragile, especially in a city where urban development was often wide open without regard for protecting aesthetics, especially in outlying boroughs like Staten Island.

An Armageddon had been threatening the college: the seemingly inevitable development of an eighteen-acre plot to the immediate west of the main campus. This largely undeveloped site had been an Augustinian monastery and school for boys. The school had closed quite a time long ago and, before doing so, had approached Wagner College about buying the land. This happened at the time when Wagner was in its worst financial condition and, instead of buying additional land, was planning to rent out some of the acreage it already owned.

Instead of Wagner taking possession, a real estate developer bought the property with plans to build high-density rows of attached townhouses, a not uncommon residential configuration in the outer boroughs of New York City. Such a neighboring community would downgrade the bucolic, rural character of the college.

The Augustinian property was at the college's gateway. In its current undeveloped condition, it provided the buffer that contributed to the metamorphosis that parents described. The drive from the bottom to the top of Grymes Hill would no longer create the transition from city to rural life once the developer removed the forest of trees and littered the hillside with housing.

I was chagrined, but helpless. The developer owned the land, had the zoning rights, and that was that.

The early 1990s were not the best years for housing developers and this project seemed to be in limbo. Although the housing development appeared inevitable, the delay that was being caused by bleak economic times contributed favorably to Wagner's recovery.

Then, a miracle happened.

The developer of the Augustinian tract declared bankruptcy and defaulted on what was described as a seventeen-million-dollar loan he had with a New Jersey savings and loan that had also just gone bankrupt. The land had been taken over by the Federal Deposit Insurance Company. This was the era of the savings and loan bank failures when hundreds of small S&Ls were going under; the result of having made too many bad loans.

Wagner had another chance to protect its perimeter, and it would be the last time that chance came about. But the trustees would have to agree to acquire the property. A growing contingent of the board thought Wagner had all the land it needed and certainly shouldn't be buying more land under any circumstances.

The Augustian property perimeter is highlighted above, to the immediate right of Wagner's main campus.

Even though my primary motivation in wanting to acquire the land was to prevent its development and thereby protect the college's rural atmosphere, we also needed additional athletic playing fields. Wagner was a residential college with an NCAA Division I athletic program, yet there were only two playing fields that were dominated by football and baseball. All other sports, including virtually the entire women's program, had to wait until football and baseball completed their daily workouts in order to start their practice.

The new students we were recruiting came from high schools where sports like lacrosse, soccer, and field hockey were commonplace, and they expressed disappointment that Wagner's limited availability of playing grounds was preventing these sports at Wagner. The Augustinian property included a spacious lower level that could be relatively inexpensively cleared and turned into playing fields for these popular sports. The more sports programs available to residential students, the more there is for them to do. The more there is to do, the greater inclination they will remain at Wagner through graduation.

We contacted the FDIC to learn of their plans for the Augustinian property they now owned. They indicated that they would probably be auctioning the parcel to the highest bidder sometime in the not-too-distant future as they do with all properties they take over by foreclosure.

The trustees were not surprised or otherwise unaware of my opinion that acquiring the property was an important part of the College's future. Thus, I was relieved when Don Spiro, John Lehmann, Bob Evans, Bill Reynolds, and others were drawn to the prospect of acquisition. But what would it cost and where would the college get the money?

Other trustees asked me how this fit as a priority when compared against everything else being proposed — like a recreation center and a football stadium — like renovated dorms — like a performing arts center.

Either/or didn't apply in my view. Wagner needed all the resources that competing institutions already had. Forgoing any of these critical resources was like asking whether a brain was more important than a heart or lungs. All three organs are prerequisites to life. Anyone required to pick one over the other wouldn't survive.

The second time around Augustinian acquisition opportunity was untimely, and Wagner really couldn't afford to buy the land. But we equally couldn't afford not to buy it. This opportunity had been passed over once before, and if the college demurred again, there wouldn't be a third opportunity. It was now or never. Failure to acquire this property would forever handicap the future of the College. We had to do it, even if we couldn't afford it.

Thank goodness the academic year had started with such a massive enrollment uptick. With that surge came a new set of financial projections going forward that demonstrated to the trustees that the College was on an impressive track to greater financial wherewithal. Had the school year opened with yet another modest growth of several dozen students, the board almost certainly would have vetoed the acquisition of additional land.

Since we were going to need money immediately, and had already incurred too much debt, the only solution was that someone buy the land and gift it to Wagner, or that we use unrestricted endowment, what little there was, with a commitment to reimbursement in the years ahead. There was time in years to come to build an endowment. There would never be another time to protect the College setting.

The FDIC moved quickly and announced a December auction at Staten Island Borough Hall. If Wagner was interested, we had to appear at the auction with a certified check for the opening bid of $2.9 million.

The board vote to acquire wasn't unanimous, but it was adequate to proceed with the auction bid on the condition that our bid not exceed four million. If other bidders were willing to pay more, they would become the owners.

The auction took place in late December a few days before Christmas. The event was remarkably informal, taking place in a hallway in the borough hall next to a bank of pay phones. To my alarm, a large number of people appeared with the prerequisite certified checks for $2.9 million. There were going to be competing bids that would push the price up.

As it turned out, not all the bidders were intending to pay much more than the $2.9 million starting price. There was some bidding, and the price crept up nearly an additional million. Wagner's bid of $3.75 million, just under the four million board mandated limit, won the day.

The acquisition proved both a Christmas present for the College, but also for Staten Island.

In an editorial in their December twenty-sixth edition, the *Staten Island Advance* editors applauded Wagner's purchase. In addition to commending the college for a "shrewd calculation," the editors saluted Wagner's town and gown responsibility.

our opinion *Excerpted from the December 26, 1994 Editorial Page of The Staten Island Advance*

Wagner's gift to Island was vote of confidence

Wagner College gave the rest of Staten Island an early Christmas present this week. The Grymes Hill institution dug deep to come up with the necessary money to buy the site of the former Augustinian Academy across Campus Road.

It wasn't a lightly made decision.

But Wagner President Dr. Norman Smith made a shrewd calculation in weighing the costs of purchasing the property versus the costs of letting the south face of Grymes Hill fall to developers - although he says the correct decision was so obvious as to be a "no-brainer."

The Wagner administration understands that a big part of the school's attractiveness to the out-of-town students craved by colleges is that it is an anomaly. Wagner, with its large, tree-lined hilltop campus, offers students the full ex-urban, small-town college experience in the midst of the world's busiest city. That's a tough combination to beat for families choosing a college, and it's one reason Wagner has been successful.

"I've known families who came here from Connecticut who said they were ready to turn around two or three times on the BQE," Dr. Smith explained. But once they arrive, many prospective students and their families "can't believe a college like this could have existed within the city limits."

To have Howard Avenue lined with townhouses would spoil forever that critical feature of Wagner College, and almost certainly would have cost the college far more in the long run.

The best part is that Wagner's interests coincide with Staten Island's. To put it bluntly, and with no disrespect to those who build or live in townhouses, but there are too many of the things around. The last place we need more is on one of the borough's most magnificent hillsides.

Wagner's acquisition of the Augustinian tract is for the express purpose of preservation. In time, the college might utilize the property in keeping with its mission and the setting, but the land will be kept for posterity.

Wagner will ask the city to waive the back taxes, considering Wagner's status and aim in acquiring the site. We hope the city agrees that Wagner has done the entire community a great service by preserving this site, despite holding out no hope of deriving financial benefit from it. And we hope all our elected officials will press this point home in their dealings with the incoming administration at City Hall.

"Wagner President Dr. Norman Smith made a shrewd calculation in weighing the costs of purchasing the porpery versus the costs of letting the south face of Grymes Hill fall to developers. The best part is that Wagner's interests coincide with Staten Island's. To put it bluntly, and with no disrespect to those who build or live in townhouses, but there are too many of the things around. The last place we need more is on one of the borough's most magnificent hillsides...the land will now be kept undeveloped for posterity."

There was one more glitch, unfortunately.

It turned out that in addition to squandering the seventeen-million-dollar development loan made by the S&L intended for the Augustinian townhouses, the developer also failed to pay real estate taxes, which had now grown to $1.3 million.

I contended that as a nonprofit, there are no real estate taxes, and that if Wagner had bought the Augustinian property the first time around, no taxes would ever have accumulated. Now that the College has taken the land off the market and is preserving it forever, shouldn't these taxes be forgiven?

Thankfully, the *Advance* editors immediately supported that argument. Obtaining tax forgiveness, however, wouldn't be easy and maybe not possible.

I went to Mayor Giuliani, who didn't want to get involved because his wife, Donna Hanover, was a trustee of Wagner.

Hmmm.

It had never occurred to me that Donna's relationship to Wagner could turn out to be a liability. Donna, too, explained that were Rudy to grant tax clemency, he could be criticized for a conflict of interest.

We launched a campaign for tax forgiveness and enjoyed advocacy throughout Staten Island. Guy Molinari, the borough president — and Wagner class of '49 — was a very strong political influence in New York City, having delivered the Staten Island vote for Giuliani.

Staten Island's state senators and representatives also all advocated tax forgiveness. And the media support helped.

No one seemed to be opposed, but no one appeared to know how to make the tax forgiveness actually happen. After nearly a year of lobbying, we were notified that the massive tax obligation had been taken off the books.

In retrospect, I consider the Augustinian acquisition as one of the most important and enduring achievements of my presidency.

Norman Smith

Lacrosse and field hockey were added to the sports program, enabled because of the availability of playing fields on the Augustinian tract.

Wagner vs. Princeton struck me as the right kind of company to be keeping. Columbia, Yale, and even Harvard were among other competitors who would now annually visit Wagner to play.

Year EIGHT 1995–1996

Chapter 28
Admissions "FOUR-peats"

Like a fine Swiss timepiece, admissions was now annually delivering an impressive cohort of new students. For the fourth consecutive year, the freshman class in the fall of 1995 exceeded projections, and the total enrollment had now reached 1,750—although this was up only seventy-five students from the previous year's level of 1,675. Freshman attrition was still proving to be a problem that had not been resolved.

To the extent that retention may have been impacted by the lack of recreational facilities and campus life, we were several years away from having a solution in place. But we were at least on our way. Although there hadn't been a groundbreaking or even a board green light to proceed, we were letting the world know that we had a plan and intended to have a recreation center in a few years. A few years, though, is too far away for a typical undergraduate student who spends only four years in college.

The growth to 1,750 completely changed the campus atmosphere.

Wagner felt energized because it was. Financially, there were also great benefits. The '95- '96 operating budget was up an additional three million from just last year, and, amazingly, a 20% discounting level was being maintained at a time when many colleges were well into forgoing a over third of their income. The additional funds that enrollment realized enabled an aggressive effort to catch up with decades of deferred maintenance. We had focused the past summer on residence hall upgrades, especially with improvements to the residence hall bathrooms.

The era of the Internet and email had arrived, and it was time for Wagner to join in if it was going to keep up with its competition. A not inexpensive but essential milestone occurred in 1995 when Wagner opened its website, www.wagner.edu, which included an email address for all faculty, staff, and students. This was only three decades ago from the time of this second edition, yet it is hard to remember daily routines before the Internet and email. My first seven years at Wagner were without these wonders, as was the case for everyone else at the college. Tech junkie that I have been from the get-go, I pushed as hard as I could to position Wagner to be as technologically state-of-the-art as possible. We wired all the dorms for Internet access via optic cable (WIFI had not yet happened). While other colleges were following suit, we were no longer going to be among the laggards.

Although the college was financially solid at this point, having posted seven consecutive years of fiscal operating balance, and especially given a ten-million-dollar annual improvement over just the past three years, I was troubled that our bond debt continued to be haunted by an interest rate that was several percentage points above the going rate for a mortgage. As a result, we were paying upward of $700,000 more in interest rates than we would for a conventional mortgage of the same size. Buying back the bonds, though, would be expensive since the bondholders were enjoying a windfall they would not forgo unless paid a premium.

The debt was vexing, but more of Year Eight's effort, on my part at least, was in search of the thirteen million needed for the sports center and football stadium projects. David and I met daily to exchange notes.

Don Spiro and I were also frequently on the telephone trying to match giving opportunities to donors. David, though, reminded me about a basic tenet of fundraising that we both knew to be reality. That is, any goal requires some major gifts at the front end. A campaign to raise, say, $50 million, requires a couple of $10 million commitments up front. Our modest $15 million goal would require at least one contribution at the five-million-dollar level.

Once again, the *Staten Island Advance* was heralding the continuing upward surge affirming the remarkable Wagner metamorphosis.

As an excerpt from a September 24, 1995 article reports:

"In his eighth year as president of Wagner College, Norman Smith can recite an impressive list of achievements: The college budget is once again in the black; its enrollment is up; and the campus dorms are full of resident students from nearly two dozen states.

When Smith took over at Wagner, its complex of dormitories overlooking New York harbor was largely empty. More than 70% of its students were from Staten Island or Brooklyn. But today the student ratio is reversed. Less than 30% of Wagner's students are Islanders.

The college also has raised its endowment, mostly through tracking down and convincing graduates of Wagner to contribute. And Wagner is actively competing with some of the top small residential colleges in the country.

Fall 1995 enrollment at Wagner is up for the fourth consecutive year and the administration sees the growth as a positive indicator of how far the college has come over the last decade."

Wagner College: Small-town flavor in heart of big city

Dr. Norman Smith

Smith stresses broad liberal arts education

ADVANCE STAFF REPORT

Dr. Norman Smith glances out the window of his office at the panoramic view of New York Harbor and the Wagner College campus spread below.

Turning to a reporter he commented that the average term of a college president is five years. "I guess I'm over the hump," he said.

In his eighth year as president of Wagner, Smith can recite an impressive list of achievements: The college budget is once again in the black; its enrollment is up; and the campus dorms are full of resident students from nearly two-dozen states. The college also has raised its endowment, mostly through tracking down and convincing graduates of Wagner to contribute.

And Wagner is actively competing with some of the top small residential colleges in the country.

Smith's formula for success concentrates on promoting a

PLEASE SEE SMITH, PAGE A 25

■ Enrollment up for fourth straight year

By DIANE C. LORE
ADVANCE STAFF WRITER

ADVANCE PHOTOS ■ MIKE FALCO

A Wagner College student relaxes under a tree as the college's Main Hall serves as a stunning backdrop.

Fall enrollment at Wagner College is up for the fourth consecutive year, and administrators see the growth as a positive indicator of how far the college has come over the last decade.

Enrollment for 1995-96 is 1,753 students, up from 1,675 last year, 1,585 for 1993-94, and 1,369 in 1992-93. Of the students currently enrolled, a total of 1,505 are undergraduates. The students represent 23 states and 28 countries, an indication of the geographically broader appeal of Wagner.

The increase in enrollment has also translated into increased revenues for Wagner. The college reported revenues of $33.4 million, up $10 million since 1992-93.

"We continue to successfully swim against the tide facing so many small, private residential colleges today," said Wagner College president Dr. Norman Smith, who is in his eighth year at the helm of Staten Island's oldest institution of higher education.

The college was founded in 1883 in Rochester as a seminary of the Lutheran Church. In 1918, Wagner College moved to its present campus on Grymes Hill, the original estate of steamship magnate Edward Cunard. The Cunard mansion, built in 1852, on soil originally transported from England as ballast on Cunard liners, is still used by the college for administrative purposes.

HIGHER EDUCATION

Since Wagner's arrival on Grymes Hill, the campus has added classroom buildings, a student union, library, gymnasium, dormitories and other facilities. Two years ago, the college purchased the 18-acre campus of the former Augustinian Academy, a nearby (though not contiguous) property off Campus Road. That acquisition brings the Wagner campus to 105 acres.

When Smith took over at Wagner, its complex of dormitories overlooking New York Harbor was largely empty. More than 70 percent of its students were commuters from Staten Island or Brooklyn, reflecting Wagner's traditional appeal as a "local" school. But today, the student ratio is reversed. Less than 30 percent of Wagner's students are Islanders.

The reversal is partly due to an ambitious recruitment and marketing strategy Smith has pursued at high schools up and down the East Coast, that touts Wagner as offering the best of both worlds — a "small town" residential college with a bucolic campus, that's located in the heart of New York City, the entertainment and financial "capital" of the country and the world.

The geographic diversity of Wagner is "good for Staten Island," Smith maintains, because it presents the Island (and New York City in general) in a favorable light. "Everyone is down on New York, but when our students leave Wagner and return to their hometowns, they bring with them a whole new view of

PLEASE SEE WAGNER, PAGE A 25

September 24, 1995 front page **Staten Island Advance** ***heralds Wagner's successes***

In his capacity as co-chairman of the campaign, Don Spiro surveyed the list of million-dollar prospects only to find that most of the alumni donor prospects and trustees were 1960s baby boomers who were still in their fifties and, in most cases, funding tuitions for their children's college education. They weren't quite ready to be giving away their millions. We needed to find someone a little farther along who had already put his or her family through college.

John Lehmann, Al Corbin, Martha Megerle, and Peggy Reynolds were among those supporters of the College who might be able to consider lead gifts, but none were particularly drawn to athletics. Martha was committed to the science center, Megerle Hall, which had been named for her deceased husband. And Martha had already committed a ten-million-dollar bequest to the college's endowment. Peggy and Bill Reynolds appeared to be drawn to the theatre department and would likely be more receptive to helping build a performing arts center. Al Corbin promised a bequest but declined committing to a major sum while still alive.

John Lehmann had not been an athlete and was more interested in other projects, including a business school.

Bob O'Brien and John Meyers were too young, although very successful. They were both meaningful donors, but as Bob once told me, "I'll be giving at Don's level when I'm his age."

As the first year of the campaign was coming upon us, we had not yet locked in a five-million-dollar gift and then, thankfully, Don once again took the lead and pledged five million dollars in the form of a challenge. Another five million had to be found to match his gift and give us the lion's share of the money needed to proceed with construction.

Don and Evelyn had already established themselves as the most generous benefactors in the history of Wagner College. Their gifts to enable the renovation of Spiro Hall, the establishment of the college's first student computer center, the opening of the Parise Fitness Center, and the establishment of an endowed scholarship fund represented millions, including Wagner's first gift that exceeded one million dollars.

This five-million-dollar pledge was that much greater a first for Wagner. I shudder to think what the first eight years, and for that matter, beyond, would have been like had it not been for Don and Evelyn. I undoubtedly wouldn't have been able to keep the college's head above water without them. There were a lot of key people who contributed to Wagner's success story, including Susan's admissions miracles, Kevin Sheehy's cheerleading, Al Corbin's financial interventions, and Martha Megerle's quiet support — but we were all sitting on the Spiros' shoulders.

Don and Evelyn, far more than anyone else, saved Wagner College.

Throughout the eighth year, I was also pondering the state of the College's academic program and particularly the weaknesses of the freshman year that were probably causing the high attrition rate.

Why couldn't all first-year students build the kinds of roots that theatre students, nurses, and athletes had built? We rarely lost theatre students because they were fully engaged with a faculty that gave them undivided attention and kept them busy seven days a week.

I had been reading more literature about innovative college programs typically characterized as "the first-year experience." Such programs included directing senior faculty into offering more freshman courses and helping them become inspired about a major they might not have otherwise considered. There were programs that included experiential components, thereby keeping students too busy to become bored or disenchanted with their college experience.

My discussions with the faculty and Gary, who was doing yeoman's work as provost, brought me to the realization that the college now needed an academic leader who was familiar with undergraduate academic innovations like first-year programs and could develop a model that would fit Wagner.

Gary, finally, was a theatre guy — a great manager, but not a broad-based curriculum expert. He had kept everything calm and orderly since taking on the provost's job, but we needed another Mort Rozanski — someone who could create an academic program for Wagner that would distinctively bring attention to the college while also retaining the top-rate students that Susan and her staff were now routinely enrolling. Wagner needed a niche.

To get that niche, Wagner needed a provost who had *been there done that,* so we didn't have to reinvent the wheel.

I consulted with the faculty leadership, all of whom agreed that Wagner did indeed need another Mort Rozanski.

So, at the end of the academic year, Gary announced his return to theatre, with accolades and genuine gratitude for holding the fort together.

Gary would move on to chair not only theatre but also the entire arts program, where he continued through to retirement in 2022.

Year NINE 1996–1997

Chapter 29
No Vacancy—SRO

It sometimes felt like an eternity, yet in only eight years Wagner College had evolved from an under-enrolled, mostly commuting student body of less than 1,200 students to a full-to-capacity, mostly residential college.

The fall of 1996, the beginning of year nine, opened with over 2,000 for the first time since the baby boom years of the 1960s, thirty years previously.

Of particular satisfaction to me was the fact that the dorms were full — no vacancies anywhere. Harborview, the tower that nearly became a nursing home, was now the most popular student residence among freshmen.

The 250-student surge over last year also represented a stronger yield rate, perhaps because we also started becoming more generous with grant aid. That most of our competitors were now discounting in the mid-thirties to nearly 40%, we concluded that staying at 20% could be pricing ourselves out of the market. Too many departing students cited the cost of Wagner and, even though tuition was competitively low at only $21,100 (tuition, room, and board), students and their families were becoming that much more influenced by the size of their scholarship. So, we had upped the average grant to 28%. Even with the higher discount rate, net revenues surged once again and the 1996-1997 operating budget grew to $36.2 million, up nearly 3 million more than last year and over 13 million more each year than four years ago.

The problem now was that annual surges in revenue were going to end starting next year. For each of the past four years, the new student surge pushed one year at a time, from just the freshman year to the freshman and sophomore years, to the first three years last year, and now all four years this year. Next year, even with another large freshman class, all four years were now covered, and the bottom-line enrollment would be about the same. Therefore, except for the added monies from a tuition rate increase or giving, there would be no bottom-line surge because the 2,000-student capacity would be growing once again to, say, 2,200 students. We couldn't accommodate 200 additional students if we wanted to.

The full-to-capacity status did not go by unnoticed and came at an opportune time for Middle States accreditation and for NYC Department of Education scrutiny. Wagner had almost all good news, and received congratulations from Middle States for what they called ***commendable and impressive performance that exceeds all expectations.***

The full-to-capacity status also energized the trustees to push for quickly matching Don's five-million-dollar challenge. Virtually everyone who could respond did, including some pleasant surprises. Bill and Peggy Reynolds released a Parker Trust gift of one million dollars. John Lehmann paid $500,000 for the entrance atrium. Bob O'Brien, Fred Lange, John Myers, Bob Evans, Greg Knapp, Tom Moles, and Fred Williamson were also six-figure donors.

By the end of the fall, over $10 million had been pledged, which for Wagner, was a lot of giving — an unprecedented amount of giving, in such a short period of time. David Long, though, was getting close to the end of his short return. He warned me, upon agreeing to return, that he would probably only stay for a couple of years. He informed me that as soon as he completed the sports center campaign, which he saw being wrapped up by the end of the current academic year, he would be returning to Saratoga Springs and his wife Jody — for good.

Everyone wanted David to stay, but we also knew we had been lucky to have had him on board for the second tenure. He set such a high bar, though, that many trustees wanted to deal with no one else but David. He was as close to irreplaceable as anyone could be.

David Long, along with Susan Robinson and the miracles she accomplished in admissions, ranks at the top of the list of those senior officers at Wagner who made the greatest difference to Wagner's success or failure. He was exactly the right person at exactly the right time. My presidency wouldn't have survived the early years without his stature and advocacy. David's very persuasive ability helped keep the college moving in the right direction and making the right decisions, especially with respect to the importance of a fully equipped campus being more important than endowment. His ability to cite the Skidmore success story as a model that Wagner should be emulating was the most effective argument presented to the Wagner trustees.

The football stadium was under construction during year nine and was scheduled to be ready for use with the start of the fall 1997 football season. All the football trustees were very excited about finally seeing a permanent football stadium. Trustee Tom Moles, '65, managing director of J&W Seligman, recalled his football days 30 years earlier. The coach had told him that the college planned to build a stadium before his graduation. It took more than 30 years after earning his degree to see that promise fulfilled.

The football construction was also getting everyone excited about the sports center. Although we were still a few million short of the goal, it would be great if we could break ground in the spring and have the summer and fall weather to make progress. Otherwise, we would have to wait until the following spring and miss a year. The board agreed that ten million dollars was enough to get underway, and we proceeded to give Stanmar the green light to get the project started. For the first time in over forty years, a major building was underway on the Wagner College campus.

But for the second time in five years, we were faced with conducting searches, once again, to replace two Wagner legends. We needed to find another Rozanski-like provost and another Long-type fundraiser.

Remembering the problems of a long commute, I early on made the case for housing a provost. Many residential colleges provided housing not only for the president, but also for the provost. If Wagner were to provide a provost's house, the ability to recruit a superstar would be greatly improved. Furthermore, the college would benefit if both the president and the provost were always in the vicinity of the campus.

A few trustees proposed building a house on campus. That didn't strike me as advisable for several reasons, most notably that there were a lot of other buildings and renovations still outstanding. A provost's house under construction could become a symbol of bad administrative priority setting. Additionally, housing that is on the immediate campus in the daily traffic patterns of students, faculty, and staff can be an intrusion into the private life of senior officers that many top candidates reject. The President's House at Harvard is so centrally located, for example, that no Harvard president in modern times has ever lived in it.

The most desirable homes were those along the ridge of Howard Avenue that, like Wagner College, overlooked the New York City skyline. The house I had been renting for the past nine years was the grandest on the street, but was not for sale—well, not for reasonable sale. The owner had a vision of building three or four houses on the nearly three-acre site and considered the land worth over five million dollars.

I learned that a classic 1960s ranch house with a circular driveway on a substantial lot about three doors over from me was about to be available for sale. Siblings who had inherited the house were anxious to liquidate. If we could get a good price, the house would be a great investment and might someday become the President's House should the house I was renting no longer be available. With the help of a prominent and well-connected real estate executive, we made an offer of $600,000 for the house and, to our surprise and joy, it was accepted.

I had thought we would have to offer more. Had the house been put on the market, it would have sold for much more. We bought the house with a mortgage, resulting in a modest annual expense.

I suspect today the house is worth several million. Like the Augustinian property, it was a timely and great buy for the college and, sure enough, has today become the President's House. My former house is now an Italian American cultural center.

The search for a provost went well. Unlike previous external searches, the pool of interested candidates this time around was large and impressive. The good news about Wagner had started to circulate within the higher education community. Top academicians that wouldn't have touched Wagner with a hundred-foot pole five or six years ago were now seeing the college as having a future they might want to be a part of. It was an exciting prospect and being so close to Manhattan was also a draw for many of the top candidates.

Most small, private residential colleges are in places like Elmira or other upstate New York and New England enclaves. A lot of the best candidates coming forward were from these rural locales and expressed a desire to be closer to a major urban center — exactly the rationale we were successfully using to attract students to Wagner instead of those same upstate venues.

The search culminated in February with the unanimous selection of Richard Guarasci, Dean of Hobart College in Geneva, New York. Previously, Guarasci posted two decades at St. Lawrence College in Canton, New York, where he evolved from instructor to Associate Dean of Academic Affairs. A native New Yorker, he grew up in Brooklyn about twenty minutes from Wagner. But for nearly three decades, he had been in rural upstate New York and was very excited about the prospect of returning to his roots.

Guarasci appeared to be a bona fide Rozanski replacement in every way. What most excited me was that at both St. Lawrence and Hobart, he had overseen well-regarded and successful first-year programs corresponding exactly to Wagner's need. We talked extensively about the problem of first-year retention at Wagner and how much we needed a model that could resolve the continuing attrition rate. Guarasci struck me as knowing exactly what had to be done.

Recognizing that I had been at Wagner for nearly a decade, Guarasci inquired as to my intentions. I presumed he was concerned that my departure might bring forward another president he didn't find as agreeable, but I also suspected that he was interested in succeeding me.

I responded that I had no immediate plans to leave, but that search firms were approaching me and that many presidents see their tenth year as a time when they start thinking about a new chapter. I told Richard that he was a logical successor, especially after a couple of years at Wagner as provost where he could make some impressive breakthroughs, most notably improving student retention with a first-year program that could become a national exemplar.

With the endorsement of the faculty and the trustees, Richard's appointment was announced. He arrived in time for the beginning of my tenth year at Wagner.

The search for a David Long clone proved more challenging. Finding a legendary fundraiser who could pick up where David left off was a very tall order. Every college, and for that matter, every nonprofit in America aspires to locate someone who can take the lead in finding them a hundred-million-dollar endowment in a couple of years.

I suspect that the overwhelming number of fundraisers who take on a lofty expectation of that proportion fail. Finding the few who can make something meaningful happen is extremely hard and especially daunting for enrollment revenue-dependent institutions like Wagner.

We found Ivana Pelnar-Zaiko. She had most recently been director of development at Rutgers University's Newark campus, but I was most drawn to her prior position as director of major gifts at the University of North Carolina-Chapel Hill where, as director of the University capital campaign, she reportedly oversaw the realization of a $400 million goal.

But although Ivana had overseen an impressive, major capital campaign at a major university with a massive fundraising infrastructure, people with experience in large universities were not always able to translate that performance to a smaller setting with fewer staff and less budget. A Harvard admissions recruiter's skills wouldn't be transferrable to Wagner. Harvard doesn't have to sell itself the way Wagner does. Similarly, a Harvard fundraiser may be spoiled by the cornucopia of blindingly wealthy Harvard alumni.

Could Ivana find comfort at Wagner? I did send her to meet most of the major donors to date, including Don Spiro, Peggy Reynolds, and Bob O'Brien. None said no, although Bob and Don reminded me that she wasn't David Long. Who was?

I began to worry that Ivana might be walking into a continuing David Long trap. We discussed the David legacy, and she expressed an understanding with a sense of confidence that she could handle the situation.

Ivana was a very exuberant person. She had a strong German accent and a PhD in musicology. Martha Megerle would have loved her but was now ailing and not receiving any visitors.

As year nine ended, groundbreaking for the Spiro Sports center took place. Ivana had arrived in mid-semester, and one of the first projects she undertook was the launching ceremony of the sports center construction site.

She did a very professional job; the way a major university would have handled the affair. She had chrome shovels made for all the groundbreaking major donors, embossed with dedication wording.

Some of the donors expressed concern about the amount of money we were spending on the digging of a first hole, but it was the first time anything like this had happened at Wagner in over forty years.

Year TEN 1997–1998

Chapter 30
A Tenth Anniversary Worth Celebrating

As expected, admissions once again delivered a capacity freshman class for the fifth consecutive year. But the four-year growth into each class ended with last year's enrollment. Fall 1997 opened with 2,036 students, up only thirty-six from the previous year, but that three dozen exceeded the capacity of residence halls, and we had to start renting apartments off-campus.

The beginning of my tenth anniversary year opened with just about everyone feeling very good about the College and about the future. The recreation center construction was underway. While much of the existing gymnasium was being expanded, a lot of interior demolition work was necessary to prepare the existing footprint for the expansion. This was going to make for an awkward period for Walt Hameline's athletic program. What little Wagner had in the way of athletic facilities was now gone for this year and the following year. Walt's staff operated out of portable housing in the adjacent parking lot. The basketball team was practicing off-campus on rental courts and playing their home games at the CUNY-Staten Island campus. No one seemed troubled with the disruptions because the light was at the end of the tunnel. A great day was ahead. Everyone was pumped.

Richard Guarasci had arrived with the start of the academic year. The faculty was very excited about having a provost who brought national stature. Richard walked into a particularly good situation, and he was the first to admit it, at least to me. "There is no vitriol anywhere within the faculty," he would tell me, "I have never seen anything like this in my entire career." There was no reason for vitriol. For ten years, each year had been better than the year before. Student quality had improved. Resources had improved. The spirit of can-do optimism couldn't have been more omnipresent. And there were sixty-five new faculty members, all of whom had been hired during my first decade.

I had the luxury, which many presidents never get, of meeting every final faculty candidate before they were offered the position. I never challenged the academic credentials of these selections, presuming their faculty colleagues had thoroughly satisfied themselves in that respect. My concern was whether they appeared to be teachers who could inspire undergraduates.

A major flaw in higher education, it has seemed to me throughout my career, is that too many college professors really don't like to teach all that much and some aren't very good at it either. The American Association of University Professors once surveyed the entire American professorate and discovered that 75% of all college professors place scholarship and research as more engaging to them than teaching. College professors are unique in not necessarily having to take even one course in how to teach to teach.

While I tried to keep my vetoes to a minimum, a few mistaken choices were prevented. On the one occasion I was talked out of a veto, my doubts proved correct, and the faculty who had been advocates shortly thereafter admitted to me that they had been wrong. They were impressed with credentials that distracted them from assessing the professor's disinterest in teaching undergraduates. Luckily, they discovered their oversight early enough to cut losses short.

At my request, and with our mutual agreement, Guarasci moved quickly to develop a first-year program and, in doing so, developed a four-year curriculum that would heavily emphasize experiential learning and learning communities around a liberal arts core. As he kept me abreast of his efforts, he would repeatedly praise faculty cooperation. While Guarasci was busy renovating the academic program, the big story of the fall was the opening of the new football stadium. From my vantage point, it had exceeded expectations. I had wanted the stadium to look like a stadium, not a set of aluminum bleachers. To that end, the contractors had erected a brick frame along the front base of the stands that gave the entire structure a sense of stature.

Norman Smith

After forty years of renting bleachers, Wagner College, an NCAA national champion football program, finally had the stadium it had been promised as far back as anyone could remember. The effect on alumni self-esteem couldn't have been exaggerated and added to the optimism that the college was finally happening.

Everyone was thrilled with the stadium, modest though it was. The surrounding track also added to the overall elegance of the setting.

Fred Lange, '53, a recent addition to the trustees, had made a six-figure gift to the stadium and we named the track in his honor. I liked Fred a great deal. He was head of his own financial investment firm and, among Wagner alumni, came the closest to being the College's version of Warren Buffett. He lived the life of a gentleman farmer in northern New Jersey, from where he also ran his investment firm.

And, he had the largest train set I had ever seen. It took up an entire expansive basement of his home.

He loved Wagner sports and would take a leadership role on the board that included treasurer.

My tenth anniversary year also marked the long overdue renovation of the library. Libraries are always viewed as central to the academic credibility of a college or university. Wagner's library, while not unsubstantial, was shabby.

Built in the mid-twentieth century, little looked improved since the day it was opened. On the one hand, it was centrally located immediately adjacent to the iconic Main Hall. But the neglected interior suggested, albeit incorrectly, the low priority that scholarship might represent at Wagner, arguably reinforced by the construction of sports facilities.

Finally, we got to work on this overdue project, and bought a lot of the furnishings at a Macy's furniture clearance sale where we purchased an inventory of leather sofas and chairs for the main reading room of the library.

Some may have argued that my approach with respect to the library was cosmetic and not substantive, but the reality was that the upgraded library had now become an appealing place for students to study.

The library was sumptuously carpeted. The furniture included plush leather sofas. All the reading tables were mahogany wood with upholstered leather seating.

The use of the library almost immediately skyrocketed, as there was now a new venue within the campus where serious students could go when the dorms and student center were too distracting. In retrospect, I should have moved on this improvement much earlier.

Once upgraded, the Library became a popular student venue, especially on evenings and weekends.

Throughout the college, this tenth anniversary year had a culminating aura.

Early in the year, Professor Bill Murphy rendered an idealized illustration of Wagner College at this pinnacle and, as always, he delivered a masterpiece that included what the college would look like when the sports center, under construction, was finished.

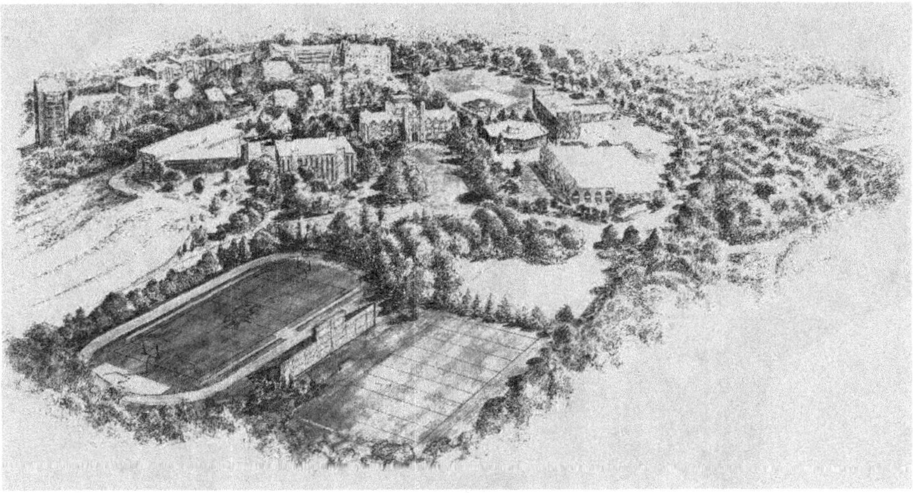

Professor Murphy's campus rendering

With everything going so well at Wagner, and being widely recognized for its breakthrough performance, I was more frequently being approached by executive search firms for rather impressive presidencies throughout the United States. I was becoming torn about the prospect of moving on. Many of my most respected colleagues outside Wagner were advising me to depart on a high note. Yet there was something to finally being able to enjoy the laurels of being on top of a success story. Most of the first ten years were very stressful. The last four years had been gratifying. But being president during this tenth year was a pinnacle hard to walk away from.

The trustees who shared the first decade with me had become family, as had so many members of the college community including Lyle Guttu, who was like a brother to me. There was a great deal I would miss were I to leave.

At the 1998 commencement ceremonies that marked my tenth anniversary, Don Spiro surprised me by intervening in the program to cite the occasion of my anniversary milestone. He, along with other trustees, led by Kevin Sheehy, presented Susan and me with citations and gifts honoring the achievements of our first decade.

Don Spiro and Kevin Sheehy salute Susan and me for the achievements of our first decade at Wagner.

The decade had posted pretty incredible outcomes:

Enrollment had grown from 1,188 to 2,035

Tuition discounting had dropped from 55% to 30% resulting in a near tripling of NET students enrolled.

SATs had increased from 788 to 1050

Fiscal operating balance for ten years

Sixty-five new faculty members

Twenty new trustees

Residence Halls were full to capacity when they were nearly empty 10 years earlier

All residence halls had been renovated

All classrooms had been renovated

Campus wide computerization including Internet and Email

$30 million in donations had been realized including the first million dollar and multi-million-dollar gifts

The ground were beautified including brick walkways and Victorian lamp posts

The adjacent Augustinian land had been acquired enabling additional playing fields for new sports including lacrosse

The first Unconditional Accreditation with commendations for leadership

Vinnie Amese took our family portrait following each spring commencement. This tenth anniversary shot was especially gratifying and memorable.

Vincent Amese

Commencement 1998 also featured the awarding of honorary doctorates to Peggy Reynolds, who with her husband Bill had now become leading trustee advocates, and to trustee Donna Hanover, who as first lady of New York City was a powerful advocate for the college.

Year ELEVEN 1998–1999

Chapter 31
TOP TIER !!

Last year's tenth anniversary struck me as being just about as good as it could get. Wagner had hit every home run anyone could have imagined after just a decade, if not more than could have been believed possible. From this point forward, the outcomes already achieved gave virtually everyone a sense of optimism that anything was possible.

The sports center expansion was a visible sign of what was yet to come, although not as easily as I had expected it would be. Stanmar, the designer and contractor, was encountering difficulties dealing with New York labor unions. Most of their past projects had been in more rural settings where they could minimize costs by employing non-union labor. They had wanted to proceed similarly with the Wagner facility, but I had dealt with the wrath of big-city unions before and didn't believe it possible to complete as ambitious as project as a 90,000 square foot facility without union involvement.

My suspicions proved accurate from the start. The first step of the construction was demolition of some of the existing Sutter Gym structure. This was relatively unskilled work and Stanmar proceeded to use some non-union contractors they had found. Within days, union representatives were on campus demanding that their people be used, or they would begin to demonstrate, which could embargo the delivery of goods to the college, including food, as other unions would honor the picket line. Stanmar acquiesced, only to learn that the labor unions demanding the work were without available personnel to send to the job. That didn't deter the union representatives, who then said they would send trainees they would recruit, none of whom had any experience in demolition. Thus, we had to double the workforce in order to underwrite unskilled trainees.

Although the construction progress was more problematic than I had hoped it would be, enough had been accomplished by the fall of 1998 to create an aura of excitement. Stanmar was predicting that they would have the project, or at least the stadium court, completed in time for part of the basketball season.

That fall delivered Wagner another big present. Each year at that time, *US News and World Report* issues its best college rankings based on the previous year's outcomes (actually, the past five years are averaged). When we opened the edition, lo and behold, Wagner College had been elevated to the top tier of their regional rankings. In just one decade, Wagner had climbed from the very bottom to the very top. I was told by *US News* that no other college in *US News* history had ever made that long of a journey from one extreme to the other.

Admissions was overjoyed with the top tier ranking, as well they should have been. As much as I was and am a critic of the *US News* rankings and their powerful influence nationwide, I was resigned to the reality that I couldn't fight City Hall. Until the truly powerful colleges and universities find some way to diminish the *US News* influence on prospective students and their families, the little guys like Wagner were going to be either victims or beneficiaries. Wagner was now a beneficiary. Making the case for Wagner from this point forward was much easier to do. The college would no longer have to field questions from parents about the rankings. "Top tier" said it all.

The *US News* ratings don't go by unnoticed anywhere in the higher education community. I started receiving notes and phone calls from presidential colleagues throughout the United States. "What are you going to do for an encore?" was the most frequently asked question. Many were reminding me that a decade is a great presidential tenure, and that maybe the time had come to move on to the next plateau.

The achievement also didn't go unnoticed by the *Staten Island Advance,* which shortly thereafter published its ***Bravo to Wagner College*** editorial.

Bravo to Wagner College

Nearly lost in the welter of late-summer commotion in this borough was a piece of very good news that bears emphasis.

Wagner College has always been something of a well-kept secret among college-bound students outside of Staten Island. It has a jewel of a campus, and unlike most other college campuses, Wagner's offers breathtaking views of the New York Harbor region, from the Manhattan skyline to the New Jersey Highlands, with the Verrazano-Narrows Bridge as a centerpiece in a perfect composition. It's no wonder that it's a favorite location for photographers. And Wagner also has New York City itself, and all the cultural treasures it holds.

But a college, of course, is more than a campus, and Wagner has much to offer in other respects. Its physical plant, from traditional buildings to modern structures (including a new fieldhouse under construction) is everything a college student could ask for. And its vibrant college atmosphere, nurtured by a core of bright and engaging professors, has always been conducive to learning and intellectual exploration.

But somehow, Wagner has never gotten recognition for its assets. Suffice it to say that the perception outside the Wagner community seldom paralleled the intense satisfaction within it.

That could be changing, at last. U.S News & World Report, in its report, 1999 Best Colleges, ranks Wagner College in the "top tier" among 200 private and public colleges and universities of all sizes (but not including those offering doctorate degrees) in the Northeast region (from Maine to Maryland). That ranking is based upon a wide array of factors, ranging from graduation rate to freshman retention, faculty-student ratio, class size, SAT scores, the percentage of freshman applications accepted and the extent of alumni involvement.

Wagner president Dr. Norman Smith, who has been the driving force behind the effort to upgrade the school's good name and put it on the educational map, said he was "surprised" and "elated" to have finally drawn this national attention from a respected authority on academic institutions. He should also be proud.

Now, to go along with its first-rate campus, location, atmosphere, Wagner's acquiring a reputation to match. Congratulations to Dr. Smith and all those in the Wagner College community for their well-deserved, enhanced prestige.

Editorial Page of the Staten Island Advance Saturday, September 19, 1998

Excerpted from BRAVO TO WAGNER COLLEGE
"Now, to go along with its first-rate campus, location,* [and] *atmosphere, Wagner's acquiring a reputation to match. Congratulations to Dr. Smith and all those in the Wagner College community for their well-deserved, enhanced prestige."

A sobering moment in the otherwise euphoric autumn of 1998 was the sudden death of Bill Reynolds. Bill and Peggy had both joined the Wagner board of trustees and had become important advocates to me. I was devastated by the prospect of no longer having Bill's influential wisdom to persuade the board to continue investing in a better Wagner College instead of closing down further infrastructure development.

Bill was among the few trustees who had not graduated from Wagner. Because so many were Wagner alumni, I sometimes thought that efforts to elevate the college were hampered by alumni trustees who had not attended the kinds of colleges Wagner should aspire to become. Too many alumni trustees were declaring that Wagner was now on top and there was no need to make additional investments. Instead, all such money should build an endowment. To the contrary, Wagner College remained a work in progress.

As venerable Coach John Wooden once said, "A winning team doesn't stay that way, it either gets better or worse." My continued view was that Wagner shouldn't sit on its laurels. Virtually all other colleges with which Wagner was now being ranked had facilities and resources that Wagner remained without. We needed to seize the opportunity to cement the college to its top tier.

Bill Reynolds had fully concurred with my view and encouraged me to 'stay the course.' A George Washington University Law School graduate, Bill had a broad view of what it took to compete in American higher education and, as the former chairman of Litton Industries International, he also knew that successful businesses had to invest in themselves to be competitive and optimize profitability in the longer run. Most important, Bill had the stature and presence to win his argument among his fellow trustees. Peggy was also a very intelligent, worldly, and refined trustee who understood that a first-rate college had to be competitive.

Bill was not the sole trustee advocate for continued investment in campus development, but he was in the forefront along with Bob Evans and John Lehmann. I saw Bill as my "spare" chairman of the board should Don Spiro decide it was time to step down. Don was two years away from the twelve-year term limit invoked on Wagner trustees. Bill struck me as the trustee who could most effectively take the baton from Don when the term limit required Don's retirement. Now Bill was gone and no longer waiting in the wings.

In addition to a powerful trustee advocate, Susan and I had also lost a friend who was very much a part of our extended family. Bill and Peggy had frequently invited us to visit them at their winter home in Ocean Reef, Florida, and they had hosted us at Gulfstream Racetrack where they had an owner's box. Bill's lifelong avocation had been horses, and, in retirement, he owned racehorses kept at Gulfstream during the winter season, and at Belmont during the summer. In New York, Bill and Peggy had a home just off Fifth Avenue near the Metropolitan Museum of Art. They were living the life that Susan and I would have loved to duplicate but knew that educators, even at the college presidential level, would never earn the money required.

Peggy invited me to speak at a memorial service for Bill in Manhattan, which I was honored to do. Thankfully, Peggy promised she would stay on the board and noted how much Bill had enjoyed becoming part of the Wagner family. He had not been that attached to George Washington University, which surprised me since its president, Steve Trachtenberg, an old friend, was pretty good at finding alumni jewels like Bill. GWU's oversight was to my benefit, and I didn't encourage Stephen to take Bill away from me.

Bill's death, though, did reignite my thinking about my future at Wagner. Kevin Sheehy, John Lehmann, and Don Spiro were coming up on their twelve-year term limits. Al Corbin had passed away. The core leadership that had backed my first decade was coming to the end of their era. Additionally, Richard Guarasci had hit the ground running and was now in his second year as provost. I sensed that he was not forgetting my indication that he was likely to be my successor when the time came.

I was beginning to think about the end of the road, but only if the next chapter offered me was truly exciting. Don Spiro and John Lehmann, my chair and vice chair, both understood. But my search for a new chapter wasn't going to deter me from accomplishing as much as I could for however much longer I would remain. With the sports center coming to completion, a number of other projects loomed that I already had underway.

Bill and Peggy had both been very interested in my desire to build a performing arts center. With a nationally top-ranked theatre program, along with a choir and band, there was a lot of student involvement in the arts, and such a building would perfectly complement the new sports center if sited on the opposite side of the Sutter Oval. In my visits to comparable colleges, virtually all either had such a facility or were in the process of building one. I had been particularly impressed with a just-opened facility at Muhlenberg College, a sister institution to Wagner, both of comparable size and Lutheran historic roots.

Moving theatre and music to a new facility would free up Main Hall to become the academic center for the liberal arts core of the college. I also wanted to see the business, education, and nursing programs in more worthy facilities than the awful Campus Hall, a 1950s dormitory that had been turned into faculty offices and classrooms. We tried to upgrade the interior, but it just didn't seem possible to make this building *feel* gravitas.

Development and alumni relations were also in Campus Hall — a very unattractive place for alumni and donors to visit. My goal was to renovate North Hall, a small, attractive house near the admissions offices that housed the music faculty. This could be a suitable development and alumni center.

The admissions facilities were particularly troublesome. The operation was divided into two small houses. Interview and reception rooms dominated one house, while the staff and operations were in the other. Especially during winter months or in inclement weather, admissions counselors would have to bundle up to leave one house to visit prospects and their families, or even just need an applicant's file, in the other. My solution was to join the two houses by building a central reception area between them.

Cunard Hall, a centerpiece mansion that housed the registrar, business office, and financial aid, was in disrepair and needed work both externally and internally. The Hall, named for its original owner, Sir Edward Cunard, had no good reason for being named Cunard Hall as the Cunards had never been associated with Wagner. The rear of the house was most typically used as the entrance and needed reconfiguring to look less like a back door.

And there was the Augustinian building, a massive H-shaped structure that, while gutted, was still salvageable. I thought it could be a grand home for the business, education, and nursing programs, while also maybe providing, on the upper floors, some needed additional student housing.

Bill Reynolds would have advocated the need for all these undertakings. Don Spiro, John Lehmann, Bob Evans, Peggy Reynolds, and Kevin Sheehy were among the remaining trustees who would also agree. But they were increasingly becoming lame ducks as the end of their twelve year terms were imminent.

There was plenty left to do if Wagner was going to remain top tier.

In addition to the sports center moving toward completion, other advances in my eleventh year included the launching of a three-year classroom upgrade program enabled by a $100,000 per year donation from Richmond County Savings Bank. Bank President Mike Manzulli had been an advocate of the college for years and volunteered the contribution. The first phase upgraded all the classrooms in Main Hall.

$300,000 Grant from Richmond County Savings Bank Enables Major Classroom Renovations to Main & Spiro

AFTER *(right)*
& BEFORE *(below)*...

Main Hall classrooms had not been refurnished in decades and thereby offered only seat-and-tablet accommodations for students that were often far to cramped for adult-sized users. The renovations have furnished all first floor classrooms with tables and chairs that permit multi-use configurations including conference table seminar settings. Also included in the renovations are carpeting in order to improve accoustics, new window shades that better enable multi-media presentations and new paint.

Serendipity knocked on the doors of Wagner College this past fall when the recently-established Richmond County Savings Bank Foundation granted the College $300,000 to renovate classrooms in Main and Spiro Halls. "We're once again very grateful to Richmond County Savings Bank," said President Smith. "Bank President Michael Manzulli and his team have been long time supporters of Wagner including coming forward to install an Automatic Teller Machine (ATM) in the Student Union for students and staff. The grant will go a long way to greatly improve the College's teaching conditions." Students and faculty immediately applauded the change, noted Wagner Provost, Dr. Richard Guarasci. "The new rooms set a much more professional tone and greatly improve the conduciveness of our classrooms," affirmed Dr. Guarasci. "They'll be especially useful for seminars and for the learning community component of the revised undergraduate curriculum."

Wagner College Link Winter 1999

Chapter 32
The Wagner Plan is Launched

From the moment he arrived as provost little more than a year before, Richard Guarasci dove into working with the faculty to fashion an academic approach that could give Wagner College a distinction that would draw academic stature and retain the higher quality students we were now successfully recruiting, but too often losing before graduation.

Guarasci's ideas were based on his previous experiences at St. Lawrence University and Hobart College. He had headed the first-year program at St. Lawrence and shared many of my views, including the belief that involvement was a key to student engagement and retention. Too often, colleges save the best for last while freshmen are subjected to survey classes that lack the magic necessary to excite them.

Many colleges had already discovered the importance of the first year since it is when the newly enrolled student is most uncertain about whether he or she has made the right college choice.

One of my more frequently repeated tenets, attributed to Benjamin Franklin, illustrated how the premise was not necessarily an innovative one, but venerable.

Tell me, and I will forget.
Explain and I will understand.
But if you involve me, I will learn.

Guarasci assembled the faculty and engaged them in a complete redesign of the undergraduate program, which he called "The Wagner Plan." The first-year students were assembled into learning communities of about two dozen students each. These groups were shepherded by a team of faculty members who would stay with the community throughout the first year. The faculty teams included all the college's most popular, and often most senior, faculty members. Some of these senior professors previously had not taught anything at the introductory level and were therefore unknown to the freshmen. By meeting these senior faculty in the first year, more students would be motivated to return for their sophomore, junior and senior years.

Another distinction of the Wagner Plan was the mandatory experiential involvement in the first year. Every student would have some sort of off-campus assignment. Guarasci called upon Professor Julia Barchitta, another of the stellar veteran nursing professors, to become dean of this component. Julia somehow located hundreds of student experiential assignments throughout Staten Island and beyond, all aimed at broadening student horizons while keeping them busy and engaged.

Although the Wagner Plan had yet to fully prove its effectiveness, it was distinctive, and Guarasci was successful in promoting it nationally throughout the higher education community. As a member of the board of the American Association of Colleges and Universities, he was able to win accolades from AACU that put Wagner's academic program into the national spotlight. *Time* magazine's College of the Year award for Wagner in 2002 was mostly the result of the Wagner Plan's fame.

In the decades since my departure in 2002, the Wagner Plan has been heralded as a significant breakthrough that was the key to the college's enrollment surge and turnaround.

The Wagner Plan most certainly deserved distinction, but these accounts have left the impression that the doubling of enrollment to capacity, along with other such breakthroughs, was the result of the Wagner Plan.

As already recounted, enrollment capacity was realized years earlier.

The Wagner Plan was implemented to provide students with a distinctive and rich academic experience that better rooted their commitment to staying at Wagner for four years. The college's surge in enrollments adversely affected student retention, particularly among first-year students. With the enrollment growth came a much more demanding and academically rigorous student body that expected more than Wagner had been providing in earlier years.

The success of the College that preceded the Wagner Plan made its implementation possible. Once the plan was implemented, Wagner was in a better position to secure the prior enrollment breakthroughs, and to that end, the Wagner Plan was and continues to be very important.

In this edition, I have added an "epilogue" Chapter 39that covers events that occurred after my departure in 2002 when it was reported that enrollment growth, and other vital signs of progress, did not take place until the implementation of The Wagner Plan.

That is not the case, as I have documented already.

The College had doubled to capacity and tripled in enrollment revenues years, not to mention being cited as one of the top ten regional colleges in New York State, long before The Wagner Plan was introduced.

Chapter 33
After Forty Years, A New Building

The spring of 1999 marked a most transformative moment in Wagner's evolution. For the first time in four decades, a major new facility was about to open. Sometimes, such culminating moments don't live up to expectation, but that was not the case with the Spiro Sports Center. In this case, the finished product exceeded expectations. The Stanmar Corporation had come up with a wonderfully designed facility that in every way took advantage of its showcase location.

We had made it a point during the design phase to visit as many facilities as possible to learn what worked well for others and what they would have done differently now that they had been using the facility. One particularly attractive Stanmar-designed sports facility we visited had put the fitness center at the front of the building so that it was easily accessible to all students, especially non-athletes. Wagner's building copied that design and showcased the expansive room with massive windows that overlooked Sutter Oval, the iconic main quad of the college. While running on a treadmill, everyone had a beautiful view that emulated a sense of running outdoors.

The swimming pool was similarly well lit with massive windows looking out onto park-like grounds. Too many indoor swimming pools are in echoing caverns of cinderblock. Wagner's was sited so that everyone walking into the facility saw it. This would be a great place for admissions to culminate their campus tours.

We dedicated the Sports Center on June 5, 1999, tying it in with the annual alumni reunion weekend. Sometime earlier, everyone agreed that the building should be named for Don and Evelyn Spiro, even though we had already named the building immediately next door for them a few years earlier. Don was happy with the prospect of the facility being called the Spiro Sports Center.

In addition to a wall of windows, the pool featured a teak-wood ceiling.

The grand exterior exceeded all expectations.

Everything associated with the opening of Spiro Hall, including Spiro Hall itself, was first class.

David Long's successor, Ivana Pelnar Zaiko, had taken personal charge of the afternoon dedication, which was followed by an evening gala dinner party on the floor of the new basketball court. Her oversight resulted in as professionally run a day as we could have hoped to have.

The evening gala was particularly elegant and conceptualized at a level I hadn't experienced since my years at Harvard.

Ivana's big university experience was being put to good use for this first new building at Wagner in over three decades.

My daughter, Caroline, far left, and Haylee Gaw, Don and Evelyn's granddaughter, help with the unveiling of the Spiro Sports Center while three other Spiro grandchildren join in.

Don seemed especially pleased with the dedication day, including that borough president Guy Molinari, a class of 1949 classmate of Don's, declared the day to be Don and Evelyn Spiro Day throughout Staten Island. Ed Burke, Guy's chief of staff and a Wagner alumnus, made the Spiro Day presentation at the dedication.

Ed Burke, '80, left, presents Don with the Spiro Day citation.

The Sports Center itself set an entirely new standard for Wagner. No other facility on the campus came close to the quality of this new building, and I could see the reaction of awe in the eyes of many — including those trustees who put endowment savings ahead of campus development. Don was especially struck by what a difference this building represented to the college.

As an NCAA Division I program, Wagner was in the college athletic big time, but was probably the smallest college in all of Division I sports. Before the Spiro Sports Center, Wagner had the worst facilities of any Division I program.

This new building didn't catapult Wagner to the top of the hill, but we were now respectable. So much so that the Northeast Conference (NEC), Wagner's athletic affiliation, opted to have the conference championship basketball tournament at Wagner for the first time ever.

Of all the NEC schools, Wagner's location in New York City made the tournament most accessible to national media. Since the winner of the championship had an automatic bid to the final sixty-four teams of the NCAA basketball tournament, the potential for some valuable publicity was always a goal, and Wagner's convenient location might make it a reality.

The tournament was so successful at Wagner that the NEC wanted to make it the permanent locale for the annual event. Other NEC member colleges objected, citing home court advantage.

But when the tournament took place at the more remote schools, major media coverage was nearly nonexistent.

Chapter 34
An Athletic Question

Since arriving at Wagner more than ten years before, I had been struggling with the College's placement in college athletics. As the smallest college anywhere in the United States with an NCAA Division I program, many major universities and national sportscasters contended that Wagner had no business being in Division I. Division I schools like Notre Dame, Ohio State, USC, and Michigan spent more on their football teams than Wagner entire operating budget.

Many nationally prominent sportscasters would concoct unflattering references to schools like Wagner, one calling Wagner a "cupcake school" that should be in Division III. In fact, most colleges with which I wanted Wagner favorably compared *were* in Division III. Regionally, the schools best suited as Wagner 'comparables' included Drew University in New Jersey, Haverford College outside Philadelphia, and Hamilton College in upstate New York.

My favorite grouping was the Centennial Conference, a Division III collection of fine Middle Atlantic colleges that would be great company for Wagner from an academic stature perspective. The Centennial

Conference includes Johns Hopkins University and Washington College to the south; Haverford, Bryn Mawr, and Swarthmore in suburban Philadelphia; Gettysburg, Franklin and Marshall, and Dickinson in middle Pennsylvania; and Muhlenberg and Ursinus, also in Pennsylvania. From a team-travel point of view, all were located relatively close to Wagner. Wagner would be an attractive place for the members of this league because of its New York City connection.

The Northeast Conference, Wagner's grouping, had a membership that really didn't align with what Wagner was trying to be. The NEC included Rider University in New Jersey, perhaps the most comparable to Wagner, and Fairleigh Dickinson University in New Jersey. Then there was Robert Morris College way out in Pittsburgh; really too distant for small colleges to be sending dozens of teams. Mount St. Mary's in Maryland was also too far away. St. Francis College in mid-Pennsylvania was remote. More troubling to me was the state universities, including SUNY-Albany and Central Connecticut State University. These institutions were Goliaths competing among David-sized members.

Moving to another Division I conference didn't seem very promising because none was interested in adding a 'cupcake school' like Wagner. Financially, we probably couldn't have kept up in any other conference, although I was drawn to the Colonial Conference that included great institutions like William and Mary, America's oldest college, and some high-visibility and urban-center institutions like Northeastern in Boston, Drexel in Philadelphia, George Mason and Old Dominion in Virginia, the University of Delaware, and Hofstra on Long Island. All these schools were richer than Wagner, but we offered the New York City connection.

We made a few overtures, but there wasn't much interest.

There was no alternative to the Northeast Conference. We would have to wait until the likely decision from the NCAA that might inevitably someday realign Division I, mandating small colleges like Wagner to join their peers in Division III. Moving to Division III, at least under the existing rules, would be a very painful and destructive process for Wagner in the short run. That is because the NCAA mandates that a college must completely purge itself of all Division I scholarship students before it can compete against Division III schools.

It could take Wagner up to six years from the year it stopped recruiting Division I athletes to see all of them complete their time at the College. Those years would be very difficult, especially considering the fact that the largest portion of the student body were athletes. No new Division III student-athletes would be interested in Wagner during this period of limbo because they wouldn't be able to compete for their entire college career.

Additionally, Walt Hameline would lose most of his staff quickly, as Division I coaches would consider Division II or III jobs to be a step backward. For that matter, Wagner might lose Walt, who was a highly regarded senior statesman of the Division I athletic director community.

Since we were in Division I and couldn't do much about it, there were some plusses that Wagner capitalized upon. Of greatest interest to me was the company Wagner could keep outside the Northeast Conference membership. Not all games were played only against NEC members, and Walt was very successful in fielding competitors who were great company to keep. Except for football, Walt annually scheduled baseball, softball, basketball, and lacrosse matchups with most of the Ivy League, hosting Harvard, Yale, Columbia, and Princeton at Wagner.

I always made it a point to take lots of pictures when these matchups occurred and those were the photos that appeared in the admissions publications — always making sure that the photo prominently displayed *Harvard* as much as it did *Wagner*.

Now that we had a respectable basketball facility, Walt Hameline was in the position to recruit a basketball coach who might be able to create a Cinderella team for Wagner that could make it to the NCAA championship playoffs. The winner of the NEC was guaranteed a spot among the final sixty-four teams, although the NEC seed was typically sixty-fourth, and matched in the first round against the top seed. An NEC winner had never gotten past the first round of the tournament, causing sports pundits to call for the removal of the conference's automatic bid. There were some conferences, like the Big Ten, where all ten teams could probably defeat the best team in the NEC. But there was excitement in being listed among the sixty-four final teams in the country and, on occasion, a smaller college got through the first round and beyond.

The Spiro Sports Center parquet floor basketball court may not have been Madison Square Garden, but it changed everything for Wagner College and made recruiting a top coach possible

Seton Hall University in New Jersey became a national contender when P.J. Carlesimo was coaching there early in my Wagner tenure. P.J. had been the Wagner basketball coach before moving to Seton Hall. Other smaller colleges including Gonzaga University have also had success in the NCAA finals.

One plus about basketball is that fielding a winning team isn't all that costly. It was the one sport, unlike football, where a smaller college, if they could field ten great basketball players, could defeat much larger universities.

Walt had a talent for recruiting great coaches and, as always, he rose to the occasion. Little time passed before Walt called to report he had located someone who might fit along the lines of my vision. Walt located Dereck Whittenburg, the assistant coach at Georgia Tech for the past five years. Fifteen years earlier he had been part of the legendary North Carolina State University team that in 1983 had defied the odds and won the NCAA national championship under the stewardship of legendary coach Jimmy Valvano.

But that was fifteen years ago and Whittenburg, now in his mid-thirties, had rattled around an array of jobs, starting with being drafted by the Phoenix Suns. After that, he took assistant coaching jobs at George Mason, West Virginia, University of Colorado, and Long Beach State, until he went to Georgia Tech where he had been for five years. Walt saw something in Dereck that might well be what Wagner needed to become the next Cinderella team of the NCAA. Upon meeting him, I couldn't judge whether he was a great coach, since I had no expertise, but I loved the guy.

Dereck was my role model of what I thought a college coach should be. Contrary to Knute Rockne's declaration that "winning isn't everything, it's the only thing," Dereck realized that most college athletes, even in Division I, weren't going professional and that they had to make their four years in college more than just basketball. They had to prepare for an alternative future.

As much as we all wanted to get Wagner in the final sixty-four, Walt and I also wanted to do it the right way; that is, as the result of a coach and a team that represented what college sports should be. Dereck was exactly what I had been hoping Walt would find, and we enthusiastically brought him on board realizing that if he was successful in taking Wagner to the 'big show,' we would probably lose him to a bigger job shortly thereafter. But Walt was used to bringing on talented coaches who saw Wagner as the gateway to better opportunities. I understood, sharing the same inevitabilities with the senior officers we had recruited to Wagner.

Dereck was hungry. He wanted to be a head coach as much as we wanted a head coach with his background. He had been passed over for far too many years and was now probably wondering if he would ever get the call. Although Wagner may have been in the cupcake rankings of Division I, at least it was Division I, and we were in the biggest sports media market in the country. And we finally had respectable facilities to field a potential championship team.

Dereck wasted no time in building his Cinderella team. His first move was to redirect recruits he had been working on for Georgia Tech to instead try to interest them in Wagner. That was a tall order, but he pulled it off, drawing in a number of top picks that Georgia Tech had also wanted.

Walt and I welcome Coach Whittenburg to Wagner.

Dereck asked for my help in closing the deal since the parents of these recruits were very concerned about their children's future. He would bring the families up to Wagner, and I would meet personally with them, making the case for the opportunity Wagner presented off the basketball court. My involvement probably wasn't key to the decision, but maybe helped make the case that Wagner cared about ensuring that its athletes were building an alternative Plan B should professional sports not happen for them.

Dereck successfully recruited some superstars that first year and, over the next four years, would build Wagner into a basketball power within the NEC.

Three years into his head coaching position, in 2001–2002, Wagner was an opening round contender in the Madison Square Garden NIT. In his fourth year as coach, the year after I left Wagner for London, those first-year recruits would take Wagner to the NCAA first-round national championships.

As usual, though, the NEC champion, Wagner, was matched against the number one seed and lost in the first round. That first round championship game for Wagner resulted, as I had suspected it would, in Dereck being offered the head coaching job at Fordham University.

Wagner couldn't match the Fordham salary, and we lost him.

Year TWELVE 1999–2000

Chapter 35
Wagner's Quiet Renaissance

It's a nice problem to have, but it is a problem nonetheless. The fall of 1999 surprised us with more freshman students than we had really wanted or could adequately accommodate. Wagner was now full beyond capacity. We now faced, for the first time, having to control growth, which is harder to do than it sounds because yields were increasing unpredictably each year. Colleges like Wagner have to admit more students than they expect to enroll. Except for Harvard and comparable institutions, most other colleges must admit three to four times the number of students than they can handle because most admits will not accept the admit offer. This is because most college-bound students apply to four or five colleges and are accepted to at least three or four of them thereby declining most of their admit offers.

Wagner had become so hot, especially after being ranked a top-tier college, that more admits were citing Wagner as their number one choice. There was no way we knew exactly how many more of the admits would enroll, so we kept admitting about the same number as prior years. When a higher proportion accepted the admit offer, we had too many new students.

Over 500 freshmen arrived at Wagner in September 1999. Our first problem was housing them. We had known we were going to be overloaded several months earlier since deposits were required in May and tuition had been due in August.

Fortunately, we were able to find some apartments, owned by Donald Trump, across the street from the college. The apartments were among the first in the Trump empire and had been owned by Donald's father. Trump once told me that when he was a boy, he would be assigned the weekend job of emptying quarters from the pay-as-you-go washers and driers.

I knew the Trump apartments were not a permanent solution, but for the time being we at least had someplace to accommodate the overflow. We offered the apartments to upper-class students because we wanted the freshmen closer to campus for their first year. This worked well, as many seniors were drawn to the prospect of having a bona fide apartment with kitchens and living rooms.

The admissions surge also demonstrated, as had been the case for some time, that admissions was on automatic pilot, giving Susan a sense that she could depart to become president of the Snug Harbor Cultural Center on Staten Island. Susan was overdue to take on a position that would permit her to excel in her own right.

Snug Harbor's array of cultural venues, including a concert hall (the second oldest in New York after Carnegie Hall), a band shell, a theatre, a children's museum, a modern art gallery, and a botanical garden, provided a complementary cultural experience for our daughter Caroline that we considered a plus.

Snug Harbor gets a new president

■ Susan Robinson, president of the Staten Island Symphony and associate provost of Wagner College, is the first Islander to hold the post

By LISA MEZZACAPPA
ADVANCE STAFF WRITER

Susan Robinson, president of the Staten Island Symphony and associate provost of Wagner College, has been named president and chief executive officer of Snug Harbor Cultural Center, Livingston, and will be the first Islander ever to hold the position.

Dr. Robinson's appointment was approved by the board of trustees last night after a six-month search from a pool of 61 applicants nationwide, according to search committee chairman Monroe J. Klein. The eight-person committee consisted of members of the Snug Harbor board.

"Many candidates had outstanding qualifications, but Susan Robinson covered more of the bases than anyone else," Klein said. Dr. Robinson's "vision" for the future of the facility and how its goals could be accomplished were most impressive, he added.

"The entire committee is unanimous on that."

Dr. Robinson holds a doctorate degree in education from Harvard University, a master of arts in special education from Columbia University Teachers College, and a bachelor of arts degree in psychology from Skidmore College.

She succeeds David E. Kleiser, former Snug Harbor president and chief executive officer, who resigned his position in April after a tenure of nearly five years. Dr. Robinson will assume her new post Nov. 1. Her annual salary will be $95,000.

"I have had a lifelong interest in and love for the arts that began in my childhood," she said, noting that she studied music and dance before pursuing a career in academia and administration.

"It's the first time the Harbor has ever appointed a president within the borough. She understands the community of Staten Island, which is important for providing programs of interest

Dr. Susan Robinson

Staten Island Advance September 24, 1999

In addition to losing Susan, year 12 marked another loss. Kevin Sheehy stepped down from the board of trustees, having completed his term limit of twelve years. Kevin had been a key behind-the-scenes operative within the board, often lining up advocacies when the board differed, especially on spending money for campus improvements versus endowment. He was also an unflappable upbeat cheerleader.

Thankfully, he could be re-elected after a one-year moratorium, as there was no rule against that. The year he would be away was untimely, and his absence would be felt.

Although I had mixed emotions about the term limit, especially when it required the loss of someone like Kevin, it did make sense, as it is almost impossible for any board not to re-elect a trustee who has been around for over a decade. The rule did allow a way to involuntarily remove trustees whose performance fell short.

Year 12 also marked another round of applause from the *Staten Island Advance* that, once again just before Christmas, sent along a particularly gratifying front-page feature with accolades that included:

FROM BOTTOM TO TOP TIER IN A DECADE

Excerpted from the Staten Island Advance Monday, December 20, 1999

WAGNER COLLEGE'S QUIET RENAISSANCE

Bigger donations, better students stream in as the Grymes Hill college's reputation soars

By MARJORIE HACK
ADVANCE STAFF WRITER

Wagner College is a school on the move and it's shooting for nothing less than a place among the national stars of higher education.

After years of wallowing in the backwaters of academe--and in red ink--the school is beginning to realize a return on its investment in Dr. Norman Smith, a Toronto-born educator who was named president of the College in 1988.

Though he arrived on the 105-acre, Grymes Hill campus unheralded at the tender age of 41 - fresh out of a deanship at the Kennedy School of Government at Harvard University and untested in any president's seat - he has clearly risen to the challenge of running a $40 million-a-year educational operation.

Smith said his first visit to the campus yielded such a clear vision of what Wagner College could be that his business and marketing plan for the school almost wrote itself.

"I was struck by the campus and what it wasn't," said Smith recently, recalling that he nearly shuddered after his first Ivy League-jaded glimpse revealed private cars parked in rag-tag fashion all around the school's main lawn, which itself was void of grass because the football team used it as a practice field. "It was a sea of mud," said Smith. Not these days. Thanks to about a $30 million investment in any number of improvements - from new faculty hires to engraved trash receptacles - the rough-edged look is history. Now, there are discreet parking lots and newly tilled athletic fields. The walkways are being painstakingly bricked over and an $11 million, state-of-the-art sports facility has been constructed, with the help of generous alumni like Donald and Evelyn Spiro.

The Association of American Colleges & Universities recently cited (Wagner's curriculum) as the best in the country.

Classrooms have been carpeted and refurnished and the school has made a major commitment to keeping pace with the latest in computer technology.

In sharp contrast to 25 years ago, the residence halls are full and paying for themselves, and most of the school's 1,800 undergraduates hail from somewhere other than Staten Island.

But it's not just the physical plant that's been spiffed up. Last year, the Institute of Mind and Body Research at Harvard University's Medical School chose Wagner's undergraduate science students to conduct the basic research component of a nationwide project investigating the effects of emotions on a person's physical health.

With the help of new provost Dr. Richard Guarasci, the undergraduate curriculum has been completely overhauled and last summer the American Association of Colleges and Universities cited the school's new, experiential approach to liberal arts as the best in the country.

And for the second year in a row, *U.S. News and World Report* placed Wagner in the "top tier" of colleges and universities in the North.

We've hired 80 new faculty since I've been here, said Smith, noting that among the 200 instructors now on board, the head of the school's music department graduated from prestigious Williams College, the head of the history department graduated from Johns Hopkins University and was a professor at Vassar College, and the head of the biology department also taught at Dartmouth College.

Harvard University's Medical School chose Wagner's undergraduate science students to conduct the basic research of a nationwide project investigating the effects of emotions on physical health.

" I see this school as a (potential) Swarthmore, a Haverford, an Amherst," he added. While students and faculty say they don't feel like they're among the elite just yet, they say the school is on its way. "It's made huge strides in becoming more of an Ivy League school" said senior business major Christina Rosensteel from Hanover, Pa. She is a golfer who chose Wagner over places like Villanova, the University of North Carolina at Wilmington and Longwood.

"There have been fundamental changes, said Christopher Catt, a native Californian now in his fifth year as producer and head of the school's theater department. The differences include theater classes that are more academically oriented and training-based, less personal politics in the way lead roles in the school's musical productions are cast, and a school administration that is committed to a higher profile for the department.

The turnaround to an institution that is emerging as a regional powerhouse is evident almost everywhere, and it's all due to Smith, say those associated with the college.

"There have been major, major changes," said Walter Hameline, Wagner's athletic director and football coach, who has worked at the school for about 20 years and now operates from a spacious, light-filled aerie above the fitness center instead of from a cramped desk in a storage closet. "It all started to take place when Norman came on board."

"On Staten Island, we have a new synonym for excellence and the synonym is Norman Smith," said Kevin Sheehy, a Tottenville High School biology teacher who is a Wagner College alumnus and a 13-year veteran of the school's board of trustees. "The ascent is remarkable."

"This place is beginning to look like a shiny, new penny. He's [Smith] got a goal and he's going for it," said Ms. Rosensteel.

U. S. News & World Report placed Wagner College in the "top tier."

"They've got the right idea. They need to continue with the right ideas," said Aaron Smith, a sophomore from Albany who plays quarterback and tight end on the school's Division I football team.

As noteworthy and pervasive as the changes are to those who frequent the somewhat secluded campus, they remain a well-kept secret on Staten Island.

Smith contends that he and his staff are in regular touch with Island high schools when it comes to freshmen recruiting, but he admits that the makeup of Wagner's student body has shifted dramatically during his 12 years at the helm - from 75 percent of the students calling Staten Island and Brooklyn home in 1988, to 75 percent coming from elsewhere these days.

"It's flipped," said Smith who is clearly not troubled by the change in demographics. "We have significantly upgraded our academic standards. We have started to create a buzz and the better students are coming to us. We want to think beyond the Staten Island world."

"Smith maintains that the school is not out to turn its back on Staten Island teens. It's just that he believes the caliber of student Wagner is looking for now is top-drawer, and serious students everywhere usually choose a college outside their immediate neighborhoods, - within a 4-hour travel distance - rather than sign on for more of the same for another four years.

Wagner is shooting for nothing less than a place among the national stars in higher education.

Today the bulk of the College's students come from upstate New York, southern New Jersey and the Bucks County area of Pennsylvania. But while Smith may not be going out of his way to discourage Staten Island residents from enrolling (he notes that they are still the single largest cohort on campus), he is clearly trying to distance Wagner College from the land mass on which it's perched. In fact, students say they rarely heard the words 'Staten Island" when they were being recruited.

"You heard 'the city,' not much about Staten Island," admitted Aaron Smith. Hameline concurs. "I don't think you sell Staten Island to a prospective college student. You sell New York," he said.

Norman Smith won't apologize for that tack either. He said that for the past four years, the school's marketing has been "heavily into visuals. There's this beautiful, bucolic setting, but it's also contiguous to the city. We're the grand compromise."

Publications used to market the school to prospective students and to big money contributors are filled with photos - many taken by Smith himself-of campus turrets and towers that soar majestically against a backdrop of the Manhattan skyline. Photos of off-campus, Staten Island locales are few and far between.

Students also say that Smith's no-nonsense personality makes for a campus atmosphere that is tightly controlled and more straight-laced than many. "They crack down on everything. Some people try, but they limit it [partying] said Scholz.

While President Smith might take issue with some of the student gripes, he too agrees there's still work to be done - about 10 years' worth - before the school is where he envisions it. For instance, though more than 10 percent of the students at Wagner major in theater and the performing arts, the school's only theater is in a building that dates from the 1920s.

Smith said now that the Spiro Sports Center is up and running, he is turning his attention to a theatrical upgrade. To this end, he is holding preliminary planning meetings with architects with an eye to constructing a new performing arts center directly across the quad from Spiro.

He also notes that the residence halls need to be refashioned to keep pace with the demands of today's students. "Apartment-like living," he notes.

The turnaround to an institution that is emerging as a regional powerhouse is evident almost everywhere, and it's all due to (President) Smith, say those associated with the College.

All of which means he will probably be digging even further into the pockets of Wagner alumni like Spiro, a 1949 graduate and chairman emeritus of the Oppenheimer Management Corp.; John Myers, a 1967 graduate who is now president and chief executive officer of General Electric Investments Corp.; Bob O'Brien, a banker at Credit Suisse/First Boston, formerly of Banker's Trust, who put together the $29 billion financing-package for Henry Kravitz's leveraged buy-out of RJR Nabisco in the 1980s; and Kurt Landgraf, chairman of DuPont Europe.

The list is quite impressive. "They have been the fuel behind what has happened," said Smith. That made be so, but before Smith Started knocking on their doors, hat in hand, they were very low-octane. "There is a tremendous amount of money," said Smith, who scoured lists of some 17,000 alumni shortly after assuming his post, rolled up his sleeves and began a wooing process that is paying off.

With his wife, Dr. Susan Robinson, now at the helm of the Snug Harbor Cultural Center, Smith 53, says he can see finishing out his career at Wagner. He said he is periodically contacted by search firms looking to set him up elsewhere, but he admitted that he has made many close friends among the Wagner faculty and has nothing to prove by going elsewhere.

"I've been at Harvard," he said. He continued: "I might [stay]. If everything continues to evolve as productively over the next 12 years, I'd be hard-pressed to find a more interesting job."

FROM BOTTOM TO TOP TIER IN A DECADE

Excerpted from QUIET RENAISSANCE

Wagner College is a school on the move and it's shooting for nothing less than a place among the national stars of higher education. After years of walling in the backwaters of academe – and in red ink – the school is beginning to realize a return on its investment in Dr. Norman Smith who was named president of the College in 1988.

For the second year in a row, US News and World Report placed Wagner in the "top tier" of colleges and universities in the North.

"We've hired 80 new faculty since I've been here," said Smith, noting that among the 200 instructors now on board, the head of the school's music department graduated from Williams College, the head of the history department graduated from Johns Hopkins University and was a professor at Vassar College and the head of the biology department also taught at Dartmouth College.

Harvard University's Medical School chose Wagner's undergraduate science students to conduct the basic research of a nationwide project investigating the effects of emotions on physical health.

While students and faculty say they don't feel like they're among the elite just yet, they say the school is on its way.

The turnaround to an institution that is emerging as a regional powerhouse is evident almost everywhere and it's all due to Smith, say those associated with the college.

"There have been major, major changes," said Walter Hameline, Wagner's athletic director and football coach who has worked at the school for about 20 years. "It all started to take place when Norman came on board."

"On Staten Island, we have a new synonym for excellence and the synonym is Norman Smith," said Kevin Sheehy who is a Wagner College alumnus and a 13-year veteran of the school's board of trustees. "The ascent is remarkable."

Smith admits that the makeup of Wagner's student body has shifted dramatically during his 12 years at the helm – from 75% of the students calling Staten Island and Brooklyn home in 1988 to 75 percent coming from elsewhere these days.

"We have significantly upgraded our academic standards. We have started to create a buzz and the better students are coming to us. We want to think beyond the Staten Island world."

Even with accolades like the *Quiet Renaissance* story, the board was increasingly leaning toward resting on the laurels to date and ceasing any further investments or improvements except to endowment.

Kevin Sheehy's departure, along with Bill Reynold's death, not to mention Don Spiro's and John Lehmann's looming term expiration, would collectively make some of my unfinished aspirations harder to realize, if not impossible. Additional housing appeared to be the first victim. The building of the Spiro Sports Center had created some trustee fatigue about building projects, contrary to my hopes that it would do exactly the opposite.

The surge in enrollment revenues had changed the balance sheet in a way that had earned an S&P bond rating of AA+, which, in turn, yet again permitted debt refinancing at a lower rate. But this was still not enough to justify, among most trustees, a new mortgage for housing. Part of the problem was that trustees and major donors had been enabling the financing of these ambitious projects, and each new project struck them as another inevitable request for a major donation.

On the positive side, the stock market was in an unprecedented high-tech surge in the late 1990s that was creating blinding overnight wealth. Even my personal holdings of Microsoft, Intel, and Cisco Systems were going through the roof. There were months when I was making more in the stock market than from my salary. Many of the trustees were doing that much better than me and had stock appreciations they could afford to donate to Wagner.

Richard Guarasci, now in his third year as provost, forwarded an idea to address the housing shortage. Since fundraising for housing isn't that easy to realize, most colleges take out mortgages because additional housing generates additional income that can pay the debt. But Wagner trustees felt the college had enough debt from the bond issue and shouldn't get any deeper than it was, even if new revenue would be realized.

Richard recounted a housing solution that worked at Hobart College. A company called Capstone built housing, at their cost, on the Hobart College campus, which they owned for twenty-five years. After that, the housing would revert to college ownership. All the college had to do was provide the land and guarantee full occupancy rental income throughout the first twenty-five years. During that twenty-five-year span, the college would incur no additional debt. That sounded like an idea that might work for Wagner. But the trustees once again demurred. The sentiment for any additional capital project, even housing, was of minimal interest.

Several exciting projects elsewhere around the college were also taking place during year 12, funded from a two-million-dollar trust that had irreversibly been designated for capital projects and therefore couldn't be refused because it wasn't endowment directed. The least glamorous of the projects was a much-needed new roof for the Union.

On the glamorous side was the installation of brick sidewalks with Belgian block cobblestone curbs funded by Peggy Reynolds from a gift of Cisco stock that she donated when the stock was at a peak price of over $80 a share. A year later, that same stock, had it not been liquidated, would be worth about $15 a share.

Peggy had attended a theatre performance and, upon departing from the front doors of Main Hall, tripped on one of the many cracks in the asphalt oval. The walkways throughout the campus were crumbling asphalt. Decades of winter weather had created potholes and chasms that really made them a hazard to pedestrians. Peggy's gift enabled most of the problem to be corrected in a way that also dramatically beautified the campus. Thankfully, this was not a project that could be rejected by the new generation of Trustees as Peggy insisted on the need for the walkway upgrade and would not give the money unless it was spent in that way. I similarly could not be criticized for soliciting a donation that should otherwise have been directed to endowment.

There is no question in my mind that this upgrade transformed the campus into an entirely different stratosphere that contributed to its *Princeton Review* status as one of the most beautiful colleges in the USA.

The brick walkways enabled by Peggy Reynolds transformed the college into one of the most beautiful in America, according to the Princeton Review.

The walkways also brought more interest in using Wagner as a television and movie setting when a prestigious, private school location was needed. Wagner's proximity to New York City was a plus that made it that much easier for production companies to set up. I had been promoting this opportunity with film companies for years and once had succeeded in drawing a Martin Scorsese-produced movie to the campus (*Naked in New York*) that starred Jill Clayburgh, Kathleen Turner, Tony Curtis, Eric Stolz, and Ralph Macchio.

Wagner turns into Harvard for cameras

By DAVID MARTIN
ADVANCE STAFF WRITER

Wagner College became Harvard University and Andover Academy for Hollywood yesterday for an upcoming feature film, "Naked in New York."

The film features Eric Stoltz, star of "Mask" and "Memphis Belle," as Jake, an aspiring New York playwright who struggles to maintain a relationship with his college love, Joanne. His sweetheart is played by Mary Louise Parker, who starred in "Grand Canyon" and "Fried Green Tomatoes."

The film opens as young Jake is being dropped off at the front door of Andover Academy on a fall day — except the front door is actually Main Hall at Wagner.

In another scene, an older Jake, now played by Stoltz, is running across Harvard's campus to the school's theater. The actor is actually sprinting across the oval in front of Main Hall to Cunard Hall.

Other stars in the movie are Tony Curtis, who plays a Broadway producer who befriends Jake out of college; and Kathleen Turner, as a star in Jake's first off-Broadway production. Jill Clayburgh and Timothy Dalton have small feature roles in the movie, and Martin Scorcese is the executive producer. None were on Staten Island yesterday.

Wagner College will provide the backdrop for about three minutes of screen time, Ms. Bardnan predicted. The movie is currently slated for a September 1993 release from Fine Line Features and Pandora Features.

"We picked this site as an exterior location because within an hour outside of Manhattan, this is as close as we could get to a New England look without going to New England," explained Julia Bradnan, the assistant to Daniel Algrant, who is directing his first feature film.

Ms. Bradnan said they scouted five other colleges around New York City before selecting Wagner as the two-school site.

After dark, the cameras filmed inside the college's Main Hall Theater, which was picked to represent a theater workshop class at Harvard.

Actor Eric Stoltz is filmed at Wagner College for a scene in the feature film "Naked in New York"

Actor Ralph Macchio meets with a group of foreign jounalists.

"We picked (Wagner College) as an exterior location because, within an hour of New York City, (Wagner) is a close as we could get to a New England look without having to go to New England. (We) scouted five other colleges around New York City before selecting Wagner College (as the most similar to Harvard and Andover.)"

Wagner was the setting for a Martin Scorsese movie that called upon Wagner to be Harvard University.

With the walkways finally presentable, Wagner was much more photogenic.

The popular HBO series, *The Sopranos*, used the Main Hall Sutter

Oval setting to portray the military school where Tony Soprano sent his problem son.

The pinnacle production, though, was *The Education of Max Bickford*, a CBS television series starring Richard Dreyfuss as a college professor in a prestigious New England small college. The series was filmed almost entirely on location at Wagner, and the campus exteriors were used extensively and lushly to capture the aura of a top-shelf private college. Unfortunately, the show was not successful in the ratings and was cancelled after only one year, even though regulars included Academic Award winners Peter O'Toole and Marcia Gay Harden, along with David McCallum of *The Man from Uncle* fame.

Academy Award winner Richard Dreyfuss drops by my office while filming* The Education of Max Bickford *on the Wagner campus.

Nevertheless, for that one year, Wagner was on primetime network television weekly, which may have helped bring attention that resulted, the following year, in being voted the most beautiful college campus in

America by the *Princeton Review.*

Yet another project that Peggy underwrote was the renovation of North Hall, a large house that had once been a girls' dorm and was subsequently used by the music faculty, into an alumni and development house. I had proposed we do this in honor of Peggy's deceased husband, Bill, which she thought would be a wonderful gesture.

Reynolds House was one of many old houses in the center of the campus that really needed work, both outside and inside. We desperately needed a fundraising and alumni center that corresponded to the lofty ambitions of the college.

Reynolds House
The new home of alumni and fundraising

Until everything was centralized in Reynolds House, most of the development and alumni staff had been in the horrible Campus Hall, along with the business, nursing, and education faculty. Campus Hall was not only decentralized but represented a most uninspiring place for alumni and donors to visit. As a result, the vice president for development, David Long, had long ago joined me in the Union executive administrative offices while the entire staff was on the other side of the campus. Managerially, that didn't work very well.

The Reynolds renovation would hopefully inspire the need for improving the rest of the buildings in this central area that included the original Sir Edward Cunard mansion and the two yet-to-be-attached admissions houses.

If all three projects could be completed, this area could become one of the most picturesque areas within the main campus.

To my disappointment, the Reynolds-funded projects were not being received as well by some trustees, contrary to just about everyone else's point of view. The pro-endowment faction was persisting and increasingly prevailing.

Next year, 2000–2001, would mark the twelve-year term limit for board chairman Don Spiro and board vice chairman John Lehmann. I shuddered at the prospect of losing both because several of the endowment-oriented members were in the forefront of Don's thinking for who should succeed him.

The pro-endowment trustees were seeking to change what had been a standard operating procedure, and a very successful one, for my entire presidential tenure. Throughout my first twelve years, I enjoyed relatively free rein to solicit monies for whatever would improve the College. Trustees were satisfied with all the improvements as long as a donor was paying for it.

The Megerle family, for example, wanted to fund improvements to the Megerle Hall science labs, since the building was named for their patriarch. That sounded reasonable to me, and to the trustees, and that is where the Megerle money typically went. The board never approved or disapproved a gift as a condition to accepting it. Don Spiro would routinely come forward and decide where he wanted his money spent. We would lay out an unranked shopping list of the most pressing needs that would only be possible with a gift. Don would decide which one made the most sense to him. Never did the board second guess Don's gift designation or inform him that the gift would only be accepted if it went to endowment.

Because the needs were compelling, the prevailing view of the board of trustees was to let the cards fall where they will. But that was changing. Most of the gifts realized throughout the first decade, which exceeded thirty million dollars, would never have been realized if endowment had been the only acceptable gift designation.

Although no longer a trustee, Kevin would visit my office frequently and share my latent frustration with the gift restrictions that were being imposed. He missed being a trustee, and we started counting the months together before he could be re-elected.

Kevin and Elaine remained close friends, and he and I decided that we would take our wives out for a Valentine's Day special dinner foursome followed by a Bobby Short concert at Susan's Snug Harbor. That Valentine's afternoon, as I was awaiting his arrival so we could drive off to pick up the ladies, Kevin never showed. He had just died of a heart attack while participating in a faculty-student basketball game at his Tottenville High School. He had pushed himself harder than he should have. Doctors later reported that he could probably have been saved had the school been equipped with a defibrillator. These devices have become more commonplace since then and can now often been seen in public areas near fire equipment.

There were promises to rename Tottenville High School in honor of Kevin. That never happened. However, a bronze plaque was set into the wall of the Wagner College Student Union terrace remembering the penultimate alumnus who Kevin truly represented.

With Bill Reynolds, Kevin Sheehy, and Al Corbin now deceased, and with Don and John leaving in a year, my front offensive line was crumbling. The new generation of prevailing trustees informed me that, in the future, I was expected to change the minds of any donor wanting to contribute to anything other than endowment. From now on, if Don Spiro or anyone else wanted to donate money for a theatre, or a roof, or a computer center, or a sports center, or anything, the gift would be declined unless they agreed to fund the endowment.

Wagner still had too many outstanding needs to close all future development and focus only on endowment. Conventional wisdom has long proven that endowments come most usually from bequests. Many major donors want to see the results of their giving — and endowment isn't anything one can show off.

While I was busy continuing my efforts to upgrade the college's resources, Richard Guarasci was refining the Wagner Plan. Early indications were that the first-year program was improving student retention. Guarasci was active in national education associations, where he was successfully bringing attention to the Wagner Plan.

I was happy to have him lauded as the architect of the Wagner Plan and I did whatever I could to give credit where credit was due, just as I had previously done for David Long in fundraising, Lyle Guttu in community spirit, Christopher Catt and Gary Sullivan in theatre, Tony Carter in business, Walt Hameline in athletics, and Susan Robinson in enrollment, and others.

My view of good leadership has always been to share success with those who were key to enabling the outcome. Some warned me that giving everyone else credit might have some concluding that I was not doing anything to make anything happen. That seemed implausible to me.

In the end, the best leaders are those who can surround themselves with able people. After ten years of building, with many potholes along the way, Wagner had become an institution that could assemble exemplary professionals.

Guarasci was also busy preparing for next year's Middle States on-campus, once-a-decade reaccreditation evaluation. The provost typically chairs an internal self-study, and Richard was taking that lead as Mort Rozanski had successfully done ten years earlier. Every indication was that we would walk through the process since nothing but good news had marked the ten years since the last time Middle States visited.

We also faced replacing Susan Robinson, following her departure to be president of the Snug Harbor Cultural Center.

Angelo Araimo, whom Susan had hired to be director of admissions, had been assuming greater responsibility and was being groomed over the years to become a vice president for enrollment.

As year twelve was coming to an end, a new era was underway, which may have had something to do with the new millennium.

We were now in the year 2000.

The new generation of trustees with their endowment-only policy was taking the wind out of my sails.

Of course, their mandates would be obeyed, but I wouldn't stop trying to appeal. The college needed additional housing, a business school, a performing arts center, and the Augustinian building renovation.

My days may be numbered, but my message would continue to be that John Wooden was right. To paraphrase, winning teams don't stay that way unless they continue to invest in getting better.

In Wagner's case, while endowments are great to have, basic facilities and resources are more essential. Wagner's work in the latter area was not yet done.

Year THIRTEEN 2000–2001

Chapter 36
The Road Not Taken

Superstitions like a black cat, a ladder, spilt salt, or the number thirteen don't usually jar me. The only reason I am inclined to avoid walking under a ladder is to prevent having something drop on me. So, I didn't think all that much about the fall of 2000 launching my thirteenth year as president. In retrospect, there *may* have been something to the number thirteen superstition.

Most noteworthy about the beginning of year thirteen was that it would be the last for Don Spiro and John Lehmann as trustees, and as chairman and vice chairman. Don and John had been my rocks for well over a decade, and I just couldn't see life at Wagner, for me, without them. Don was still chair, but it was clear that he was systematically transferring power to many of the pro-endowment trustees with whom I philosophically differed about the immediate priorities and needs of the College.

The fall 2000 class once again exceeded expectation and it was becoming time to start admitting fewer students, because too many of them accepted our offer of admission. My call for additional student housing was falling on deaf ears.

Even the Capstone proposal that would require no investment by the College except to relinquish ownership for the first twenty-five years failed to interest the Board of Trustees. I saw no problem with the Capstone project, as the College would continue to realize all the tuition income and would only forgo the housing income, which would otherwise have gone to a mortgage.

The board, however, just didn't want to do anything else to the campus. However, they did agree to undertake a campus master plan study, perhaps to have their view — that nothing else was needed — affirmed by experts. We hired a firm named H2L2 that had undertaken comparable master plans for some of the most highly regarded small colleges in America, including Haverford and Swarthmore.

The prevailing new trustee sentiment was that the College was full, if not super saturated with students, and, if that was the case, nothing more needed to be done because no additional sales were needed. It was true that the application rate kept soaring, fueled by a top-tier status that was climbing even higher.

Not only was Wagner now on the top tier in the northeast, but it also was a top ten college in New York State, where there were over one hundred private colleges and universities.

As it would turn out, H2L2 pretty much agreed with me and submitted a report listing everything that Wagner needed to be competitive with other colleges they had advised. The report was not well received, and the board 'tabled' it.

Instead, the board forwarded a proposal that over the next two years, twenty-four million dollars should be found and added to the endowment. Finding twelve million a year for each of the next two years struck me as a tall order for Wagner and set the stage for a moratorium on addressing any other outstanding need, including student housing.

This ambitious endowment-fundraising goal wasn't the timeliest initiative given what was happening in the stock market. Since the fateful April 14th crash earlier in the year, over five trillion dollars in market value had been lost, most notably in the high-tech sector where stocks like Cisco and Intel had been decimated.

How fortunate for Wagner that Peggy Reynolds had donated her Cisco stock before the crash. Had she hung on to the stock, or, for that matter, had Wagner not sold it to underwrite the Reynolds House and walkway renovations, the value would now be under $250,000; $750,000 of its value would have disappeared.

A lot of people were feeling much poorer suddenly. Locating $24 million worth of endowment this year and next year represented about the worst time to raise money since the 1929 stock market crash, especially since most major endowment gifts come from bequests which require the death of the donor before the funds are realized.

I leaned against Peggy Reynolds and John Lehmann, sharing with them my frustration with the way in which the brakes had been put on Wagner College's future.

John was especially annoyed. "Those guys just don't get it. They've never run a business. I have had to fight bankers my entire life. They want belts and suspenders and don't want to take any risks. No business, except banks and accounting firms, can succeed with that kind of attitude."

Peggy rightfully observed, "If only Bill was still alive. He could make them understand." But, alas, Bill was gone. Peggy, though, bless her heart, pledged five million dollars to the endowment, hoping that we could get the mandated goal behind us quickly and get on with progressing the college.

A positive highlight of year thirteen was the Middle States team that visited that spring and enthusiastically recommended the reaccreditation of the college. They heartily commended Wagner's progress since their last on-site evaluation, a decade ago.

Excerpts from their evaluation report included:

"The board of trustees hold the president and senior staff in high regard and have complete confidence in their abilities to manage the institution."

"Everywhere at the college we find vigor, confidence, and an eagerness to work towards the future."

"The senior management team is strong and well respected."

"President Norman Smith is a strong visionary who has assembled a competent and trusted senior management team, and a board of trustees who are capable of significant gifts and who want the college to succeed and prosper."

"The visiting team commends Wagner College for its significant progress in the last decade."

All these accolades had a downside, though. Expectations were rising everywhere, especially among faculty and students. Since many needs remained, which I continued to remind the board of trustees, a new culture of complaining about what wasn't getting done was beginning to emerge. I was hearing from the campus community:

"If Wagner is top tier, why isn't there enough housing on campus?"

"When will the faculty be paid top-tier salaries?"

"If Wagner has the best musical theatre program in the country, why are they still without a bona fide theatre and still have to perform in a high school auditorium?"

"The athletes now have their top-tier building, but what about the choir and band that always must perform off campus because there is no recital hall at the college?"

"The business program is the highest enrolled in the college with over half of all majors, yet the faculty is housed in the crummiest building, a former women's dorm. When will this top-tier college get a business school worthy of its stature?"

The answer to all of these questions was not one I wanted to abandon. The trustees, at least for the foreseeable future, had closed the door on addressing any of these issues — at least until $24 million had been deposited into the endowment.

The one exception was a gift that was not reversible. Henry Pape, a classmate of Peggy Reynolds, had noticed the announcement of the renovation of Reynolds Hall, the former North Hall, and how it had been named in honor of Peggy's husband, Bill. He called me from his retirement home in Florida to tell me how he remembered Peggy *(nee)* Bambach and also how he had once lived in North Hall, which is now Reynolds Hall. He invited me to visit him the next time I was in Florida. Peggy's gift to honor Bill had inspired him to do the same kind of thing at Wagner for his recently deceased wife.

I did go to Florida to visit Henry. He lived very modestly in a two-bedroom apartment that looked like it had been built in the late 1950s or early sixties. I didn't know how much he was thinking of spending in memory of his wife, and, according to board endowment mandate, I proposed an endowed scholarship program that could be named the Pape Scholars. To no surprise, Henry didn't think that sounded as good as a building with her name on it, just like what Peggy had done. I explained to him that the board of trustees sought gifts that would strengthen the endowment, and I tried to compare the Pape Scholars to Rhodes Scholars.

He asked if there were any buildings like Reynolds House that needed similar upgrades. There were several that he remembered because they were also in the same part of the campus. Cunard Hall was one he recalled. And there were the two admissions houses that needed to be connected, although I also advised Henry that the trustees had postponed any such project until the endowment was larger. Henry said he would think about it, and I returned to Wagner College empty handed. A couple of weeks later he called me and asked me what, exactly, a renovation of either Cunard or the admissions houses would look like. A local architect, Michael DeRuvo, had already developed a concept for the admissions houses. A family friend, Michael had volunteered the sketches.

I went to Don Spiro contending there was little hope of getting anything from Henry Pape unless it emulated what Peggy had done for Bill. Don was sympathetic and authorized me to continue talking to Pape about the admissions house but advised that I should aspire for a gift exceeding the cost of the renovation so some of it could go into the endowment.

Estimates for the DeRuvo project were about $500,000 to build the connecting structure. The amount was modest, because the actual structure was little more than a platform that created a one-story connector to the two houses. In addition to extending the porch to connect with the twin porches of the two separate houses, the extension provided for a large central reception and waiting area, and for two interview rooms at the rear of the addition.

To accommodate the trustee mandate, my plan was to propose the same one million dollars for the project that Peggy had donated for Reynolds House. That way, $500,000 of the gift would go to the endowment. I had no idea whether Henry Pape was thinking of a million-dollar gift, but that would be my starting point. If he demurred, I would return to the scholarship proposal.

Henry seemed very comfortable with the price and was particularly happy that the facility would be adjacent to Reynolds House. So we went ahead with the admissions house, calling it Pape House.

The renovation made a beautiful difference and finally gave the College a front office atmosphere that admissions should represent.

Additionally, the admissions staff now had a workable facility that allowed them to keep their coats in the closet throughout the winter months.

The renovated Pape Admissions Center didn't look like two houses had been joined together. The connecting centerpiece created a building-long front porch with a new central entrance into a reception center. Anyone who had not previously seen the two separate houses would have assumed that the building had been originally built in this singular configuration.

The growing trustee resistance to my agenda of continued physical improvements to the campus was beginning to discourage me and, in doing so, was stimulating my receptiveness to search firm presidential opportunities elsewhere.

Late in midsummer of 2001, a search firm called to ask if I had any interest in going to London, England. The American University there was looking for a new president. Susan and I had always loved our trips to London, and we had already taken Caroline there on several occasions. Each time we were there, we dreamed about how great it would be to live in London.

The American University in London might well be the only British opportunity that would ever come my way.

The road not taken...

Before the new generation of trustees put the brakes on all campus development, Peggy Reynolds had provided a gift to hire an architect to conceptualize a performance center that would include a Broadway-class theatre, a recital hall for band and choir, a dance studio, rehearsal rooms, and faculty offices. This facility would have been sited on the northwest side of Sutter Oval, facing the new Spiro Sports Center.

The structure had a Lincoln Center aura to it and would have made a powerful statement for the college, but alas, the project was aborted because of the trustee shift to endowment-only giving. If only the board had been populated by as many theatre alumni as had been the case with former athletes, I think it likely that this structure, like the Spiro Sports Center, would have become a reality.

Over two decades later, the building has not been realized and would probably cost three times as much.

Year FOURTEEN 2001–2002

Chapter 37
9-11

With the prospect of moving to London emerging as a possibility, the fall of 2001 was beginning to feel like the beginning of my final year as president of Wagner College. The new year was opening routinely. We no longer worried about enrollment and whether enough students would show up.

Instead, we worried that we wouldn't be able to accommodate everyone. Even though tuition, room, and board were now $27,500 *(then quite a sum),* there didn't seem to be anything deterring students who wanted to attend the top-tier college of New York City.

We were, however, faced with 83% of all students wanting to live on campus, which far exceeded available housing. We were renting as much as we could find nearby and off campus, but it wasn't proving to be an ideal situation. The apartments we were leasing were scattered throughout apartment complexes that extended for blocks in all directions. Typically, families unrelated to Wagner rented other apartments in the same complex, and many of them weren't happy about college students living next door to them. Most of the college students felt the same way about the families. I kept appealing for the construction of additional housing but wasn't making any progress.

Classes were underway on Tuesday, September 4, the day after Labor Day, although most students had arrived the week before for orientation programs. The weather was beautiful that September. It was a great time of the year for new students to acclimate to what would hopefully be their home for the next four years.

We would get only a week of bucolic campus life before a massive balloon burst.

The following Tuesday, September 11, continued what had been a week of consistently beautiful weather.

I was in my office having a cup of coffee when Lyle Guttu came rushing in, telling me to turn on the television. A plane had just crashed into the World Trade Center. I looked out the window and, sure enough, I could see a billow of smoke on the horizon where the World Trade Center was located.

The television broadcasts were all reporting that they didn't yet know what kind of plane had slammed into the building. One network reporter was suggesting that a private plane must have crashed as had long ago once happened at the Empire State Building.

Although it seemed inconceivable that a professional commercial pilot could have made a mistake like that, the size of the hole and the intensity of the flames suggested a plane larger than that of a typical private plane.

Everyone on the floor had assembled in my office, as I had the only television set. No one was prepared for what would happen next. When the second plane crashed into the second tower, we felt as if our building had just been hit. The news commentator's first reaction was to express astonishment at the uncanny "coincidence" of lightning striking twice in the same place. Pretty quickly, though, the other reporters realized that we weren't witnessing any coincidence. What just happened was deliberate. Some group or country had just attacked both World Trade Towers.

Then, in came a report that something similar had just happened in Washington DC, and that the Pentagon may have just had an airplane crash into it. Panic was quickly setting in. What was going on? This only happens in the movies!

Lyle started getting calls from the residence staff, particularly in Harborview, which had a heads-on view of the World Trade Center towers. Since it was still early in the morning, most students were in their rooms. Virtually all the Harborview students were freshmen that had only been at the college for a week or so.

Everyone was in a state of panic and wanted answers that no one had. With no one knowing anything, there was every reason to fear the worst. Is the USA under attack by a country that had declared war? Is another plane heading for us?

For the next hour, until the towers collapsed between 10:30 AM and 11 AM there was less a sense of hiding from potential attacks and more of a fixation on what was happening.

It became clear that many people above the two crash sites were trapped. There was talk about trying to get everyone to the roof. A lot of the trapped people were calling for help from their cell phones, and their voices were being broadcast.

Then we began seeing people jumping to their deaths, all being broadcast live by the television networks.

When both buildings went down, the prevailing sentiment was sheer terror.

Wagner had a direct view of Manhattan and the World Trade Towers. The Harborview student residence hall, to the left of the above photo gave the freshmen a heads-on view of the horror. I took this photo with a telephoto lends which does make Manhattan look closer than it actually is.

For the rest of the day, we weren't sure exactly what to do and what not to do. Most everything was being closed and we were being advised, essentially, to stay put. We were trying to keep calm, but parents were calling up about their sons and daughters realizing how close they were to the nightmare that might not be over.

"What is the College doing to ensure that they are not going to be attacked?" we were being asked by panicking parents. An understandable question that had no reassuring answer. We had never had a security meeting to plan for an airplane slamming into the

College's buildings. Many parents said they were on their way to get their child out of harm's way, although they might have trouble getting to Wagner as all bridges onto Staten Island were closed. We were hearing reports that all bridges and tunnels throughout New York City had been closed. It seemed that we were 'trapped' on Staten Island for the time being.

The following morning began somewhat calmly but didn't stay that way for long. The media continued to be without the answers everyone sought, and there was speculation that further terrorist attacks were plausible. We were hearing rumors of trucks full of explosives being driven over the Verrazano Bridge, timed to blow up in the middle of the bridge. By now, though, some of the bridges had been opened, but with inspection teams checking all vehicles.

We realized there was little point in trying to keep the College up and running during this panic, so we closed, knowing that with over 70% of our students being from out of state, most were going home to get away from New York City. We remained closed for the rest of the week but concluded that life had to go on.

We announced that the college would reopen for the semester on Monday, September 17. Most public officials were calling upon everyone to return to their routines in life. To do anything else, everyone contended, would mean that the terrorists had won.

But would everyone return? Would anyone return?

We really didn't know.

Hopefully, the parents of our students would agree that the only solution was to get back to routine. To our relief, all but one or two students were back for the following Monday, and the semester proceeded without any additional interruptions — except that the world was very different now than it had been the week before.

By the middle of the following week, we discovered that the Wagner community had been victimized by 9-11. Many Staten Islanders worked in the World Trade Center. Many Wagner alumni worked there too. Don Spiro's corporate headquarters were in the World Trade Center, but below where the airplanes crashed. Everyone from Don's OppenheimerFunds got out but the offices were, of course, destroyed.

We were learning that too many of our alumni were not as lucky, as was the case with the sons and daughters of some of our trustees and close friends. For the next month, attending memorial services for Wagnerites and Staten Islanders who died that day was an endlessly recurring event.

But life did go on ... and Wagner survived relatively unscathed, except emotionally.

Another consequence of 9-11 wasn't as human but was meaningful. The college's marketing message heavily relied upon the twin towers as Wagner's iconic and metaphoric connection to the Big Apple. As the largest buildings in Manhattan, along with their location at the bottom of the borough (and therefore the closest to Staten Island), they were the most prominent landmarks that could be seen from the Wagner College campus.

The recently updated admissions view book displayed at least a dozen photographs featuring views of the World Trade Center. The twin towers had become Wagner's way of making the point that top-of-the-ladder opportunities were within reach of the college. Even the dramatic final moment of the Phil Dusenberry video panned from the Wagner main campus over to Manhattan — which was dominated by the World Trade Towers. We had just printed a two-year supply of admissions view books, and it now appeared that the entire supply had become obsolete overnight. Trying to sell Wagner College based on its proximity to the World Trade Center would now be more poignant than exciting ... and maybe even a deterrent.

The World Trade Center had meant much to me. On my fiftieth birthday, five years earlier, Susan and Caroline took me to Windows on the World, the top-floor restaurant where diners felt like they were hovering over Manhattan while eating. My first attempt to bring John Lehmann and Don Spiro together occurred over lunch in that same dining venue. John and Don would then lead the board for the next decade. Now, the towers were a symbol of tragedy.

PAGE 12 WAGNER COLLEGE LINK ■ WINTER 2002

Wagner mourns the victims

■ **Paul Qualben '44** lost his son, Lars ■ **Edith (Feller) Haack '58** lost her son-in-law, Rob Lenoir ■ **Al '61 and Chris (Zullo) Palladino '64** lost their son-in-law, Dennis Cook ■ **Daniel C. Coughlin '65** lost his brother, John ■ **Paul M. Britton '66** lost his sister, Marion ■ **Janet Y. (Schuttler) Wassmuth '66 M '70** lost her son-in-law, Richard Mhyre ■ **Richard C. Bartels '73** lost his brother, Carlton ■ **Linda S. Fiore '73** lost her brother, Michael Fiore ■ **Alan K. Jensen '74** lost his life ■ **Brendan Ryan '75** lost his brother, Matthew ■ **John E. Connolly '76** lost his life ■ **John Leinung '76** lost his stepson, Paul ■ **Rayna Upton-Haigh '76** lost her brother, Allen Upton ■ **Michael DeRienzo '87** lost his life ■ **Lisa DeRienzo '87** lost her brother, Michael '87 ■ **Joseph J. Hasson '91** lost his life ■ **Christopher T. Hasson '92** lost his brother, Joseph '91 ■ **Victoria L. Hasson '92** lost her brother, Joseph '91 ■ **Nancy DiFranco-Levy '93** lost her brother, Carl DiFranco ■ **Rose Errico '93** lost her brother-in-law, Danny Libretti ■ **Mary "Victoria" (Rowley) Higley '93** lost her husband, Robert ■ **Timothy J. Finnerty M '94** lost his life ■ **Michael J. Clarke '96** lost his life ■ **Joseph Doyle '99** lost his life ■ **Michael F. Cammarata '00** lost his life

The faces of Wagner alumni lost

Michael Cammarata '00 · Michael J. Clarke '96 · John E. Connolly '76 · Michael DeRienzo '87 · Joseph Doyle '99 · Timothy J. Finnerty M'94 · Joseph J. Hasson III '91 · Alan K. Jensen '74

Michael Cammarata '00, youngest MVP in Wagner history

Huguenot (SI) resident Michael Cammarata, 22, had been on the job only nine weeks when his company, Ladder 11, Manhattan, was called to the scene of the World Trade Center attack.

He left a message on his father's voice mail just before 9 a.m., saying he was heading to lower Manhattan because an airplane had hit the Twin Towers.

"Just tell everyone I'm all right," were his last words to his family.

Born in Grymes Hill (SI), he moved to Huguenot (SI) with his family in 1989. He was athletically gifted from a young age. He was a South Shore Little League All Star competing in the Little League World Series in 1991.

He played junior varsity for Tottenville High School while he was still a student at Bernstein Intermediate, and was on the New York Sharks Bantam A team, traveling in the U.S. and Canada.

Mr. Cammarata made the varsity team as a sophomore at Tottenville High School, winning sportsman of the team. As a junior in 1995, he won best defenseman title while playing club ice hockey for Tottenville, and was an assistant captain and an All Star for the New York Ice Hockey Association.

At Wagner, he was named Rookie of the Year in 1996, and in 1997 was the youngest named MVP in Wagner College history. That year his team received the Metropolitan Collegiate Conference Championship title. They made the championship game again the next year.

Mr. Cammarata was sworn in as a firefighter on May 3 of last year.

(Reprinted from the Staten Island Advance)

Michael J. Clarke '96, played on the hockey team

Michael Clarke, a firefighter, was last seen in the lobby of Tower 2 on Sept. 11. He was laid to rest on Oct. 10.

Mr. Clarke is survived by his father, his brother Jimmy, sister-in-law Kim and his niece and nephew, Tiffany and Jimmy.

A 1996 Wagner graduate, Mr. Clarke played on the Wagner hockey team and coached the St. Joseph by-the-Sea High School hockey team.

Alumnus Michael Hoffman said: "His last day was spent doing what he loved best: serving his community."

John E. (Jack) Connolly '76, worked his way through college

John E. (Jack) Connolly, 46, and his wife, the former Dawn Ann O'Brien, would have celebrated their 15th wedding anniversary on Sept. 27. But the assistant vice president at Euro Brokers was working on the 84th floor of Tower 2 on Sept. 11.

Mr. Connolly was born and raised in New Brighton (SI), and graduated in 1972 from St. Peter's Boys High School. He earned a bachelor of science degree from Wagner.

He had worked his way through college as a bartender at the former Denyan's Hofbrau, Stapleton (SI), where he was affectionately known as "Slice" because he could down several pizzas at a glance.

After they married, the couple moved to Redondo Beach, Calif., for a year, to pursue Mr. Connolly's business opportunities. They moved to Allenwood, N.J., five years ago.

Mr. Connolly worked at the New York Daily News for a short time as an accountant, but left to pursue a career on Wall Street taking a position as a money broker for Tullets, now known as Tullets & Tokyo, where he spent 13 years. Seven years ago, he began working at Euro Brokers.

An accomplished athlete, Mr. Connolly enjoyed golf and softball.

In addition to his wife, Dawn, his brother, Kevin, and his two sisters, Marie and Eileen, he is survived by his daughter, Dineen Ann, 11, and his two sons, John Patrick, 8, and Patrick Liam Craig, 6.

(Reprinted from the Staten Island Advance)

Michael DeRienzo '87, Tau Kappa Episolon brother

Born in Great Kills (SI), Michael DeRienzo was a 1983 graduate of St. Joseph by-the-Sea High School, Huguenot (SI). He was a member of Tau Kappa Epsilon Fraternity at Wagner, where he graduated with a bachelor's degree in business administration in 1987.

Mr. DeRienzo began his career at U.S. Trust, Manhattan, where he worked for five years before transferring to Cantor Fitzgerald.

His close relationship with his sister, Lisa, was made even closer when their mother, the former Joan Cunningham, died in 1997.

The Saturday before Sept. 11, he went down to Spring Lake, where he often went to read on the beach. He stopped by Staten Island on the way the home. This mix of social and solitary events typified his life.

Mr. DeRienzo was a skier and an avid runner who ran the New York City Marathon in 1996. He recently returned from a trip that included France, Italy and London. He also traveled this year to Tibet, where he did some climbing, said his sister.

He had planned to attend a religious retreat in Morristown, N.J., and run the Dublin marathon.

In addition to his sister, surviving is his father, Michael, a retired city Police Department sergeant living in Florida.

(Reprinted from the Staten Island Advance)

Joseph Doyle '99 star pitcher for the Seahawks

Three minutes before the first plane hit Tower 1, Joseph Doyle, 25, was sitting at his desk on the 101st floor talking on the phone with his brother, Billy. Most of the time, the two brothers were too busy at work to talk, but that morning they were chatting about Joey's fantasy football league and laughing.

It is a conversation Billy Doyle, 29, will never forget. He hung up the phone, only to find out moments later that a plane hit his brother's building.

He immediately screamed, "My brother! My brother!" and dialed his number. The phone just kept ringing.

A government bond supervisor at Cantor Fitzgerald for the last three years, Mr. Doyle was a devoted son, brother and uncle.

Born in Eltingville (SI), he moved with his family to Annadale (SI) 20 years ago.

He played in the South Shore Little League and Babe Ruth League and was a starting pitcher for St. Joseph-by-the-Sea High School, where he earned Staten Island Advance and Daily News All Star honors.

Mr. Doyle again starred in baseball as a pitcher for Wagner College, where he earned a partial scholarship and graduated with a degree in business administration. He was known as "the bulldog" on his college team.

(Reprinted from the Staten Island Advance)

Timothy J. Finnerty M'94, coached the basketball team

Timothy J. Finnerty received his master's degree from Wagner in 1994.

He was a bond broker for Cantor Fitzgerald on the 105th floor.

Mr. Finnerty was an assistant basketball coach at Wagner until 1994 and recently coached 7th- and 8th-grade teams at St. Catherine's Church in Glen Rock, N.J.

In May 1998, he married Theresa. They met while they were undergraduates at the University of Scranton.

Mr. Finnerty enjoyed golf and cooking lasagna for his wife.

Joseph John Hasson III '91, gregarious and energetic

Joseph John Hasson III was born on March 2, 1967, and shared a loving childhood with his sister, Victoria and brother, Christopher.

A 1991 Wagner graduate, was known for his gregarious and energetic personality.

On September 19, 1997, he married his wife, Mary. They enjoyed dining in one of their favorite Bay Ridge restaurants or taking exotic vacations.

Their son, Joseph John Hasson IV, was born on Father's Day, June 17, 2001. When asked about his son, Mr. Hasson would take his photo from his wallet, kiss it, show it, then kiss it again before he put it away.

Alan K. Jensen '74 magna cum laude graduate

Alan K. Jensen, 49, was a member of the Class of 1974. On Sept. 11, he was working on the 96th floor of Tower 2 as a vice president in trust administration for Fiduciary Trust International.

A resident of Wyckoff, N.J., Mr. Jensen was married to the former Martha Moore and the father of two sons, Billy, 13, and James, 10. He was born on Staten Island on March 19, 1952 to Ingrid and Grover Jensen and graduated from Staten Island Academy High School.

At Wagner, he majored in business administration and minored in history, graduating magna cum laude. He was inducted in the Delta Mu Delta Honor Society and Phi Alpha Beta History Honor Society.

Wagner Link Winter 2002

Many more losses would emerge throughout the rest of the academic year, but the early reports of Wagner deaths were staggering in their number.

Chapter 38
Cheerio, Wagner

In October, less than a month since 9-11, the London presidency search was moving along quickly. I had become very interested and learned that they were also interested in me. I was invited to visit members of the search committee who were assembling in Manhattan to meet the first round of candidates.

The first interview went very well. The chairman of the board of trustees was British and knighted. Sir Cyril Taylor reminded me of Rex Harrison's portrayal of Professor Henry Higgins in *My Fair Lady*. He was very animated, outspoken, and opinionated, but we seemed to be fundamentally getting along.

The search committee was moving on a fast track and invited me to London at the end of October. I similarly got along well with everyone there and was enchanted with the prospect of living in London. What a wonderful global experience this would be for Caroline's adolescence.

In one of the shortest search processes I have ever experienced, I was offered the job on the spot, which I happily accepted, returning to New York to inform the board of my decision.

The entire search process lasted little more than a month. American searches typically last a year. I like the British way. I could see that Sir Cyril had no patience for elongated processes, and while there was a wide-reaching sense of involvement among the London faculty, staff, and trustees, he was clearly in charge, and the decision was going to be made quickly.

Sir Cyril also quickly announced my appointment, almost before I could get back to the United States to inform the trustees. Don Spiro and John Lehmann, I sensed, were almost relieved to learn that I was moving on to something I really wanted. Peggy Reynolds was elated. She and Bill had lived in London for years on the famed Montpelier Square in Knightsbridge, the fictional home of *The Forsyte Saga* families. Had it not been for unfavorable tax treatment of Americans in England, I suspect Bill and Peggy would never have left London.

Susan was elated although also torn. Her Snug Harbor presidency had called upon her to be out and about on Staten Island on an almost nightly basis. She had become a prominent cultural leader, and she loved the civic and art milieu. When not participating in an evening recital, sporting event, or other function, I often accompanied her to maintain a college tie to the community.

All these obligations, however, meant we were rarely home. We learned the hard way, contrary to prevailing feminist ideology, that young children miss out when both their parents are chief executive officers. For too many years we had been dependent on sitters, nannies, and tutors to do for Caroline what at least one of us should have been there to oversee.

Things were going to be different in London. From this point forward, Susan intended to give her undivided attention to Caroline for however long that seemed necessary. Thankfully, she was looking forward to the prospect although she was going to miss Snug Harbor. But Caroline, now ten, left us with only seven or eight years before she would be off to college. Each of these remaining years was precious.

I reported my departure to Bob O'Brien, who had taken over Don Spiro's chairmanship. Bob was then head of Credit Suisse First Boston

— a mega-job — but among the remaining trustees, he ranked with John Meyers of GE Investments as among the few trustees who could come close to Don's stature. Whenever Bob visited the college, he would wander through the campus seemingly very pleased with how good the place looked. In fact, he would usually compliment me.

At the same time, though, Bob was among those trustees who advocated, to my disappointment, putting the brakes on any additional campus development, including housing, until a larger endowment was realized. I didn't agree, but it no longer mattered. My approach to what would work best for the future of Wagner College, as had been the case for the past decades and a half, had now come to an end.

The *Staten Island Advance* ran a front-page story in the November 6 edition announcing that both Susan and I were leaving our joint presidencies. The other story dominating the front page that day was a follow-up on Ground Zero at the 9-11 site, a tragedy less than two months old that was still understandably the top daily story throughout New York City.

Sir Cyril was anxious to have us move to London as soon as we could break away from Wagner, and he proposed arriving in the next month or so. Upon consulting with Bob O'Brien, he thought it preferable if we could stay through the academic year, another eight months, and have our departure include what he called a "victory lap" that would culminate with commencement where Susan and I would both receive honorary degrees.

I was a little surprised that Bob wanted to conduct a national search for my successor. Richard Guarasci aspired, as was expected, to succeed me. Outside candidates needed a level playing ground, or so Bob surmised. He asked me to contribute by staying on as president until after the search had decided on my successor. I agreed to remain through June, also because Caroline would be better served if she finished her school year without a midyear relocation.

Richard Guarasci seemed to recognize the appropriateness of a national search, knowing that such processes are inevitable to give the entire college community a sense of having participated in the decision.

Richard had built a considerable following after nearly five years at Wagner that would be difficult for anyone else to overcome.

As expected, after months of meetings and interview stages, the board of trustees opted for Guarasci at their spring meeting.

No one was surprised.

Except for the presidential search, the rest of the academic year was relatively low keyed as the college prepared for a transition of leadership.

Several gratifying newspaper articles recounting my years at Wagner were being published. One that meant a great deal to me came from Jack Minogue, the sports editor of the *Staten Island Advance* who had often been at odds with me as I would advocate academics ahead of athletics, including among athletes.

His article seemed like an acknowledgment that I had been right, and, at times, he had been wrong.

The Staten Island arts and cultural community selected Susan and I to be the joint recipients of their highly regarded annual Neptune Award for leadership and contribution to the arts. This was also Snug Harbor Cultural Center's opportunity to salute the short, but well-regarded presidency of Susan Robinson.

Susan had taken on the massive and complicated job at a time when funding sources were drying up, especially from municipal and state sources. Yet the advances made in her short tenure brought much new attention and stature to the Center.

Although not successful, Susan had tried to persuade the New York Philharmonic orchestra to use Snug Harbor as their summer Wolf Trap or Tanglewood venue.

She liked to think big ... as did I.

Staten Island Advance
SATURDAY, APRIL 20, 2002

Smith leaves a legacy with Wagner athletics

Outgoing college president made a profound impact on improvements in Seahawk facilities and academic gains

By JACK MINOGUE
STATEN ISLAND ADVANCE

When Norman Smith leaves Wagner College for England and American University of London some time next month, he'll leave a sports legacy.

Undoubtedly, some Staten Islanders and some coaches who have had to deal with Smith's formulas for financial aid will take exception to that statement.

The coaches, almost all of whom were not at Wagner when Smith became president 14 years ago, can be forgiven for their reaction, but Staten Islanders who were here then are guilty of short or selective memory.

"I remember Norman's first day," Wagner athletic director and football coach Walt Hameline said yesterday. First, Hameline was told budgets had to be cut to save the financially floundering institution.

Then, Hameline took Smith for a tour of Sutter Gymnasium. Sutter, with its two squash courts and tiny weight room beneath the basketball court was the sum total of recreational facilities for the student body — and really, the school's athletic facilities.

"The staff," Hameline remembered, "was downstairs painting the lockers." The football "stadium," was aptly named Fischer Field. It was just that — an open field surrounded by the remnants of a cinder track, something from that sport's dark ages. The football surface was in such bad condition in the mid-1970s that one of the team doctors warned the administration that the field could cause players' injuries.

The baseball and softball teams shared Willetts Field with the softball diamond and its cutouts in baseball's centerfield.

On spring mornings and fall afternoons, it was beaten up when it tripled as the football team's practice field.

Occasionally, Smith's manner rubbed people — even sportswriters — the wrong way, but in retrospect, he had more vision than any of us, and that vision proved contagious. Just ask Donald Spiro who donated the millions for the new gym and football stadium.

Spiro Center upset some in the community who were looking for an arena, something which could seat 5,000 spectators. Not that we have anything here — not even Curtis-St. Peter's on Thanksgiving eve or the SIHSL basketball tournament — which could come close to filling that size facility.

Smith's vision, though, was for something more: A picturesque gym which seats 2,500 and recreational facilities for the student body. There's a pool. There's an exercise room, a free weight room, and an aerobics room which students use from early morning until the facility closes. And, there are actually offices for members of the athletic staff who were bumping into one another in the old gym.

Fischer Field, a football "stadium" each fall when temporary seating was installed, is now a real stadium with permanent seating for 3,000 and with lockers, a weight room (which gets athletes out of the rest of the student body's way), an equipment room, and a trainer's room beneath the stands.

There's an all-weather track around the football field. The latter can now be maintained because there's a sprinkler system built in. And there's a practice field behind the stadium which is now lighted, courtesy of Elsie Love. Willetts Field is now strictly a baseball field with an infield and outfield not beaten up by softball and football.

And, except for those who would be in favor of high-rise apartments being constructed down Howard Avenue to Clove Road, this community owes Smith who had the vision — there's that word again — to purchase the former Augustinian Academy.

That's where Wagner's women's softball players and the men's and women's lacrosse teams practice and play now (although women's lacrosse plays its matches at the football stadium), and that's why green is the predominant color at the bottom of Howard Avenue. Surely, Title IX colored Smith's thinking, but in the last decade, Wagner has added six sports for women — soccer, volleyball, golf, lacrosse, swimming and water polo — and lacrosse for men.

Full-time athletic staff has nearly doubled to 25, and part-timers and grad assistants now exceed 60. This at a school where in the last stages of the Bob Hicks football era, Hicks was refused a single grad assistant.

One more item, perhaps most important of all. A month ago, U.S. News and World Report's cover story surveyed 303 colleges and highlighted what it called America's Best College Sports Programs — at a time when it was revealed that zero percent of basketball power Cincinnati's players earned degrees.

The magazine compared overall graduation rates to scholarship athlete graduation rates. Out of those 303 schools, Wagner ranked 15th: 80 percent of those who received athletic financial aid graduated as compared to 72 percent of Wagner's general student body.

If, as Norman Smith's critics claim, he was indifferent to athletics, then future generations of Wagner athletes can only hope the next administration is as indifferent.

Excerpted from Athletics Legacy column

When Norman Smith leaves Wagner College for England and the American University in London sometime next month, he'll leave a sports legacy.

Occasionally, Smith's manner rubbed people – even sportswriters – the wrong way, but in retrospect, he had more vision than any of us and that vision proved contagious.

Just ask Don Spiro who donated the millions for the new gym and football stadium. Smith's vision was for a picturesque gym which seats 2,500 and recreational facilities for the student body. There's a pool. There's an exercise room, a free weight room and an aerobics room which students use from the early morning until the facility closes. Fischer Field, a football "stadium" each fall when temporary seating was installed, is now a real stadium with permanent seating for 3,000.

And except for those who would be in favor of high-rise apartments being constructed down Howard Avenue to Clove Road, this community owes Smith who had the vision – there's that word again – to purchase the former Augustinian Academy.

One more item, perhaps most important of all. A month ago, US News and World Report's cover story surveyed 303 colleges and highlighted what it called American's Best College Sports Programs at a time when it was revealed that zero percent of basketball power Cincinnati's players earned degrees. The magazine compared overall graduate rates to scholarships athlete graduation rates.

Out of those 303 schools, Wagner ranked 15th: 80 percent of those who received athletic financial aid graduated as compared to 72 percent of Wagner's general student body.

If, as Norman Smith's critics claim, he was indifferent to athletics, the future generations of Wagner athletes can only hope the next administration is as indifferent.

At the Wagner Commencement ceremonies, Susan and I were both awarded honorary degrees and the *Staten Island Advance* wrote a most flattering *Graduating with Honors* feature.

Graduating with honors

■ **Dr. Norman Smith, Wagner College's longest-serving president, bids a fond farewell during emotional commencement exercises at the Grymes Hill campus**

By JODI LEE REIFER
ADVANCE STAFF WRITER

ADVANCE PHOTO ■ IRVING SILVERSTEIN

Dr. Norman Smith, outgoing Wagner College president, and Dr. Susan Robinson, his wife and a former dean at the school, receive honorary degrees. Speaking is Dr. Robert O'Brien, board chairman.

The man credited with turning a little-known college in debt into one of the country's notable liberal arts institutions, bade farewell to Wagner College yesterday at his 15th and final commencement exercises.

On a sun-soaked morning, Dr. Norman Smith, Wagner's longest-serving president, conferred degrees on 546 graduates in the grassy center of the campus. He, along with his wife, Dr. Susan Robinson, and Dr. John Myers, were awarded Doctor of Humane Letters honorary degrees.

"I am thrilled to finally be an alumnus of Wagner College," Smith told graduates, who were clad in black robes. "For you it took four years, for me it took over 14 years," he joked.

Smith arrived at Wagner in 1988 at age 41, when the Grymes Hill school's main lawn was void of grass because the football team used it as a practice field. Enrollment stood at about 1,200, hundreds below capacity, and the average SAT score for incoming students was 800.

Today the institution boasts first-class facilities, a more distinguished faculty and a student body of greater geographic diversity. Enrollment swelled to over 2,000 pupils and the average SAT score for applicants rose to 1140. Wagner was recently cited by Time magazine as one of the four most notable liberal arts colleges in America for 2002 for first-year programs.

Graduate Kimberly Almeida, hailing from Chilestown, R.I., selected Wagner because of its proximity to Manhattan and rising reputation. The marketing major hasn't decided if she will remain in the city or return home to pursue her career.

"We're not sure where there's more opportunities," said her mother, Jo-Ann. "I think the economy is actually on an [upswing]."

And from Montana came class speaker Kinsey Casey, who described her class as the guinea pigs for many of the changes at Wagner. Departments were rearranged during their college careers, the credit system was revamped and even the breakfast plan was overhauled.

Part of the legacy Smith leaves is his ability to harness financial support. During his tenure, well-heeled alumni such as Donald and Evelyn Spiro donated generously toward the construction of $12 million sports center named for them. Patrons like Margaret "Peggy" Reynolds made other improvements possible, said Smith.

The outgoing president, who will assume the head post at Richmond, The American International University in London, in the fall, urged Wagner graduates to become the next generation of contributors.

"Don't let go of this institution," said Smith. "From the day I got here I said, 'This can be one of the great ones.' We are well on our way."

After Smith thanked students for letting him be a part of their experience, the graduates responded with the first in a series of standing ovations for him. Minutes earlier, his wife choked back tears as she received her honorary degree.

During her decade as associate provost and dean of admissions at Wagner, Dr. Robinson was responsible for redesigning the marketing plan that brought enrollment to capacity and raised the standards of admission. She left Wagner in 1999 to become the first female president of Snug Harbor Cultural Center, Livingston.

Like her husband, she encouraged students to strengthen their bonds to Wagner. "It isn't simply getting a paycheck that should be your next goal," she advised. Graduates must think about qualitative ways to give back to organizations, said Dr. Robinson.

"Wagner will never leave my heart," she said, her voice cracking. "I will be keeping an eye on you, a very loving eye."

The third honorary degree recipient, Dr. Myers, a 1967 Wagner alumnus, touched on how the world has changed since Sept. 11 and reflected on the values his parents' generation instilled in the country. Earlier, a moment of silence was observed for victims of the World Trade Center attack.

"I was a product of the 'Greatest Generation,' " said Dr. Myers, referring to newsman Tom Brokaw's description of the young men and women of World War II. The tragic events of Sept. 11 united the country in a way his own generation had never seen. "You have the opportunity to become our nation's next-greatest generation," he told graduates.

He named leveling economic inequality, facing global warming, and making community service a standard responsibility as some of the challenges that lie ahead.

For many, the economic downturn will also be one of the challenges.

But with cameras and flowers in hand, parents expressed confidence yesterday in their children's abilities to land plum jobs.

Wagner graduate Lisa Ninnivaggio of West Islip, L.I., who earned her master's in business administration, wants to work in the financial aid area of higher education. Her mother, Charlette Ninnivaggio, said the sluggish economy could be good news for her daughter. "Enroll-ment is up at colleges, so they'll need people in financial aid."

Justin Rosenberg of Willowbrook will begin work for a pharmaceutical company on Monday. Family friend, Dr. Leah Henry-Beauchamp, said graduates like the chemistry buff should expect to see a brightening job market.

STATEN ISLAND ADVANCE

May 2002

Excerpted from Graduating with Honors...

The man credited with turning a little-known college in debt into one of the country's notable liberal arts institutions bade farewell to Wagner College yesterday at his 15th and final commencement exercises.

Smith arrived at Wagner in 1988 at age 41 when the Grymes Hill school's main lawn was void of grass because the football team used it as a practice field. Enrollment stood at about 1,200, hundreds below capacity and the average SAT score for incoming students was 800.

Today the institution boasts first-class facilities, a more distinguished faculty, and a student body of greater geographic diversity. Enrollment swelled to over 2,000 pupils and the average SAT score rose to 1140.

Part of the legacy Smith leaves is his ability to harness financial support. During his tenure, well-heeled alumni such as Donald and Evelyn Spiro donated generously toward the construction of a $12 million sports center named for them. Patrons like Margaret "Peggy" Reynolds made other improvements possible.

During her decade as Associate Provost and Dean of Admissions at Wagner, Dr. Susan Robinson was responsible for redesigning the marketing plan that brough enrollment to capacity and raised the standards of admission.

The final event before we would hop a plane for London was an early June outdoor farewell reception that followed the alumni reunion events typically scheduled after graduation. The large tent used for the alumni gatherings was still up in the Oval and had been reconfigured for an afternoon farewell. A large sign read:

CHEERIO! NORMAN, SUSAN AND CAROLINE. THANK YOU.

And, as a finale, the *Staten Island Advance*, honored us with a front-page story declaring ...

Wagner says goodbye to its renaissance man

■ During a farewell ceremony, Dr. Norman Smith receives the title of president emeritus after his 14-year tenure at the Grymes Hill college

By STEPHANIE SLEPIAN

ADVANCE PHOTO ■ JOSHUA CARP

Wagner College's outgoing president, Dr. Norman Smith, second from right, joined by his daughter, Caroline, right, and his wife, Dr. Susan Robinson, left, is presented with the title of president emeritus by Dr. Margaret B. Reynolds and Dr. Robert O'Brien, a trustee and director of the board of trustees at the college, respectively, during a farewell ceremony at the Grymes Hill campus.

There once was a time when Wagner College was near financial ruin — and it showed.

Its sidewalks were cracked, its grass was in need of some greening and its academic reputation was on the line.

That was before Norman Smith.

Today, Wagner College is home to brick walkways, a luscious lawn and a student body that has caught the attention of Time magazine.

This is after Norman Smith.

On the Grymes Hill campus, "Before Norman Smith" and "After Norman Smith" are catch phrases — the only way to describe Wagner's renaissance under his 14-year tenure as president.

Yesterday, Dr. Smith became the first person in the 119-year history of the college to receive the title of president emeritus.

This time next week, Dr. Smith, his wife, Dr. Susan Robinson, and their 10-year-old daughter, Caroline, will be settling into a new home at a new university in England. Dr. Robinson is the former president and CEO of Snug Harbor Cultural Center and former associate provost and dean of admissions at the college.

In the fall, Dr. Smith will assume the presidency of the American International University in London.

But Wagner will never be far from their hearts.

"We have spent so much time focusing on our excitement about where we are going because we don't want to face how much we are leaving," Dr. Smith said yesterday to close to 400 of his supporters who came to say goodbye and good luck. "It is a day like today that reminds us of the downsides of what we are doing."

Gathered under a tent on the grassy oval in front of Wagner's distinctive Main Hall, speaker after speaker took the microphone to praise Dr. Smith for the seeds he has planted since his arrival as president in 1988.

"When Norman Smith came in 1988, the Good Ship Wagner was floundering in murky seas," said Dr. Robert Anderson, the college's longest serving faculty member.

Fourteen years later, Wagner is steaming ahead and charting a course of success with enrollment topping 2,000 and SAT scores shooting past the 1100 mark.

The college has been cited as one of the four most notable liberal arts colleges in America in 2001 for first-year programs by Time magazine and logged a fourth consecutive year as one of U.S. News and World Report's "top tier" regional colleges.

In 1988, enrollment stood at 1,200 and the average SAT score for an incoming freshman was a lackluster 800.

"[Dr. Smith] inherited a campus that was unkempt and an institution on the verge of financial collapse," said Dr. Donald Spiro, chairman emeritus of the board of trustees who, along with his wife, donated $12 million toward the construction of the athletic center in their name.

"Norman knew what an unpolished gem Wagner was and he immediately turned his vision into reality," Dr. Spiro continued.

Dr. Smith's journey to Wagner began in 1971 when he was hired as an assistant dean of students at Drexel University in Philadelphia, where he earned a bachelor of science degree and a master's in business administration. He received a doctorate from Harvard University.

During his career in higher education, he served as executive vice president at Moore College of Art and vice president/dean of student affairs at Philadelphia University. Before arriving at Wagner, Dr. Smith was an assistant dean of the Harvard Graduate School of Education and assistant dean at Harvard's newly established John F. Kennedy School of Government.

In 1988, Dr. Smith joined the Wagner family as its 17th president and went on to become its longest serving leader.

Throughout the three-hour reception in Dr. Smith's honor, Wagner's new president, Dr. Richard Guarasci, stood quietly in the shadows, allowing the crowd to reflect on the accomplishments of his predecessor.

"Dr. Smith stands as a monument of those who have been most respected and influential in the entire history of Wagner College," said retired Surrogate Charles D'Arigo, a former trustee.

While heartfelt and at times tearful, the tribute to Dr. Smith was not without a lot of laughs, including those brought on by Ed Burke, who finally placed the blame for Howard Avenue's multiple traffic lights where it belongs.

Soon after Dr. Smith took over, he became concerned about the safety of the students crossing busy Howard Avenue. So he called upon Burke, a 1980 Wagner graduate who serves as executive assistant to the borough president.

As any good alumnus would do, Burke brought representatives from the city Department of Transportation to the site for a study and up went light No. 1 at Campus Road — not exactly where Dr. Smith wanted it.

"He called me up so animated because they were putting the light up in the wrong place," recalled Burke. "I called DOT, but they told me once it's in, it has to stay." A second DOT study resulted in the installation of a second light.

"Don't ask for a roundabout when you get to England because I am afraid you will wind up with two roundabouts," Burke laughed as he cautioned Dr. Smith.

Dr. Robert C. O'Brien, chairman of the board of trustees, who emceed the event, summed up the feelings of everyone standing under the tent: "Thank you for a wonderful and amazing 14 years."

From a platform with a banner proclaiming "Cheerio! Norman, Susan and Caroline," Dr. Smith thanked his colleagues for guiding him through the last 14 years.

"All I can say is, keep your eyes on this place for me," he said. "Together, you can take this place into the stratosphere. Keep your hearts, souls and hands on this place. We are going to miss you so much."

As the tributes came to an end, crowds gathered around Dr. Smith and his family for a final farewell.

"When London comes your way and you are my age, you say London may never come again," the 56-year-old former president said following the ceremony. "As much as I love this place, I would always wonder what it would be like if I didn't go. I've got to do this, but I am going to miss this place big time."

STATEN ISLAND ADVANCE

MONDAY, JUNE 10, 2002

Excerpted from

Wagner says goodbye to its renaissance man

There once was a time when Wagner College was near financial ruin – and it showed. The sidewalks were cracked, its grass was in need of some greening and its academic reputation was on the line.

That was before Norman Smith.

Today, Wagner College is home to brick sidewalks, a luscious lawn and a student body that has caught the attention of TIME magazine.

This is after Norman Smith.

On Grymes Hill, "Before Norman Smith" and "After Norman Smith" are catch phrases – the only way to describe Wagner's renaissance under his 14-year tenure as president.

"When Norman Smith came in 1988, the Good Ship Wagner was floundering in murky seas," said Dr. Robert Anderson, the College's longest serving faculty member.

Fourteen years later, Wagner is steaming ahead and charting a course of success with enrollment topping 2,000 and SAT scores past the 1100 mark.

"Dr. Smith inherited a campus that was unkempt and an institution of the verge of financial collapse," said Dr. Donald Spiro, chairman emeritus of the board of trustees.

"Norman knew what an unpolished gem Wagner was and he turned his vision into reality."

Chapter 39
Missteps and Lessons for the Future

Soon after I began the presidency of the Richmond American University in London, I started to hear from Wagner colleagues who were telling me that my presidency was being characterized in a negative light.

Being in London, England and dealing with another troubled institution not dissimilar to the state of Wagner College when I arrived in 1988, I was disheartened by these reports but was too distracted and too far away to do much about it.

It is not uncommon, unfortunately, for former presidents to be criticized by those who succeed them, so I guess I shouldn't have been surprised to be similarly victimized.

But I concluded that there was no way the heavily documented achievements of the 1990s could ever be successfully swept under the carpet or otherwise characterized as a failed era. There were too many faculty and staff at the College who were part of that time and remember the state of the College when I arrived as compared to the "renaissance" characterization of Wagner when I departed in 2002.

Almost all the trustees who were part of my tenure, and were the heroes of Wagner metamorphosis, were no longer on the Board as there was a 12-year limit that expelled them at about the time of my 14-year term. Many of them had died so they were unable to challenge any new version of history that was being propagated.

So, I went about dealing with the challenges of my new presidency and was fundamentally out of touch with whatever was going on at Wagner.

Also unfortunate is that all the laudatory media accounts, which you have seen for yourself in the pages of this book, were published before the era of Internet archives. To this day, none can be "Googled" as is the case nowadays for more recent media accounts. So, those accolades are all proverbial 'yesterday's newspaper' articles.

Not too long after I returned to the USA after our wonderful years in London, I came across a magazine article about Wagner that affirmed my years as president had indeed been criticized.

The November/December 2009 issue of *Change* magazine, a highly regarded higher education publication, featured 8-page story heralding Wagner's practical liberal arts and first year academic program as having been the key to the College's enrollment surge.

While too extensive to completely reprint here, opening excerpts included:

"In the 1980's and early 1990's, Wagner's leaders initiated an aggressive marketing campaign; added athletic and recreational facilities and relandscaped the campus.

Enrollments continued to decline.

What Wagner lacked was an identity that would differentiate it from all the other small, independent, liberal arts colleges.

Simply put, the college was in very serious trouble."

While there was admittedly much still to do when I departed in 2002, the above characterization is inaccurate but explained why so many former colleagues were contacting me during my years in London.

Enrollments did NOT "continue to decline" and had never been declining throughout my 14 years at the College.

When I arrived in 1988, the headcount enrollment was 1,188 full time students, mostly commuters from Staten Island and Brooklyn. When I departed in 2002, 2,200 full-time undergraduates were enrolled and over half of them were resident students from out of state.

Even more remarkable, the 1,188 students in 1988 were receiving an average 55% tuition discount thereby making the NET full time enrollment about 535 students.

The 2,200 full-time students in 2002 were receiving an average tuition discount of 35%, thereby making the NET enrollment 1,430.

So, while the full-time enrollment nearly doubled from 1,188 to 2,200 in 1997, the NET revenue enrollment nearly tripled from 535 to 1,430.

This was hardly a college ***"simply put...in very serious trouble"*** as portrayed in *Change* magazine.

The *Change* magazine article's contention that Wagner, during my tenure, lacked an identity that differentiated it from other colleges and thereby failed to attract students until The Wagner Plan's "practical liberal arts" was introduced is untrue. In fact, Wagner's identity as a bucolic campus on a hilltop overlooking the best career opportunities anywhere, namely Manhattan, was a very magnetic identity that we promoted successfully and generated enrollment surges beyond expectations.

The Wagner Plan was introduced to retain students, not to recruit them. At that time, we had more students than we could house on campus.

While distanced from the past two Wagner decades, what I gather is that Wagner's full time undergraduate enrollment peaked in my final year, 2002, at about 2,200 students and has since been in decline.

Over twenty years later, full time undergraduate enrollments appear to have significantly dropped if the website statistics I found are correct:

How many undergraduates are at Wagner College?

1,591

Wagner College is a private institution that was founded in 1883. It has a total undergraduate enrollment of 1,591 (fall 2022), and the campus size is 105 acres. It utilizes a semester-based academic calendar. Wagner College's ranking in the 2024 edition of Best Colleges is Regional Universities North, #69.

Google

My hunch is that The Wagner Plan and the emphasis on what was coined "practical liberal arts" worked against student recruitment. Wagner College is not categorized as a liberal arts college and should not have been so heavily marketed as one. It does not qualify for Phi Beta Kappa status, the honorary society for liberal arts colleges. The Carnegie Commission on Higher Education does not include Wagner among the nation's liberal arts colleges.

And most notable from an enrollment marketing perspective, studies have reported that only one half of 1% of college students major in liberal arts subjects. *(Source: National Center for Education Statistics reported 78,000 liberal arts and English Literature majors among the total of 1,836,000 majors).*

Today, as was the case when I was President, I am told that Wagner's undergraduate enrollment is one-third athletes (over 500) with most other undergraduates majoring in business, social sciences, health sciences/nursing and theatre. Perhaps the emphasis on liberal arts resulted in the enrollment decline from 2,200 when I left to what is cited as 1,500-1,600 full time undergraduates today.

To be clear, I am a lifelong advocate of a broad-based liberal arts education. Most college bound students really don't know what profession they will finally choose and, reportedly, 70% change their minds while in college. Thus, every college should require what I have always called a core curriculum, especially in the first year, that optimizes a broad array of liberal arts subjects.

However, the reality is that 99% of college students do not opt to major in liberal arts subjects like anthropology or literature.

It appears that the past two decades of emphasizing "practical liberal arts" via The Wagner Plan, along with ceasing to improve infrastructure, especially student housing, business and performing arts, resulted in a massive enrollment decline of as many as 500-700 full time undergraduates. That represents a potential annual revenue loss of at least $30 million.

As the past 21 years have all posted lower enrollments than existed up to 2002, the total revenue loss over two decades could be more than $300 million.

In 2002, when I left, I had hoped and expected Wagner would continue its upward momentum and by now be in the top 5, or even #1, among the northern regional colleges where it has every potential to be. Had the competitive instincts and strategies of the 1990s prevailed for the past two decades, that surge in ranking along with at least 400-500 more students each year would have happened.

A continued investment in infrastructure would also have been necessary for Wagner College to become number one.

One third of the enrollment today would not be athletes had we not built the Spiro Sports Center, the football field and acquired the Augustinian land for additional sports playing fields.

That should have made it a no brainer to continue to enhance facilities for other major programs like theater and business.

That didn't happen except for a relatively small residence hall, in 2010. Only recently have renovations to archaic dorms started ... at least two decades delayed. Other colleges that Wagner should want to compare to have provided apartment-like student housing for decades while Wagner remained primarily in a 1950s dormitory configuration much less competitive when today's generation of private college students have come from homes where they had their own bedroom and private bathrooms.

Instead, Wagner pursued a focused policy of building an endowment --- period --- a Trustee mandate which was launched in my final years, irrespective of my advice to the contrary, and which today (2023-24) reportedly exceeds $100 million. A very large part of that endowment were bequests from trustees and benefactors that were cultivated during the years that David Long and I sought. Those monies weren't realized until the benefactors died which occurred after David Long and I departed.

Noteworthy, though, is that $100 million, at best, generates little more than $5 million in interest income that can be spent on annual operations. Had Wagner continued upgrading infrastructure, as was happening throughout my 14 years, to create a top shelf private college in every respect, I doubt the enrollment would have dropped and could have grown to 2,500 thus generating four to five times the annual income that a $100 million endowment provides.

Note: I realize there are other revenue sources than the full-time undergraduate enrollment. As there was in the 1990s, Wagner enrolls graduate students and, more recently, online students. However, full time undergraduates are the most significant source of tuition revenues because one such student, measured by revenue, can represent eight to ten part time graduate students or on-line students. That is because graduate students and online students often take only one course at a time while full time undergraduates take four to five courses each semester and also pay for room and board if they are resident students. Therefore, a residential undergraduate college like Wagner should make the enrollment of full-time undergraduates their top priority which doesn't seem to have worked well for the past two decades.

Also disappointing is that these declines adversely affected the College's *US News* BEST COLLEGES ranking. The 2024 edition cites Wagner College as 69th among regional colleges and universities in the north. That isn't even in the top half. Over the past two decades since I departed, not only has enrollment plummeted but the TOP TIER ranking we spent ten years earning, that took the College to the TOP TEN regional colleges in New York State, has been lost.

Officials from the College have stated that the *US News* ranking is not important because research reports that only 30% of all college bound students refer to the rankings when deciding about where to apply. What is overlooked in that contention is that only 30% of all college bound students seek to attend a private college like Wagner. 70% attend community colleges and state institutions.

So, conceivably ALL private college bound students are influenced by the ranking. That was certainly the case in the 1990s when we doubled enrollments and tripled net enrollments, which contrary to the claims echoed in *Change* magazine, occurred <u>long before</u> The Wagner Plan practical liberal arts was introduced.

While I have emphasized the importance of BEST COLLEGE rankings, I am not a fan of them. I have long been among the critics of the way in which these rankings are formulated. In more recent years, as already mentioned, *US News* and other ranking agencies have come under fire and some major universities refuse to participate because they are so flawed.

All that acknowledged, though, there is no question in my mind that the rankings are much more influential than they deserve to be and therefore cannot be disregarded, especially by heavily enrollment revenue dependent private colleges like Wagner. I don't know what compelled *US News* to drop Wagner from the top tier to the bottom half of northern regional colleges and universities, but whatever it is, Wagner must do everything within its wherewithal to correct this damaging setback.

As was my feeling when I joined Wagner 35 years ago, the College has everything going for it and should be widely regarded as one of the very best in the east, if not the entire USA. But Wagner continues to be a work in progress as far as facilities and resources are concerned when compared to other top colleges. While that should be what happened after I departed, it is not too late to make the investments that will put Wagner on top of the mountain. Wagner remains a potential crown jewel in need of some additional polish.

Wagner College can return to its past successes if it brings back the kind of entrepreneurial leadership that created the 'miraculous' success of the 1990s. The roadmap to that greatness is fully documented in this book.

As George Santayana and Winston Churchill are both credited with having declared:

"Those who don't learn from the mistakes of the past are doomed to repeat them."

I would paraphrase and say:

"Those who don't emulate the successes of the past will fall short of the plateaus they are capable of achieving."

Testimonials

from those involved in Norman Smith's
five career presidencies

"Norman accepted what seemed to be a hopeless task when taking the presidency of Wagner College. He then exposed the community to his highly infectious and creative optimism and led Wagner to the top of the mountain. The entire Wagner community owes Norman a debt of gratitude."

Donald Spiro, Chairman of the Board
Chairman Emeritus, OppenheimerFunds

"Never in the history of Wagner College have so many owed so much to one man. Norman's legacy cannot be overstated."

John Lehman, Vice Chairman of the Board of Trustees
Chairman Emeritus, Vogue-Butterick

"I was struck by Norman's conviction to Wagner's boundless possibilities. As President, he inspired us all to realize that possibility."

Professor Anne Schotter, Humanities Chair

"Norman Smith's leadership has been the key to greatness for Wagner College."

Richard Herberger, Trustee

"Norman brought Wagner College to the pinnacle of success. His leadership has beautified the campus, filled the school to capacity with bright, energetic students, increased the number and caliber of faculty and brought us national recognition."

Professor & Dean Julia Barchitta, Nursing Faculty

"Norman Smith came to Wagner just when it stood at the crossroads between life and death. Under his leadership, we not only survived, but found prosperity and rebirth."

Professor Bill Murphy, Arts Faculty

"I cannot imagine a more influential or successful president of Wagner College. What miracles Norman Smith has wrought."

Professor Lewis Hardee, Theatre Faculty

"Norman brought Wagner College from a blcak and highly uncertain state to the pinnacle of excellence and distinction,"

Fred Lange, Treasurer, Board of Trustees

"When Norman arrived, Wagner was virtually dead. He saved the College."

Professor George Rappaport, Political Science Faculty

"Norman has led Wagner to an extraordinary level of success. His example is our road map into the future."

Robert O'Brien, Chairman of the Board of Trustees (following Don Spiro)
Managing Director, Credit Suisse First Boston

"Wagner College has experienced dramatic changes in the past three years since the appointment of a dynamic and talented new president, who, together with a very supportive Board of Trustees made the necessary and gutsy decisions which have resulted in the vibrant institution we find Wagner College to be. For all these successes and more, Wagner College, and particularly the President and Board of Trustees are to be highly commended."

1991 Middle States Accreditation Team Report

"The results of the past three years are nothing short of impressive, even miraculous. For all of these successes and a great deal more, Wagner College and particularly the President are to be highly commended."

1991 Middle States Wagner Accreditation Team Report

"We applaud, as loudly as we possibly can, the great successes achieved by President Norman Smith in just three short years. Words cannot adequately capture all that he has done. Suffice it to say that the evaluation team endorses the monumental achievements of the President and the College"

1991 Middle States Wagner Accreditation Team Report

"We have no recommendation for the President except to urge him to keep on doing what he has been doing."

1991 Middle States Wagner Accreditation Team Report

"President Norman Smith is a strong visionary who has assembled a competent and trusted senior management team.

2001 Middle States Wagner Accreditation Team Report

"Norman Smith is a great leader. At Richmond, he took on challenges that were daunting. He made more progress in five years than most could have thought possible. He proved himself to be an impressive visionary with exceptional managerial skills. I am privileged to have worked with him."

David McAuliffe
Richmond University London Trustee, Chair of the Finance Committee

"In my 35 years in the world of academe, I've never seen a more competent administrative leader than Norman Smith. At Richmond London, his accomplishments were superb. I was especially impressed with the respect he earned from his faculty and staff during very difficult times."

Russel Taylor
Richmond University London Trustee
Founder, The Taylor Entrepreneurial Institute

"Norman Smith assumed the Richmond University presidency at a difficult time in its history and quickly made a positive impact. As Provost, I worked closely with him and found his support and advice to be invaluable. I learned much from Norman. His outstanding financial management, business acumen and understanding of higher education, student needs, enabled him to build morale and re-energize faculty and staff. Norman has my highest regard."

Professor Jos Hackforth-Jones
Director, Sothebys Institute of Art London
Former Provost, Richmond University London

"The Middle States team, echoed by both the Board and the community, applaud the dynamic, effective leadership provided by Dr. Norman Smith."

2006 Middle States Richmond Accreditation Report

"Four years ago, Dr. Norman R. Smith was appointed Richmond's President. It was a time of challenge, with declining enrollments, fiscal deficits, and major operational questions. Some would say it was a crisis environment. The President quickly moved into action, bringing new roles into the environment, making hard budget decisions, increasing information sharing and establishing clear institutional priorities."

2006 Middle States Richmond Accreditation Report

"Richmond University has dramatically reversed a pattern of operating deficits... Much of this turnaround can be attributed to the arrival of the current President and the establishment of a new management team."

2006 Middle States Richmond Accreditation Report

"Norman Smith arrived at Dowling College too late to save a terminal patient, but that didn't stop him from exerting every effort to catch up for lost time. He is the most impressive college president I have ever worked with or known. If only he had taken over five years earlier, the College would have been saved."

Dr. Elana Zolfo, Provost, Dowling College

"Albeit too late to correct the grave mistakes of the past, President Smith's leadership energized the College community and made clear what could have been had he arrived as President in time. He was the College's first truly competent President."

Dr. Nathalia Rogers, Professor of Sociology and Chair, Dowling Faculty Council

"Suffolk University accomplished a great deal under the leadership of Norman Smith. Unlike some interim leaders, Norman did not come here to keep a seat warm. Since his arrival, Norman put a laser-like focus on elevating Suffolk's reputation. He has highlighted the excellence that exists across the university and showcased its many success stories. On behalf of the Board of Trustees, we offer our sincere thanks for Norman's excellent leadership."

Andrew Meyers, Chairman, Board of Trustees

"Norman Smith did an absolutely superb job as Suffolk University President. It was a pleasure working with him."

Richard Rosenberg, Trustee
Chairman & CEO (retired) Bank of America

"I have a great deal of respect and affection for Norman Smith. His presidency of Suffolk University is remembered very positively."

Robert K. Sheridan, Trustee
President Emeritus, Savings Bank Life Insurance
Past President, Massachusetts Bankers Association

"Of all the presidents of Suffolk University, Norman is the best. He's a real pro."

Marshall Sloane, Trustee
Founder and Chairman Century Bank

"Norman Smith accomplished more good things in his first year as President of Elmira College than what has been achieved in the prior five years combined."

Robert Morris, Chairman, Board of Trustees

"Norman Smith was a wonderful president and a Godsend to Elmira College."

Robert O'Leary, Trustee
CFO (retired) Cox Communications

Family Update

Upon returning to the USA from London in 2007, we set up residence in Philadelphia. Caroline, now 15 and beginning senior high school, enrolled in The Shipley School adjacent Bryn Mawr College. She went on to earn her bachelor's degree at Skidmore College, the alma mater of her mother and from where David Long, Wagner's fund-raising czar hailed. After Skidmore, Caroline earned her master's in fine arts at the Rhode Island School of Design. She then moved to New York City where she has worked for a number of major companies including SHOWTIME and *The New York Times*.

Susan became a founding officer of AVENUES The World School in Manhattan and then headed enrollment and admissions at the Friends Central School in Wynnewood on the Main Line of suburban Philadelphia.

I joined what was then the Registry for College and University Presidents where I served as President for several institutions including Suffolk University Boston, Elmira College and, for a very short time, Dowling College on Long Island which, unfortunately, was a terminal patient. Elmira College's trustees and faculty awarded me my second President Emeritus status. I have written several books on higher education and more recently have headed the Board Governance and

Leadership advisory team at the Registry which is composed of a distinguished cadre of retired college and university presidents who provide short term counsel to presidents and trustees.

Susan and I live in Center City Philadelphia in a high rise condominium atop the City's iconic Academy of Music concert hall. Lately, we have very much enjoyed our return to Wagner College to attend their wonderful theatre performances and football games.

Saluting Unsung Heroes

It Takes a Village is a book by Hillary Clinton, the title of which has been attributed to an African proverb, "It takes a village to raise a child." The same proverb is very well suited to my fourteen years overseeing Wagner College. A village of people saved Wagner College. There were giants like Don Spiro who were indispensable to survival.

However, gaggles of others made key contributions that were catalysts not only to survival, but to the unprecedented success Wagner realized in little more than a decade.

I wrote this book in large part to immortalize the Wagner 'villagers' who were part of the years that turned around the college, elevating it to the fully enrolled, top-tier status it achieved during my first decade as president and has sustained since my departure in 2002. I am struck by how many of these wonderful people are no longer alive. Hopefully, this memoir will keep their memory and legacy alive for generations to come.

Many trustees, benefactors, alumni, faculty, staff, students, and community leaders were cited throughout *Top Tier*, but there were many others who also helped make my presidential tenure as successful an era for the college as it truly was.

In this final section, I seek to honor those who were not cited in prior chapters but who made memorable contributions, particularly during the early years when uncertainty about the future of the college was widespread.

Al Accettola '41 —*Al was a veteran trustee prior to my arrival and in the early years of my presidency. He always wanted the best for Wagner and was an encouraging cheerleader.*

Keith Addy —*A gentlemanly chemistry professor who would be an asset to any fine college. He preceded me but was a symbol of integrity and dignity throughout my presidency.*

Kathy Ahern —*Kathy held the nursing program together after I had raided it of Mildred Nelson, Connie Schuyler, and Julie Barchitta.*

Mohammad Alauddin —*Mohammad quietly brought academic distinction to the college's physical sciences faculty. I remember him as a consummate scholar and gentleman.*

Randy Alderson —*Randy was a beloved theatre professor who died too young in the early days of the AIDS epidemic. He was one of the pioneer faculty members who made Wagner's theatre program one of the best in the country.*

Barbara Barletto —*Barbara was Susan Robinson's assistant in admissions during the boom years and then moved over to the registrar's office where she took on management responsibility.*

The College Store Team —*Jo Manzi, Patricia Coffey, and Carmela Ruggiero operated out of a warehouse room when I first arrived. The bookstore was little more than a textbook repository. We knocked down walls to create a glass-wall front to a full college store, including carpeting and Barnes and Noble reading room features. Jo, Patricia, and Carmela had a friendly and welcoming attitude that made everyone feel at home.*

Howard Braren —*Howard was a veteran fundraiser and former Wagnerian who had the respect of alumni trustees whom he inspired to become major donors.*

Richard Brower —*Richard was a terrific psychology professor whose opinions I always sought and valued.*

Cherie Caccese —*Cherie held the business office together, often behind the scenes, throughout my tenure.*

Mark Collins —*Mark took on all the toughest student problems, including alcohol abuse, and always managed to get the problem solved. He was also a great defensive football coach, student affairs dean, and a good friend.*

Geoff Coward —*Geoff took over the education faculty, under challenging circumstances, and won it new respect within the profession.*

Bob Delfausse —*Bob headed the music faculty and conducted the bands, including the pep band at football and basketball home games. With limited resources and no recital facilities, he nevertheless added much richness to the college community.*

Frank Fontanarosa and Amado "Junior" Velez —*Frankie and Junior were an army unto themselves. They were Wagner's omnipresent jacks-of-all trades. From receiving to moving stuff throughout the campus, they were always ready and enthusiastically able to make the impossible happen, including, it always seemed to me, being in ten different places at the same time. I don't know how they did it.*

Patrick Gardner —*Patrick was a passionate and talented choir director for whom I was never able to deliver an on-campus recital hall.*

Randi Graff —*Randi was a theatre alumna who won a Tony award and sang the original "I Dreamed a Dream" in the New York production of* Les Miserables. *She was a great advocate for Wagner theatre students.*

Miles Groth —*Miles was a steady, wise, and supportive professor whose judgment and opinions always meant a great deal to me.*

Christine Hagedorn —*Christine very ably oversaw academic counseling and had a remarkable skill to know just about every student. She moved on to a senior position in Bucks County Community College and now heads the Business Faculty at Rosemont College next to Bryn Mawr College in suburban Philadelphia.*

Lewis Hardee —*Lewis was the music genius behind the theatre faculty and a gentleman performing arts professor.*

Phill Hickox —*Phill staged all of Wagner's wonderful theatre productions.*

John Jamiel —*John was a great acting professor and part of the theatre dream team of faculty.*

Frank Kamenar —*Frank headed administration and finance for the last five or six years of my presidency. He was loyal, honest, and solid.*

Marilyn Kiss —*Marilyn is a student's professor. She taught languages and headed the study abroad program. She was always there for both her students and for the best interests of the College.*

Rich Kotite '66 —*A Wagner football great who went pro and went through some tough years as head coach of the Philadelphia Eagles. Rich was a big supporter and advocate for my presidency, which I greatly valued.*

Judith Lunde —*With intelligence, competence, steadiness, and grace, Judy held the president's office together for my entire fourteen years. She was a pillar who never sought any credit, and deserves much more than she ever received. When I started as president, there were three staffers in the office. For financial reasons, I cut the staff to just Judy and never needed more.*

Carol Maniscalchi —*Carol was in the president's office with Judy Lunde, when I started. For financial reasons, I transferred her to the vice president for development where she supported David Long, remaining there for my tenure and beyond. She always delivered her best.*

Tony Martinesi —*An ex-NYC cop, Tony was deputy head of Wagner security, often taking on the demanding night shifts. He was solid.*

Bob Matthews —*Bob said he was retired, but he was a leading force in community relations, especially as it related to admissions and students.*

Virginia Mendez —*Virginia took care of the president's house and played an essential role in Caroline's childhood. She was part of the family.*

Mickey Meola —*Mickey, who retired early in my presidency, was a veteran member of the buildings and grounds team who was there during those tough times helping Dominick and Stan mobilize everyone to fix up the campus.*

Ammini Moorthy —*A biology professor, Ammini was positive and ambitious. In the early years, she strongly advocated a better tomorrow for Wagner.*

Angela Moran —*Angie was yet another member of the wonderful nursing faculty who was always positive and can-do.*

Mike Nicolais '49 —*Mike and his wife, Margaret, had given up on Wagner at the time of my arrival, but reconnected to head the fiftieth anniversary of their class. In 1999, four years before my departure, they commended me and said the College would be in their will in a big way.*

Wally Pagan —*Wally, a '60s football alumnus, was part of the trustee contingent that advocated my hiring.*

Al Palladino '61 —*Al was also a steadfast advocate of my aspirations for Wagner.*

Warren Procci '68 —*Warren was on the board for the second half of my presidency. A Pasedena-based psychologist, he was a little too far away to play a leadership role on the trustees, but he was a citizen who cared about Wagner, and I wish he had been closer. He was, in my mind, a future board chairman.*

Paul Qualben '44 —*Paul was a retired Wagner college psychologist who was always there to cheerlead on my behalf.*

Zohreh Shavar —*A mathematics professor who preceded me also was an early advocate for a better Wagner. She remained a can-do advocate throughout my tenure.*

Peter Sharpe —*Peter was another great student-oriented professor who also oversaw journalism and advised the student newspaper. I always trusted his professionalism and sought his advice.*

Annmarie Sortino —*Annmarie headed the nursing faculty during my early years as president and she unselfishly permitted me to raid her department of strong faculty members like Mildred Nelson and Connie Schuyler, and later Julia Barchitta.*

Paula Tropello —*Paula was one of my favorite nursing professors whom I didn't poach for other jobs at the college. She was always a joy to be around.*

Mary Lou Ulriksen —*Mary Lou took care of everyone's copier needs facing dozens of faculty and staff who all needed something copied immediately. She was never ruffled and always greeted everyone with a smile.*

JoAnne Venturella —*JoAnne ran the mailroom and the copy center. She, too, was solid in every way with a brassy, upbeat spirit that had everyone enjoying the mailroom visit. Her husband, Tony, was an extraordinary pianist who played at all of our house holiday parties.*

Rich Vitaliano —*Richie headed security while also serving as head coach of the baseball team. The campus decorum was a testimony to his professionalism and hard work.*

Ed Wendel —*Ed was an education professor who had once been vice president for academic affairs long before I came to Wagner. He was one of my most valuable historians among veteran Wagnerians. He was also a champion for change he considered long overdue. He was very charismatic and positive, reminding me of a Boston political leader of the mid-twentieth century. Curiously, his wife, Kathy, looked remarkably like Jackie.*

Roger Wesby —*Roger headed the choir during my last four or five years. He was—and continues to be, I would presume—a very talented musician and a very dedicated professor. He brought the choir to all of my major donor parties, including during the holidays.*

There were many others who cared about and made important contributions to Wagner College's turnaround.

Those I cite in the book and this epilogue stand out in my recollections as having been exceptionally outstanding to me, especially during the very difficult early years when the future was uncertain.

ACKNOWLEDGMENTS

This recollection is rich in photographs, illustrations, and media accounts, which I believe add a critical dimension to my story.

I personally took most of the photographs of Wagner College, including the cover, during my years as president. Other photos, including those of me, were taken from my scrapbook of Wagner College memorabilia. Since many of these clippings are decades old, I am not sure who took some of the photos, and where I am uncertain, I have indicated that the photograph is "archival." Many of those archival photos may have been taken by a professional photographer whom I used frequently, Vinnie Amese. I have credited him on all photographs I remember him taking.

I am extremely grateful to Caroline Diamond Harrison, the publisher of the *Staten Island Advance*, the local daily newspaper that thoroughly reported Wagner College's developments throughout my tenure. Caroline, along with *Advance* editor Brian Laline, gave me permission to display reprints of these media accounts. Being able to do so adds invaluable credibility to my recounting of events.

Several friends and colleagues read the 1st edition manuscript before publication, helping me ensure that my recollections were accurate and of potential interest to readers not familiar with Wagner College. First and foremost, my wife, Susan Robinson, was of essential assistance throughout. Professor Vernon Howard, my friend and colleague since our days together at Harvard University, now deceased, was a thoughtful reader. Wagner trustees and benefactors Bob Evans and Peggy Reynolds, deceased, were especially supportive reviewers who have encouraged me to publish this memoir.

Wagner College's legal counsel during my years as president, John Connors Jr., and his wife Kathy were valued readers and advisors. Thanks to David Long, the Skidmore College and then Wagner College fundraising guru who was essential to the early days of Wagner's recovery. David, now deceased, read the entire manuscript, objecting only to the way in which I portrayed him as having been heroic. He was that and more.

stamats
HIGHER ED. SMARTER.

STAMATS is, in my view, the gold standard for higher education marketing and branding, a critical facet in private college success today more than ever before. I have relied upon them for three decades at a number of the most successful college outcomes I have overseen as President and their role has been key to those successes.

Guy Wendler

Past President, has my gratitude and respect for assembling professional teams of the highest quality.

Marilyn Osweiler

Senior Vice President, is the best in her profession. I have relied upon her for projects dating back to the 1980's and she has always delivered outcomes that exceeded expectation. Her decades of clients throughout the US and internationally make her expertise invaluable. Marilyn played an important role in helping me assemble the issues presented in this book.

Chris Reese

Head Designer, is a visionary artist who has created and assembled some of the most head-turning marketing images that have ever been produced for colleges and universities. His work has been key to some of the most successful turnarounds I have ever come across or been a part of.

Jason Jones

STAMATS' go-to independent photographer is my choice for being viewed as the Ansel Adams of college and university photography. I don't know how he does it, but he makes colleges look their very best and even more than that. He creates images that make prospective students and their families want to visit and see for themselves.

www.stamats.com

norman@registryinterim.com

Edited and co-authored by Norman Smith

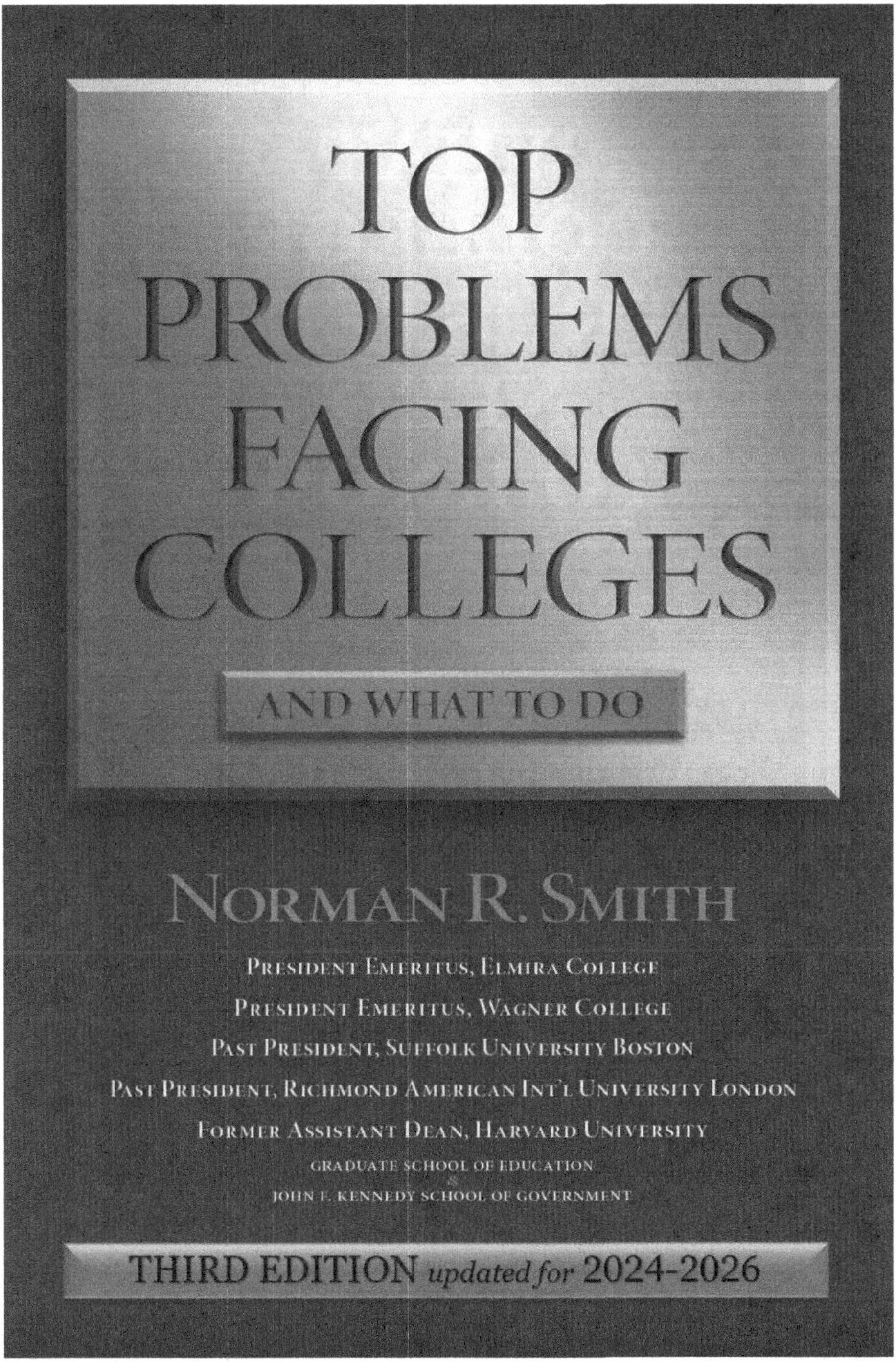
TOP
PROBLEMS
FACING
COLLEGES
AND WHAT TO DO
NORMAN R. SMITH
PRESIDENT EMERITUS, ELMIRA COLLEGE
PRESIDENT EMERITUS, WAGNER COLLEGE
PAST PRESIDENT, SUFFOLK UNIVERSITY BOSTON
PAST PRESIDENT, RICHMOND AMERICAN INT'L UNIVERSITY LONDON
FORMER ASSISTANT DEAN, HARVARD UNIVERSITY
GRADUATE SCHOOL OF EDUCATION
&
JOHN F. KENNEDY SCHOOL OF GOVERNMENT
THIRD EDITION updated for 2024-2026

Second edition published in 2019. Available from on-line book retailers including bookstore.iuniverse.com, Barnes & Noble and Amazon.com.

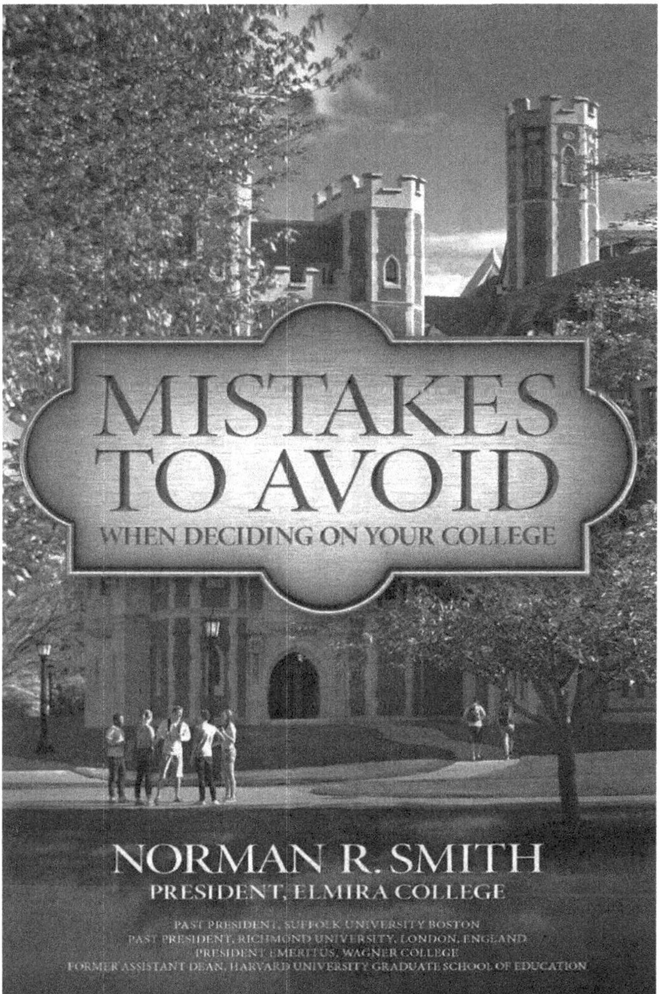

Published in 2016.
Written for high school college counselors and college bound students and their families.
Available for free download at [www.elmira.edu]() and at [www.normansmith.org]()

6th Annual Edition updated for YEAR 2000
Selecting the Right College
A College President's Advice on making one of life's most important decisions.
by Dr. Norman R. Smith
President of Wagner College

Originally published in 1994 and reprinted annually through 2000, book is now out of print, but updated in the retitled "Mistakes to Avoid." Book is periodically offered for resale at ebay.com.

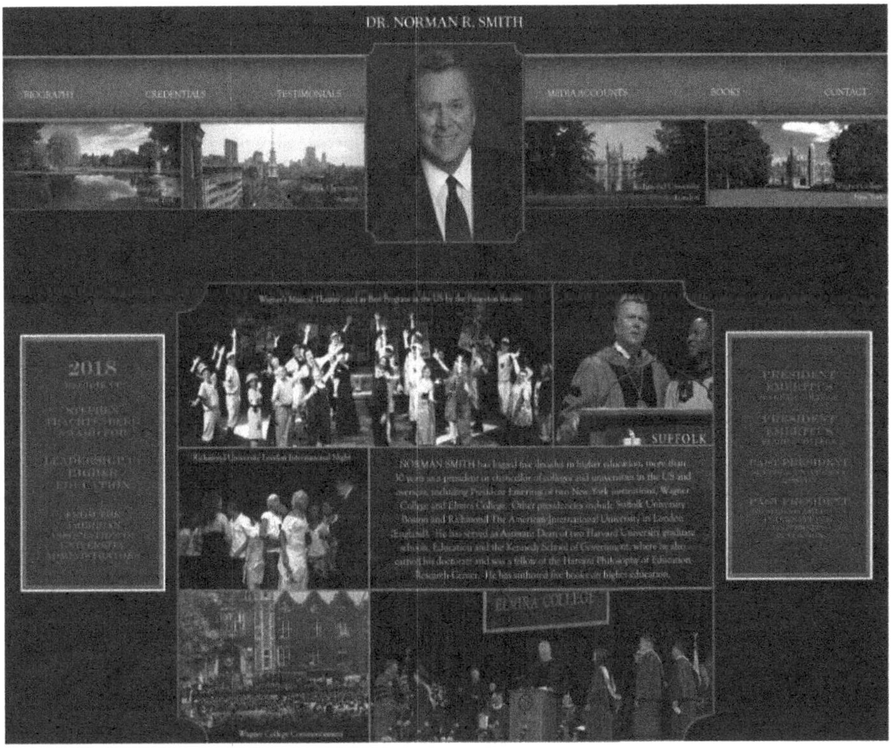

To contact the author,

go to

www.normansmith.org

Click on "CONTACT"

Printed in the United States
by Baker & Taylor Publisher Services